Language
and Faith

Language and and Faith

Studies in Sign, Symbol, and Meaning

by
JOHN A. HUTCHISON

Philadelphia
THE WESTMINSTER PRESS

PUBLISHED BY THE WESTMINSTER PRESS ®
PHILADELPHIA 7, PENNSYLVANIA
PRINTED IN THE UNITED STATES OF AMERICA

Contents

❖ ❖

Contents

Letter to the Reader

✧ ✧

As the work of writing this book approaches completion, I adopt the somewhat unusual procedure of a letter to the reader. In a sense every book is addressed by its author to its readers, and this one is no exception to the rule. Yet in some ways this relation is more true in the present instance than is usually the case. It is not a new idea, but rather a very ancient one, that philosophical and theological thinking is dialectical in character. In its proper and etymological sense, dialectic means conversation; or, as Martin Buber has been reminding us for many years, it is a dialogue. I hope that this letter will underscore this fact of dialogue between author and reader, and also facilitate the dialogue.

Speaking of more practical matters, I assume readers whose background and interests are different from my own; and I know from experience how difficult it sometimes is to grasp an idea whose human source and context are different from my own experience or are unknown to me. Hence it occurs to me that understanding and communication may be aided by a brief account of my interest in the main ideas of my book.

Permit me to identify myself as a college and university teacher whose work during the past two decades has extended over the fields of philosophy and theology (which, as I shall argue in Chapter IX, is properly defined as the comprehensive study of religion). The beginning of my interest in the subject of this book can be definitely dated. It occurred more than two decades ago when I both heard and read from Reinhold Niebuhr that religions and religious ideas might be construed as symbolic or imaginative statements of the meaning of human existence. A faith—any faith—is not primarily a speculation concerning some presumably inaccessible or remote object such as God, eternity, or heaven (though once the new context is established, these terms play an indefeasible role in Niebuhr's theology). Rather, it is primarily a way of understanding and living out human existence. The primary referent of faith, then, is not some realm beyond the stars but is man's existence in the world. This feature of Niebuhr's thought found definitive statement in his book *The Nature and Destiny of Man,* and it has become a generally accepted, though seldom fully expressed, feature of existential theology. Theologians as far apart as Tillich and Barth share this assumption. Tillich paraphrases faith as "the courage to be," that is, the convictions necessary to establish and sustain a man's existence. Barth writes that the Bible contains, not the correct human thoughts about God, but the correct divine thoughts about man. Beyond all the differences among these theologians, they all regard the primary referent of theological statements as man's existence in the world. More recently Bultmann in his *Theology of the New Testament* has developed his own distinctive interpretation of this same theme.

One aspect of this way of understanding religion is its manner of expression or utterance. With characteristic forthrightness Niebuhr said it was mythical or poetic. Early in his career, he turned upside down a well-known aphorism of Santayana that "poetry is myth we no longer believe." Niebuhr asserted that myth is poetry we do believe. In calling religious expression myth or mythical,

Niebuhr has had its imaginative, poetic, or expressive quality in mind. Myth for him means poetic or imaginative
discourse concerning the great themes of human existence.
Tillich also has consistently maintained the symbolic character of primary religious utterance against all assertions
of a literal relation of religious statement to its referent.
It is with the development of precisely this point that my
book is concerned. Taking faiths as symbolic statements of
the meaningful nature of existence, what conclusions are
thereby implied concerning religious language? This book
seeks to answer this question.

The other main source of my study may also be dated.
As a graduate student of philosophy two decades ago, I
took courses in logic and philosophy of science, thus coming into contact with the philosophy called logical positivism or logical empiricism. While I took no vows and
joined no movements, I was attracted, along with a great
many of my contemporaries, to what seemed to be a new
perspective in philosophy. Its criticism of many features
of traditional philosophy seemed to us eminently well
founded, and its spirit of critical rigor appeared as a kind
of ascetic devotion to the intellectual life.

The logical positivists made short shrift of religious language; yet even at the time, the question seemed to me
worthy of more serious consideration. During the past two
decades the philosophy then called logical positivism has
undergone a radical transformation that has brought precisely this question close to the center of critical discussion.
As we shall presently see, the old verificational analysis of
logical positivism is dead, and in its place many semantic
philosophers have developed a functional analysis. The
former sought to reduce all meaningful statements to two

types, namely, the empirically verifiable propositions of natural science and the logical rules by which these statements are made and ordered. Statements differing from these two types were consigned to the limbo of nonsense or meaninglessness. In sharpest contrast, the newer functional analysis assumes many uses of language, or as Wittgenstein has stated the matter, many language games, each with its own rules and goals. Of these many uses, it is at least possible that religion is one. Is there a distinctively religious use of language, and if so, what are its characteristics? The question has arisen in recent years in the minds of many analytic philosophers. I point out here simply that it is essentially the same question as that raised by the views of the existentialist theologians. Apparently, then, here is another meeting of extremes in contemporary philosophy.

To some readers the attempt to bring together existentialism and semantic analysis will seem not so much a meeting of extremes as an excursion into madness. On the contrary, I believe that such a relation is not only possible but of the greatest benefit to both parties. For now that the faddish novelty of existentialism has begun to wear off, the work of critical appraisal can begin. For this task the tools and the general viewpoint of semantic analysis are well fitted. Conversely, analytic philosophy needs work to do. In some of its formulations it runs the real peril of unemployment. That is to say, apart from substantive tasks of analysis, this philosophy runs the danger of narcissistic preoccupation with methodology. The analysis of religious language is one such task. The analysis of existentialist philosophy is another.

A glance at the table of contents will suffice to show the dispersive character of my book. The question arises, Is there any thread of unity in these several lines of thought, or, like Stephen Leacock's man, have I jumped on my horse and ridden off in all directions at once? Appearances to the contrary, I believe that there is a single thesis that draws these chapters into a unity, and that it can be simply and plainly stated. *My thesis is that religious language, or, as I would prefer to say, faith language, may be characterized as symbolic or expressive language used for the purpose of total life orientation.* It is well to guard the thesis immediately by the assertion that it does not prejudge either negatively or affirmatively the religious or theological significance of faith language and its symbols; to assert that their human function is total life orientation leaves open the question of whether or not they may (or must) be regarded as messages from God. Expressed in other words, I assert this thesis throughout the study as a proposition in the phenomenology of religion, and not as a proposition of theology. Around and under this major thesis all the subsidiary theses and all the argument of the book have been organized. It may be useful to the reader to have in advance a brief sketch of the argument that follows from and develops the thesis.

One particularly ironical feature of the widespread contemporary study of language and symbolism is that there is no unanimously accepted vocabulary of basic terms and concepts. Indeed, quite the opposite is true; the words by which men study the ways of words are subject to variant and conflicting interpretations. This has made it necessary for me to spend the first three chapters defining and characterizing the categories in terms of which the subsequent inquiry proceeds. These five main terms or categories are: sign, symbol, language, image, and imagination. I hasten to add that these are ideas of intrinsic intellectual interest to philosophers, theologians, and many other students of human mind and culture. Hence I make no apology for beginning here, but only for the brevity of the treatment.

Having established a context for discussion, the argument proceeds in Chapter IV to an initial statement of the main thesis, namely, that religion may be regarded as comprehensive life orientation. A faith or religion may be regarded as a path of life. Religious statements may thus be characterized as orientation statements. That is their function in human existence. I believe this to be a convertible statement; in other words, whatever statements perform this human function thereby take on religious significance. In form these statements are, in the terms of our analysis, symbolic or imaginative. Religious language consists, then, of powerful and luminous symbols by which men delineate their path through the mortal woods.

Are such religious statements cognitive? Do they constitute a form of knowing, or does such an assertion stretch the good word "knowing" beyond its elastic limits? To raise this issue as we shall do in Chapter V also perforce raises another question, namely, what is knowing or cognition? If we take as our model the kind of knowledge that occurs in natural science, then it follows obviously that religious experience and language are not cognitive. However, the answer to which we shall be led is that there are many kinds or modes of knowing, and that it is the part of wisdom in particular situations to specify as precisely as possible what kind of knowing is there involved. Although it is clearly false and misleading, alike to reason and to religion, to claim that religious experience involves ordinary informational or objective knowledge, I do believe that it does involve as an essential constituent another, different, and distinctive kind of knowing; and I shall try to show that existential philosophy as well as arts such as literature and painting can help us characterize what kind of knowing this is.

Yet if religion involves distinctive forms of knowing and saying, so too do other human concerns such as science, art, and philosophy. We can understand the distinctively religious form better by a look at these related and contrasting forms. Chapters VI, VII, and VIII glance successively at these forms of thinking and saying. The relations to religions are different in all three cases; yet all of them are significant, and much is to be learned of religion and religious language by looking at these contiguous forms of reflection and utterance.

As I have worked at the nature of religious language, I have become convinced of the importance of a sharp and clear distinction between religious and theological language. The failure to make this distinction leads to serious confusion, yet to make it leads also to some necessary qualifications as well as to the assertion of mixed forms of language intermediately located between theological language and the direct utterances of faith. With these issues Chapter IX is concerned. If I may judge from responses of friends and critics, this chapter is clearly the most controversial in my book. At this point I wish only to add two comments: first, that I would like to be taken precisely at my word in these matters, and second, that whether the reader agrees or disagrees with my distinction, he may be led thereby to further discussion of this important problem. Continuing consideration of the issue is more important than any single formulation of it.

The last two chapters, X and XI, are concerned with the application of the thesis developed in previous chapters of the book to data from existing faiths and to their forms of expression. In Chapter X the application is to the religions of the world, and in Chapter XI it is to the Bible and Biblical traditions of faith. These two applications may be regarded as a process of testing ideas in the way in which ideas or hypotheses must always be tested on relevant facts. In this connection it may be remarked that far too much of the current discussion of religious and theological language appears to take place without any slight acquaintance at first hand with the languages of actual religions.

Concerning my attempt to establish this acquaintance and relation, I wish to add that these chapters are of a preliminary and provisional nature. As this manuscript goes off to the publisher I am hard at work on a second volume on religious language which will seek to apply my main thesis in detail to the religions of the world, construing them as paths of life or different systems of life orientation. In succession I hope that there will also be a third volume dealing with Biblical symbols or images in the Western tradition.

In bringing to an end this letter to the reader, I must confess to a misgiving that has recurred repeatedly as I have worked on this book. It is, namely, that there is something unhealthy about the present widespread preoccupation with language and symbolism. Is it not better to practice communication than to be forever talking and theorizing about it? For, plainly stated, words are to talk with, and talking is for communication among persons. Is there not, then, an unhealthy subjectivism in the subject before us? Indeed, a case could be made for the view that the present preoccupation with language and symbolism reflects the tragic breakdown of communication in many areas of the contemporary world. Even further, in some aspects of logical and semantic study, theory appears as a kind of escape from the urgent problems of human practice and action.

There may well be significant truth in these negative suggestions. Yet whatever its origin or motivation, once a real question has been raised or put, there is no alternative for the human mind but to seek an adequate and satisfying answer. And this is, I must insist, a real question and not (in a libelous phrase) an academic question. It is a real question with genuinely serious implications or consequences for both human theory and human practice.

In our concern with the practical aspects of the question we shall do well to avoid two equal and opposite errors: on the one hand, a kind of messianism, both false and foolish, which claims that the misuse of language lies at the foundation of the world's ills and that a new linguistic or semantic system will usher in the new age, and on the other hand, an escapism which flees from all issues of practical significance to a "pure" intellectualism that has the same fascination as chess or contract bridge. It is a sufficient hope and a realistic one to aspire to contribute modestly to the amelioration of human problems.

Concerning the intellectual significance of our question, two observations must suffice. First, while the question of language and symbolism has sometimes been narrow, meager, and technical, if it is pursued with a lively sense of its wider implications and inclusive relations, quite the opposite is true. It then becomes one of the most humane and liberalizing questions in the contemporary world. The second observation follows from this. It is that many intellectual workers in many fields or disciplines in their various ways are concerning themselves with the question of language and symbolism. Thus, over the whole topic we may place the familiar highway sign, MERGING TRAFFIC. As is often the case in such circumstances, we must be prepared for traffic snarls, conflicting claims to right-of-way, and indeed occasional collisions. Yet the situation offers us the possibility for shared meanings, the opportunity for increasing human communication of many sorts and in many ways, if only we have the qualities of mind and heart to grasp the opportunity, to realize the possibility.

J. A. H.

Claremont Graduate School
Claremont, California

Language
and Faith

I Signals, Signs, and Symbols

✧ ✧

1. *Of Words and Man*

What is so commonplace as the words used in daily communication, yet what is so distinctively human? On the one hand, language is as common and ever-present as the air we breathe or as the earth on which we walk; but on the other hand, language in the strict and proper sense of the word is a distinctively and uniquely human phenomenon. It is so in the sense that no nonhuman species possesses language, and that all human societies of which there is reliable knowledge do possess it. So it is that Cassirer defines man as *animal symbolicum*.[1]

We begin, then, with the human fact of language. To be sure, communication of some sort extends to many of man's animal relatives. One dog barks and another answers; the mother hen clucks and her chicks respond. Indeed, the beehive and the anthill show impressive systems of communication. Current research and practice with mechanical brains and related devices has even extended the idea of communication analogically to so-called mechanical brains and other inorganic or physical systems dealt with by the new science of cybernetics.

Yet all these impressive systems of communication differ

irreducibly, and in kind, from human language and the mind that finds its primary expression in language. This difference can be indicated most readily by pointing to the fact of conscious formal structure in the syntax and grammar of human language. There is no evidence that the bird is conscious of the structure of his song or that the dog is aware of any syntax of barks. Yet man's signals of sight and sound do exhibit formal organization, so that a mistake in grammar or spelling is noticeable even though it has no practical consequences whatsoever. Furthermore, beyond syntax and grammar, there are many other levels or contexts of conscious organization that have significance in the complex business of human communication.

The emergent fact of language presupposes an altogether basic feature of the human mind and self in terms of which it becomes explicable, namely, self-awareness or self-consciousness. It is indeed this feature of man's mind which transforms animal signals into human signs and symbols, transmuting the grunts and squeaks of animal communication into human language. Let us see how this comes about.

Mentality or mind is defined by modern scientific psychology, in a broad and functional sense, in terms of anticipatory response. Responsiveness to environmental stimuli is a fundamental trait of living beings. Broadly speaking, organisms or living beings are systems capable of responding to their environment in ways promoting their own survival. Among living beings some exhibit the further feature of responding not simply to present but to future stimuli. On the basis of past experience they respond with expectations or anticipations of the future, and they do so in a manner aiming at adaptation or adjustment to environment. Thus, for example, the dog responds to the dinner pan or the whip not simply as a present stimulus but in terms of expected consequences. He does so in terms aiming at solving his problems, adjusting him to his environment, and generally promoting his survival. Such anticipatory responses may be said to constitute mentality or mind in its most general sense. Where such anticipatory or prospicient responses occur, there mind, in this broad sense of the word, is present.

In this use of the term, mind embraces not only man, but a great deal of animal life as well. Indeed, the difficult question, which happily we need not discuss here, is how far down the tree of life mind extends. How do we draw the line between mental and nonmental systems? It is sufficient to observe that, wherever they occur, mental systems in this definition of terms are wholly susceptible of biological explanation. Mind, in this definition, is a device of nature for the guidance and survival of organisms fortunate enough to possess it.

One feature of such mental systems pertinent to present discussion is what may be called a signal. Most simply defined, a signal is an object that sets off an anticipatory response. The dog's whip and pan are signals. Many natural objects ranging from the gathering clouds before the storm to changing seasonal temperatures also function as signals. Although at times such signals involve, directly at least, only a single organism, other signal situations are social, involving a stimulus in one organism to which others respond. Thus, one rooster crows and another answers; the mother cat calls and her kittens respond. Such social situations may be said to constitute the biological foundations of human language. Once more, we note that such situations appear wholly explicable in biological terms.

In this context how shall we understand the emergence of human mind and its primary and most characteristic expression in language? A fruitful suggestion is forthcoming from the observation of George H. Mead that "the self has the characteristic that it is an object to itself, and that characteristic distinguishes it from other objects and from the body."[2] To be an object to itself means in some sense to be aware of the self. Now, awareness or consciousness in its first and simplest occurrences is a kind of light to guide the organism among the objects of its environment. In this objective sense, awareness or consciousness is a general feature of animal mentality. With his animal relatives man shares this awareness of objects. But in man the light of awareness is turned inward as well as outward, producing self-awareness or self-consciousness. To be sure, self-awareness is not entirely absent from animal life, but what is peripheral there becomes central in human life.

Paradoxical as it may sound, the human self may be defined in terms of self-awareness. In other words, when awareness is turned inward, the human self comes into being. Just how or when this process occurs need not concern us here beyond the bare suggestion that it is not a simple event taking place all at once, but rather a long and complicated development. Indeed, full or complete self-awareness is not a fact, but to the end of man's life remains a hope and an aspiration.

Self-awareness, then, is the defining feature of selfhood. The self as a more or less centered and conscious system of responses is literally called into being by this new form of awareness. In becoming a self, man does not cease to be an organism. Indeed, the physical and biological aspects of his nature constitute integral components of selfhood. Yet when selfhood emerges, a radically new dimension of life with new kinds of responses opens up. Without ceasing to be an organism in an environment, man becomes something new, namely, a self confronting a world.

What are the significant features of the new situation? The range of responses of a self is far wider than that of an organism. The environment of the latter is effectively bounded by the necessities of survival or, at most, biological well-being in the immediate situation. By contrast, the self lives in a vastly wider and more complicated world. Walt Whitman's well-known lines compare this new world unfavorably to the stable harmonies of the animal's environment.[3]

> I think I could turn and live with animals, they are so
>   placid and self-contain'd,
> I stand and look at them long and long.
> They do not sweat and whine about their condition,
> They do not lie awake in the dark and weep for their sins,
> They do not make me sick discussing their duty to God,
> Not one is dissatisfied, not one is demented with the
>   mania of owning things,
> Not one kneels to another, nor to his kind that lived
>   thousands of years ago,
> Not one is respectable or unhappy over the whole earth.

The new features of the emergent human situation are rooted in a single aspect of man's mind or selfhood. It may be called self-transcendence, or simply transcendence. The etymology of the word "transcendence" discloses the root meaning of going beyond or across. Basically, "transcendence" connotes the observable tendency of the human mind and self to push beyond any fixed or given context, and to resist any total identification with, or immersion in, any fixed or given context or situation. Whereas an organism is to all intents and purposes a part of its environment, a self stands over against its world. In other words, as Reinhold Niebuhr has argued, the self has the capacity in imagination to stand outside itself. The reader may, without moving from his seat, perform an experiment to verify this power. He may in imagination stand clear of himself and look at himself. In the next moment he may stand clear of the previous moment's viewpoint and look at it as well. In some such fashion anyone may verify what Niebuhr has termed man's capacity for self-transcendence in indefinite regression.[4]

From this capacity derive many of the most characteristically human problems and features of man's life. From self-transcendence derives the self-determination that is the central aspect of human freedom. From this same source springs what has been described as man's restless energy. From it also derives man's capacity to envisage his own nonbeing, hence his own finitude and his own death.

What is most pertinent to our present discussion is that it is this same property of human consciousness which transforms animal signals into the signs and symbols of human language. Very simply stated, it is man's capacity to turn awareness upon himself and all the various aspects of his experience that enables him to be conscious of his own signals of sight and sound, and so to organize them consciously and formally. Able to stand clear of them in imagination, man can accordingly identify his signals as such, thus tearing them loose from any fixed relation to particular objects or contexts and establishing them as terms in human discourse. In some such manner as this, human language is born.

The peculiar nature of the human self in its capacity for self-awareness and self-transcendence offers a valuable clue for the equally peculiar nature of the human mind. Indeed, this mind may be most readily characterized by its relation to the self. Stated most simply, the human mind can be defined as the full cognitive activity of the self. Conversely, it can also be asserted that the self is the human mind in its agency, as it turns from thinking to doing or acting. These reciprocal assertions concerning self and mind carry several implications that are pertinent to our study and may be pointed out in succession.

First, this viewpoint provides a unitary, functional definition of both mind and self which avoids both the dualism and substantialism that have vitiated much traditional thinking on these issues. We need only mention Descartes's view of mind in body, like a bird in a cage, or as Ryle has expressed it, like a "ghost in a machine."[5] Rather than to say that man has a mind, the present viewpoint asserts that man is a mind. Mind, in short, is man thinking. The words "self" and "mind" refer to identifiable aspects of human experience, and both mind and self are aspects of man.

Second, this approach can help us to avoid the reductionism that characterizes much contemporary psychological discussion of mind. It will do so by directing attention away from the methods and models of psychological science to the factual study of the human mind in its actual existence. Surely it is a counsel of common sense to assert that mind is what it is—that is to say, what factual inquiry discloses to be true rather than what any a priori model asserts must necessarily be the case. Against all reductive explanations, which explain by explaining away, we must affirm that human mind is not less than the full and variegated cognitive life of the self.

A further controversial issue pertinent to our present inquiry lies in the long tradition in the West that the study of the mind is in a special way the domain of the psychologist. If there is any truth in the viewpoint to be developed in the present study, this assumption must be challenged. While we should continue to accept with gratitude whatever light psychology can shed on the mind, we challenge its exclusive proprietary claim, and assert that we ought to look to other sources as well. Notably we ought to look to language and culture for primary clues as to the nature of human mind. For both language and culture are common and peculiar to man. As previously observed, all men and only men have language. The same may be said of culture. Thus, it may be asserted that whatever else and whatever more man's mind may be, it is that which creates and sustains language and culture.

Our proposal, then, is to understand the human mind functionally through its distinctive activities. Language may be construed as embodied, objectified mind; hence as we gain understanding of its manifold structures and processes we will also be gaining understanding of the mind that finds expression in language. Specifically, the various kinds of language that will occupy our attention throughout this study may fruitfully be regarded also as basic aspects of the mind's life.

As the first creation of culture, through which all the other work of human culture gets accomplished, language is of primary importance here too. It is so whether we look to human culture in general or to particular culture patterns. "Language," then, is apparently a middle term between "mind" and "culture."

2. Cassirer's Philosophy of Symbolism and Culture

The relation between the three terms "mind," "language," and "culture" is a major theme in the philosophy of Ernst Cassirer.[6] Indeed, it is not too much to say that the fundamental task of Cassirer's philosophy is to understand this threefold relation. In the first place he sees an irreducible difference between what he terms "animal signs" and "human symbols." Animal signs (or, as we have called them, signals) function in the immediately given environment to guide animal behavior. Their range and function are both limited by this context of organism-in-environment. Such natural signs (or signals) point to or indicate objects that are significant in this limited context. With human symbols (or, as we shall presently argue, signs and symbols), the situation is irreducibly different. Indeed, human signs and symbols may be said to constitute a new emergent level of mind.

> In the human world we find a new characteristic which appears to be the distinctive mark of human life. The functional circle of man is not only quantitatively enlarged; it has also undergone a qualitative change. Man has, as it were, discovered a new method of adapting himself to his environment. Between the receptor system and the effector system, which are to be found in all animal species, we find in man a third link which we may describe as the *symbolic system*. This new acquisition transforms the whole of human life. As compared with the other animals, man lives not merely in a broader reality; he lives, so to speak, in a new *dimension* of reality. There is an unmistakable difference between organic reactions and human responses.[7]

The presence of the new element is revolutionary, for the human mind, in the words of Susanne Langer, is no longer simply a complicated switchboard but a transformer whose work consists of the transformation of the immediately experienced world into symbols and symbol systems.[8] The results of this "symbolic transformation" are manifold. For one thing, the human mind is separated or cut off from immediate contact with nature; man can approach his world only through the intermediation of signs and symbols. Furthermore, at the new emergent level of human mentality, symbolic activity or symbolization itself becomes an intrinsic need as pressing and urgent as daily bread and a fulfillment as delightful and satisfying as hunger appeased.

Animal signals, thus transformed into human signs and symbols, acquire many new characteristics to which we must give attention in the next section of this chapter. Here let us note that by means of the signs and symbols of the emergent human mind, the natural environment of the animal is transformed into the world that confronts the human self and mind. This world is not only wider than animal environment, and not only does it extend farther into past and future, but it also has a revolutionary new dimension of open possibility which transcends the actually given aspect of the world. This new aspect of the world is strictly correlated with what we shall presently describe as the distinction between essence and existence in man's mind. The world of free possibility opens before man's mind, which is thus able to distinguish essence from existence. This new feature of the human situation may be traced to its source, once more in the self-conscious and transcendent character of the creative mind of man.

In Cassirer's view the mind's creative activity brings into being whole series of symbol systems such as myth and religion, language, science, history and art. Furthermore, for Cassirer, these and other symbolic enterprises constitute the substance of human culture. So it is again that symbols and symbol systems constitute a middle term between mind and culture. On the one hand, they are mind at work, or objective mind; on the other hand, they constitute the living content or substance of human culture. If we look away from individual mind to the full social reality of culture, what we see is a configuration of different symbol systems that constitute its content. Culture, in other words, *is* a configuration of symbol systems. Thus, by attention to the middle term "symbol systems," we are led again to the conclusion that culture is objectified mind. This is true whether we focus attention upon a particular culture pattern—American, Melanesian, Kwakiutl, or any other—or upon the generic phenomenon of human culture. In either case, the great and characteristic works of culture are embodied mind. This relation may be traced in either direction, from mind through its signs and symbols to culture, or from culture back through signs and symbols to its source in mind. Either way the threefold relation is clear.

Although we must be grateful to Cassirer for the basic viewpoint sketched here and for the broad and humane wisdom he brings to its development, we must raise two important questions concerning his work. Whereas his Kantian idealism imparts to his philosophy its genuinely humanistic quality as well as its emphasis on the universality and creativity of mind, it also deprives him of any criterion beyond inner coherence for judging any symbol system. His idealistic epistemology leaves him ultimately no way of judging the adequacy of symbol or symbol system to referent or object. This is an issue to which we shall return in Chapter V. Second, by using the word "symbol" to cover all terms in human language, he has needlessly blurred the distinction between significantly different kinds of terms. We shall soon find it imperative to distinguish between symbols and signs.

3. Two Dualities in Human Language

Once human language comes into being it goes its own way and leads its own unique kind of life. If we wish to understand it, we must begin by observing the kind of life it leads. This observation will be furthered by noting two significant dualities in the ways of words: (*a*) the distinction between expression and reference, and (*b*) that between intension and extension. Incidentally, we must be on guard against confusing these two distinctions or dualities with each other. To begin with the first duality, human words establish and sustain relations (1) with the objects to which they refer, and (2) to the subjects or selves who use them. This latter relation, namely, the whole traffic and commerce of words with the selves who use them, is what we shall call "expression." The former relation sustained by words to the world of objects is what we shall mean by "reference."

If we understand this distinction clearly, we shall have little trouble in concluding that the second duality, namely, that between extension and intension, or between denotation and connotation, occurs as an aspect of reference.[9] In the business of relating human minds to the world of objects, words may be said to mark off definite domains in the world of objects or referents; or in other words, they have definite extensions. However, they also have a "pure" or essential meaning apart from or "above" the objective world; in a word, they possess intension or connotation.

Simply stated, extension consists of the direct relation that words carry on with their referents in the objective world, while intension consists of relations to other words or to their meanings. Thus, for example, we may ask the meaning of a word, and for the answer look it up in the dictionary, where we find its conventional intension. Or we might even ask a friend to tell us what comes to his mind when he hears the word; that is, we ask its subjective intension for him. Some textbooks of logic also list the further concept of comprehension or total intension, an idea that raises many intriguing philosophic questions.[10]

Under other circumstances, however, it may clarify a word more effectively to point to an object that illustrates or exemplifies it, or to raise the question of whether this or that particular entity is embraced by the word in question. For example, is this object really a chair? In other words, we turn from intension to extension, from a word's relation to other words to its direct relation to objects.

It is significant to note this duality in linguistic meaning against the background of signals as discussed in the previous section of this chapter. Signals simply point to or *indicate* objects, whereas human words *refer* to objects. Since the relation of reference involves an intensional as well as an extensional aspect, it is possible for words to refer to absent objects or even to nonexistent or abstractly possible objects. There is, in short, no evidence for "pure" or intensional meaning in the case of signals. There are no dictionaries at the level of animal meaning. Thus, pure or intensional meaning seems to be another manifestation of the self-transcendent character of the human mind or imagination. Furthermore, once such pure meanings or essences supervene upon the relation of signal to its object, we have also something else new, namely, extensional meaning, which in its way also differs fundamentally from the relation of indication between signals and their objects. Intension and extension are polar words; neither exists without the other. They are both emergent human meanings.

The distinction between intension and extension points to other issues such as the traditional quarrel between realism and nominalism. The Platonic realist position may be described as that which regards intensional meanings or essences as "real" in a sense similar or identical to the "reality" of physical objects. Nominalism, on the other hand, characterizes such essences as so many huffs and puffs of human breath whose most important function is to indicate or designate extension. Happily we need not enter these vexed issues beyond the assertion that our study of meaning has up to this point left us strictly neutral. It is more important to observe the actual behavior of words as they function in discourse than to liken them to other kinds of entities. Words are words, however we may subsequently choose to interpret them metaphysically.

The distinction between intension and extension will be related as our study proceeds to that between essence and existence. At this point it is sufficient to indicate the whole area of intensional meaning as the realm of essences. Conversely, an essence might be defined as a piece or chunk of intensional meaning. Extension and extensional meaning, by contrast, involve the problem of relating such essences or Platonic ideas to the world of existence.

We turn attention now to the wider duality in the ways of words, namely, to that between expression and reference, or in other words, between the relations words sustain to the selves who use them and to the objects and objective situations to which words refer. In this duality we must look particularly at expression and expressive meaning; and we begin by observing that expressive meaning is actually a wider category than literal or verbal language. There are many significant kinds of nonverbal symbols or symbol systems. For example, human selves frequently find significant expression in nonverbal symbol systems ranging from clothes or bodily movement to nonobjective painting.

Once more, expression formally characterized is the articulation, or the saying—in the widest sense of that word—of some aspect of the life of the human self by means of words or of nonverbal symbols. The double use of words for expression and reference is the basis for an important feature of the philosophy of semantic analysis. In the earlier logical positivist phase of this philosophic movement it provided the distinction between scientific or verificational meaning on the one hand, and emotive meaning on the other hand. In the more recent phases of this philosophic movement, expressive meanings and referential meanings are distinguished as different language functions or different language strata.

It is not too much to say that one of the most egregious errors of logical positivism or logical empiricism has been the assertion of an exclusive disjunction between the expressive and the referential meaning of verbal language.[11] Thus, it has commonly been assumed that if a term has expressive meaning it cannot possibly have referential meaning, and also vice versa. Along with this has gone a second assumption often even more unconsciously held than the first, namely, that to say "subjective (or expressive) meaning" is to say "individually capriciously subjective meaning." The background and context of these erroneous and misleading assertions is a positivist philosophy which takes natural science as the ideal type of all knowledge. Often it has asserted that only if terms and statements fit the model of mathematics and the physical sciences can they have genuine or referential meaning. Whatever forms of language go beyond this model have been judged to have only a subjective or emotive meaning.

These contentions will be subjects for critical scrutiny throughout our study. At this point it is enough to lay bare the unproved and "dogmatic" character of the assertion of the exclusive disjunction between expression and reference, and of the further assumption that subjective meaning must necessarily have a merely emotive and capriciously individual character. As Wheelwright has remarked,[12] the negative of "referential" is not "expressive" but "nonreferential," and the negative of "expressive" is not "referential" but "nonexpressive"—assertions that might be regarded as obvious to logically minded inquirers.

If we now combine these two terms, "expression" and "reference," with affirmative and negative values, we get four possibilities which can at least possibly be illustrated by different forms of language. It is at least formally possible to find utterance that is (a) expressive and referential, (b) expressive and nonreferential, (c) nonexpressive and referential, and finally (d) nonexpressive and nonreferential.

The wise course here as elsewhere in human experience is not to prejudge factual issues by assertions in advance of inquiry. Having defined the possibilities, let us see how many of them find exemplification in actual fact. Does a poem have referential as well as expressive meaning? Are mathematical and scientific terms expressive as well as referential? Do we use words that are neither expressive nor referential? All of these and many other questions are pertinent ones to test in actual linguistic situations.

4. Signs and Symbols

Discussion of expression and reference brings us to the problem of defining the terms "sign" and "symbol" as we shall use them throughout our study, and to some of the important similarities and differences between these two kinds of terms in human utterance. It seems clearly impossible to achieve a definition of "sign" and of "symbol" that will embrace all the variant uses of these terms in contemporary writing and speaking. Accordingly, we must adopt a convenient usage, and hold it consistently. Our primary concern here is literal or verbal language; yet as we have already seen, wider references to nonverbal systems of utterance soon open before us. *A sign may most simply be defined as a term in human language whose significant use or purpose is referential, whereas a symbol is a term whose significant use or purpose is expressive.* Thus, to cite some illustrations, the terms of mathematics and natural science are pure signs. Indeed, they are examples of signs as pure as any in actual human use. By contrast, the terms of a poem are symbols. Attention is called especially to the fact that these definitions are in terms of use or function. For example, the number "three" may have poignant expressive meaning for an individual mathematician, but this meaning is plainly irrelevant to the mathematical or scientific use of the term. Similarly the term "daffodil" is a sign to the botanist, but it is a symbol in Wordsworth's poem. What now are some significant differences and similarities between signs and symbols? The list that follows here is by no means exhaustive, but it will serve to get the main issues before us.

a. The first difference consists in their mode of occurrence to the human mind; symbols are apprehended with immediacy, whereas signs are apprehended by the mediation of discursive thinking or intellection. If we may use the term "intuition" for any form of immediate apprehension, we may say that symbols are intuited. Symbols occur to us, "strike us," or irrupt in our minds. They are data, literally *things given*—given, that is, in the mode of perceptual immediacy, or presentational immediacy.[13] Indeed, their subsequent functioning in our minds is related to their capacity to impress themselves upon us with immediacy and power. We might perhaps paraphrase Kant to say that symbols are perceived, but signs are conceived. We may also note in passing the frequent use of the metaphor of seeing for perception. It is often an extremely useful device, and surely not misleading if we are aware of its metaphorical character. How often men speak of seeing something, not in the sense of literal vision, but in the wider sense of perceptual immediacy in some act of cognition!

In this connection we must indicate briefly two prejudices that have characterized much empiricist philosophy. Early modern empiricism, as illustrated by Hume, assumed that the only kind of genuine and irreducible immediacy was that of sense data. On such a foundation Hume sought to erect his own epistemology and to launch his criticisms of other epistemologies. It is of course a well-known philosophic fact that some later empiricists such as James and Dewey greatly expanded the term "experience" to include relations and qualities other than sense data. However, it is also a fact that logical positivism or empiricism has exhibited either a marked preference for the older, stricter empiricism, or a serious ambiguity concerning the meaning of this key term. In some cases logical empiricists have moved back and forth between the stricter and wider empiricism.[14]

Here let me say plainly that I am taking a wider view of perceptual immediacy. It may be characterized as the edge of the mind's encounter with the world. The object of perception is something given and not made, discovered and not invented. Accordingly, it is at least possible that there may be other forms of immediacy than those located in sense data or the nerve endings of external sensation. If the world which our human minds encounter includes objects other than physical objects, as, for instance, other subjects or selves, it is at least an open possibility that these realities may on occasion directly impress themselves upon us in the mode of perceptual immediacy.

To widen the conception of immediacy in this manner is open to obvious dangers. How, for example, do we know for certain whether a given experience is a genuine datum rather than a projection of our own subjectivity? Are not our selves singularly prone to this kind of self-delusion? The reply is that we never do know with absolute certainty whether a particular experience of immediacy is something given or found rather than something delusively constructed and projected. Also, it may be added, we never know with absolute certainty in the case of sense data. Error is possible here as it is in other areas of the mind's life. Nevertheless, there are many tests that intelligent men apply to such situations. In symbol situations, loaded as they so often are with heavy charges of affection or emotion, such critical discrimination is as necessary as it is difficult.

The other frequent error of empiricist epistemologies follows from the first; it is to locate perception too easily, too exclusively, and too completely in particular organs of sensation, notably those of seeing, hearing, and touch. It is at least possible that perception may sometimes be an activity, not simply of my eye or ear, but of my whole integrated and functioning self. It is not just my eye that sees, but *I* who see. Such a view of perception seems necessary in order to comprehend the nature of artistic perception which in its way is as valid and irreducible a form of perception as that of the physical scientist or of the psychologist experimenting with his human subjects and their perception of color patches. Those same color patches assume a very different significance in the context of the artistic beholder's perception.

b. A second difference between signs and symbols consists in the presence in symbols, and absence in signs, of significant affective tone or emotion. Symbols are emotively charged terms; indeed, the precise quality of emotion that they elicit is fundamental to the symbol situation. In the case of signs, we have seen that whereas doubtlessly some emotion accompanies our apprehension, it is irrelevant to their function as signs. In symbols, on the other hand, this emotion has genuine relevance.

The terms "emotion" and "affection" very probably carry a deceptive and delusive simplicity. Contemporary prejudices and biases of a great many kinds have combined to lump together a very wide variety of human experiences as feeling or emotion or affection, and to classify them as subjective and noncognitive, and thus to have done with them. If our reference is to the full range of actual affective states of existing human selves, the issue is not so simple. Indeed, it may be asserted that the terms "emotion" and "feeling" are among the most perilously ambiguous in the English language.

Here obviously we cannot do more than very barely indicate the lines along which a start might be attempted in the clarification of these terms, and thus on this aspect of signs and symbols. Beginning with the affective states of existing selves and communities of selves, we may observe that they occur at least sometimes as significant forms of response to the objective world; and also that such states or responses sometimes have a significant cognitive component, even though at times it seems little more than a luminous spot in the experience of feeling. What is more immediately important for us here is to note that such experiences very often cluster about a symbol. The emotive or affective experiences are, in short, in their actual occurrence sometimes symbolically articulated, expressed, or elicited. Also in their actual occurrence they do not seem to be clearly or completely under any human rational control. Rather, such symbols appear to have their own necessity. Authentic and living symbols are thus never consciously contrived and controlled; rather, they happen in the encounter of a real self (or community of selves) with the real world. Conversely, contrived or constructed symbols and symbol systems are the unauthentic products of propagandists and advertising agencies. Furthermore, the life of authentic symbols and symbol systems consists in their continued capacity to elicit various highly specific kinds of emotive responses. When they are no longer capable of this, they may be presumed to be dead. The birth, life, and death of such symbols constitute a genuine mystery—in the precise philosophic sense of the much misused word "mystery." The affective character of symbols implies further that it is in terms of living and powerful symbols that men act. Symbols are terms that inspire action. Signs, on the other hand, are terms not in action but in intellection or reflection.

c. A further difference between signs and symbols is that signs are in no way implicated or involved in their referents. There is nothing of "twoness" about either the oral or written term "two." Such is not the case with symbols. As Tillich has written,[15] symbols participate in the reality they symbolize, meaning that symbols are themselves inextricably involved in the whole symbol situation.

This difference may be clarified by noting an implication, namely, that signs are always replaceable, whereas symbols seldom or never are so. Thus, every term in a com-

plex mathematical expression is replaceable, given sufficient time, by verbal prose. By contrast, in a well-con-
structed poem not a word is replaceable without doing
violence to the integral meaning of the symbol situation.
Wheelwright discusses this relation as one of semantic
discreteness (the difference between a sign and its referent)
and iconic signification (the relation of symbol to that
which it symbolizes).[16]

d. A sign has, ideally at least, one and only one meaning,
whereas a symbol often deliberately involves a wide variety of meanings. The ideal of univocal meaning is most
nearly approximated in such carefully controlled sign
situations as in mathematics and natural science. It is
nevertheless an ideal to be approximated as nearly as possible in all sign situations.

On the other hand, symbols often embody a wide variety
of meanings. The range of such multiform meanings is
from puns, and other similar word plays, to the widely
different intensions or connotations frequently gathered
into a single pregnant term. Often, too, a kind of conscious
and controlled ambiguity of symbolic terms adds a rich
suggestiveness to both poetry and prose. Many of these
features find illustration in nonverbal symbolisms as well
as symbolic words.

e. Still a further contrast may be made between definitional meaning and contextual meaning.[17] The former is
what we find in a dictionary or lexicon; and it is a fixed
core of meaning presumably present in every occurrence
of the word. But it is an observable fact that in many situations each particular occurrence of a word will show
nuances and differences not present in other occurrences
of it. Let us call this contextual meaning, that is to say,
meaning apprehensible in a particular context. These are

not so much different kinds of meaning as they are alternating moments or aspects in meaning. Thus, in learning a new word we fix an initial portion of meaning by definition and then seek an illustration in some use of the word. So begins a movement of alternation—a kind of leapfrog game between the two moments or aspects of meaning. A similar alternation may be observed as a man learns a new language.

Although both aspects are present in both signs and symbols, it is a safe generalization that in sign situations definitional meaning preponderates, while in symbol situations contextual meaning preponderates. Thus, in the natural sciences, once we have a clear and adequate definition of a word, we may be sure that subsequent uses will not differ significantly. In sharp contrast, the critic of poetry must assume as a major task the careful scrutiny of just how a given word functions and what it means in each particular situation.

f. As a final observation concerning signs and symbols, and as agenda for our study, we assert that the terms "meaning" and "truth" apply to both signs and symbols, but, conceivably at least, in different ways. We reject the claim of logical positivism that "meaning" and "truth" are applicable only to the propositions of science, and are specifically denied application to symbol situations. Nevertheless, we shall have to be prepared for significantly different applications of these terms to sign situations. This issue will be before us throughout our study, but particularly in Chapter V. Here let us simply remark that the terms "meaningful" and "true" are not univocal, but literally a whole package of distinguishable and variant items which it remains for us to unpack and inspect.

II Languages and Their Uses

❖ ❖

1. *What Is Language?*

In the previous chapter's consideration of signs and symbols the reader may well have felt that something important was left out. If so, he was right. It is indeed true that human language is an ordered system of signs and symbols. But the question persists: Is that all it is? Is that characterization fully adequate to human linguistic experience? What, we may well ask, is such a system for? *The answer now proposed is that a language is such a system used for some sort of human communication.* If we look from the order or structure of language to its use or function, we come directly upon the activity of human communication in one or more of its manifold aspects. Human communication, I shall argue in this chapter, is language in action or in use. Thus, conversely, a study of the human activity of communication may throw light upon the nature of language.

By the term "communication" I seek to denote the activity of discourse or saying in the widest possible sense in which it is applicable to human life. It is that activity by which an idea, a statement, an emotion, a nuance of meaning, that is in some sense "in" my mind comes presently to be "in" yours. Languages are the vehicles by which this process of communication takes place; and conversely, communication is what language is for. This is, in effect, a functional approach to language, though as we shall see in a later section of this chapter this view raises some formidable issues for us.

This approach to language involves some fairly drastic criticism of much recent and current linguistic philosophy. Linguistic philosophy has often been so fascinated with the logical and semantic structure of language that consideration of the human uses of language, if it takes place at all, is relegated to an appendix on "pragmatics."[1] To point out this fact is not to deprecate or belittle the study of structure. Indeed, logic and semantics, whatever else they may be, constitute the fundamental morality of language. However, to set structure in an active, functional human context may shed fresh light not only upon language but upon logical structure as well. It may also be pointed out that exclusive and fascinated preoccupation with structure and theory, apart from actual human use, which has so frequently characterized modern logic, often takes on the character of an escape from reality. Wittgenstein remarks that many investigators seek to examine language as they might examine a car with the motor idling.[2] Surely such study has its uses, but the good mechanic takes the car for a drive to observe the motor in action as it pulls the car along a road. The proposal here is to approach and study language in this latter way. This course follows the lead of the later Wittgenstein with his emphasis on the manifold uses of language, or as he puts it, the many "language games" which men play.

As in the preceding chapter, our study of language in action, or communication, may well begin by noting its foundation in biological nature. At this level or in this context, communication may be said to take place when a stimulus in one organism elicits a response from another organism. Thus, one dog growls and another shrinks or flees. The system of organic communication in a beehive or an anthill is often wonderful to contemplate.

As we move from animal species to man, many significant continuities may be observed here as in other aspects of experience. Like many of his animal cousins, man is gregarious. Hence, the grunts and squeaks of his vocal chords as well as the marks he makes on clay tablets or on paper function in ways similar to the interorganic signals of animal species. Nor are these organic continuities to be deplored, depreciated, or minimized. First of all, they constitute an order of facts for the redirection and changing of human practice, as the uses of psychology and medical science often show. Not least of all, if we are to take seriously the emphasis of much current theological study of man on the reality and goodness of the body, then clearly here is a body of facts that demands not only recognition but an entirely affirmative valuation. Truly, man is a living, functioning body; whatever else or whatever more he is, he is this, and his language mirrors this fact.

In the preceding chapter we located a genuine difference between men and animals in the peculiar kind of human awareness of self and world. Man is and remains an organism in a natural and social environment. However, aware of himself, he becomes a self confronting a world. It is this quality of human awareness which, supervening upon his organic signals, transforms them into the signs and symbols that are the terms of emergent human discourse and mentality. There seems general agreement in the conclusion that language is a phenomenon common and peculiar to man.[3] Here we offer an explanation of this generally accepted fact.

In a way analogous to the difference between human language and animal signals, we may observe a real difference in the manner in which human individuals are joined together in society, or conversely, in the way in which gregariousness impinges upon the individual. The human individual commits himself to his society and its tradition. One component of this tradition consists of human values or goods to be aspired to and striven for. This is to say that animal society or natural gregariousness is transformed at the distinctively human level of life into human community; and community assumes the aspect of a possibility or good to be striven for by human individuals and groups. To say "community" is to speak of free and mutual relations between human selves, relations that, conversely, are altogether basic to the selfhood of these selves. Furthermore, to say "community" is in an altogether basic sense to say "communication." It is this use of human language to which we must now turn.

2. *Language and Selfhood*

To approach language first of all as an activity is admittedly a sharply different view from that of much analytic or semantic philosophy. And to regard it as a kind of activity that expresses or articulates a human self, or significant aspects of selfhood, is to be doubly controversial. Yet this is precisely what is proposed. Many forms of semantic philosophy will respond that this is a merely subjective or emotive use of language, and regard that as the end of the matter. To the contrary, my contention here is that self-expression (or better, "self-articulation," for "self-expression" is a badly debased or ruined word) is a fundamental and unavoidable use of language greatly needing critical delineation and study.

To be sure, self-articulation must not be regarded as fully equivalent with selfhood. There are aspects and activities of a human self that are not involved in the activities of articulating or bodying forth that self in symbols, whether verbal or nonverbal. Nevertheless, the negative of this statement does seem to be true, namely, without self-articulation no selfhood is possible. Apparently, then, we must make the double assertion that a self necessarily involves self-articulation and that the same self transcends any given process of self-articulation. Expression seems to be a necessary, though not a sufficient, condition of self-hood. Here, then, we have a use of language, which, to say the least, is of elemental and fundamental importance to human selves.

Before proceeding farther, we must note briefly an error concerning the nature of human selfhood, egregiously prevalent in much modern and contemporary thinking on the subject. It may be put briefly in a figure of speech. Modern individualism in many of its diverse forms has assumed that a human self is a circle with individuality or individual identity at the center. About this center the circumference extends. The varieties of individualism range from that of Adam Smith through Emerson to bohemian individualism in the arts or to many brands of existentialist individualism. The human self, I wish to suggest, is not a circle with individuality at the center, but an ellipse with individuality and community as the two focal points. Man is inherently both an individual and a member of community. Take either away from him, and selfhood is either distorted or destroyed. Stated more affirmatively, the realization or fulfillment of both individual identity and community is essential to self-fulfillment. Both individuality and community are basic goods or values of the self. What is pertinent here is that language has an indispensable role to play in the achievement of both of these goods or goals of selfhood.

The lifelong and never completed process of self-realization or self-fulfillment begins in infancy. The baby's first emotive and expressive cries, so like those of animals, soon come to have a relation both to his own individuality and to his relation to other people and to his environment. As language begins to emerge from his infantile signals, both his relation to others and his own self-identity begin to assume the form of determinate problems. Gradually and fitfully, words and statements emerge. It is interesting to observe that the nominative singular "I" is often one of the last achievements of emerging language. Other selves and objects precede one's own self in the process of life development and self-articulation.

It is particularly important to note that in existential fact, awareness of self and awareness of objects and other selves, although always distinguishable, are never in fact separable. Neither occurs apart from the other. Rather, self and world appear to be polar or correlative concepts inescapably linked to each other. Selves, in any actual or engaged sense of the word, do not occur cooped up in their own subjectivity, but in relation to a world that includes both objects and other selves.

If we ask what kind of language expresses or articulates human selfhood, it is tempting to reply "expressive language" and let the matter rest. Yet observation of human selves shows us that all kinds or sorts of language can and do serve this expressive function. Although self-expression often does, for example, take place in the expletives of daily speech, or in the deliberately symbolic language of poetry, it is nevertheless a factual observation that some human selves find significant expression in the austerely nonexpressive signs and sign systems of mathematics and science. Once again, expression does not designate a kind of language but a use of language. It is also important to note that many nonverbal languages or symbol systems can also serve this same expressive purpose. Some selves find significant expression in the clothes they wear, others in their bodily actions or gestures, and still others in intellectual actions and activities. There is literally no fact about a man that cannot serve some expressive use or purpose. The relation between these various kinds of languages is a question we shall explore in section 4 of the present chapter.

A further question that we must press is the truth possibility and the truth claim of these various expressive languages. Logical positivism had an answer to this question as forthright as it was inadequate; it asserted bluntly that all forms of statement except those of logical and natural science possess at best only a subjective or emotive meaning.[4] The simplest kinds of expressive language, like the cries "Oh-oh" or "Ugh," offer the best examples of what these philosophers were talking about. Yet even here may it not be that one man can deceive another as to his true feelings, thus engaging in deception or falsehood? Again, do not actors daily simulate with great skill human attitudes that they do not feel, that are not part of their true or authentic personalities or at least not of their whole engaged personalities? Where there is the possibility of deception or falsehood, meaning and truth are also in some significant way involved.

Apparently even here in these most subjective aspects

of human selfhood we have some cognitive rules or stand-ards of utterance or saying. Two such criteria we have just illustrated, namely (*a*) the conformity of utterance to attitudes of the whole self, and (*b*) the conformity of ut-terance to the real self in its encounter with the world. These two categories taken together may be said to con-stitute the test of authenticity. A statement is authentic if, and only if, it does not conflict with, and does in fact articulate, significant aspects of the self of the man who utters it; and also if it expresses the life of this whole self in its engaged or active life, and not simply in a state of detachment from reality. Thus one says to another person, "This action is unlike you or is inconsistent with your personality." One speaks also of a coherent personality, or negatively, of an incoherent personality. One also some-times observes that an act or attitude clashes with factual experience.

The relation of selves to reality demands further devel-opment. As already argued, selves never occur cooped up in their own subjectivity but in relation to a world. An engaged self is a self-in-relation-to-the-world; and it is a world that includes at least other selves, physical nature, and the realm of norms or normative values which de-mand our action in accordance to them. For the engaged self or mind, a part of its experience is the apprehension and testing of facts that come as messages from the world outside the self. The apprehension of such facts constitutes not only an essential part of the mind's life, it also figures importantly in the expression or fulfillment of the appre-hending self.

All of this raises an extremely important issue relating to the possible meaning and truth of expressive statements. Many such statements, such as "Ugh" and "Oh," are obviously subjective, though even these cries of human feelings actually occur as responses to an objective situation and are adequate or inadequate to the situation and to the self's response to the situation. But as we make our way to more complex and objective forms of expressive utterance, such, for example, as works of art or moral imperative, a further question arises. Do we not find here criteria of truth beyond merely subjective authenticity?

The implications of this question will be with us to the end of our study. Are there noetic or cognitive elements or claims in the various forms of expressive utterance? Do these forms of language claim to tell us something about ourselves or our world? Are there statable and defensible ways in which the truth or falsity of expressive statement can be checked or tested? These are only a few facets of the root question of the truth or falsehood of expressive statement. At this point in our total argument it is relevant at least to indicate some of the significant ways in which the claim to cognition or noesis occurs in expressive language. Such statements may in the first place claim to convey or communicate a direct insight about some aspect of the self or the world. Lyric poems frequently make such claims. Again, the subjective attitudes of real, engaged human selves involved as they are with real facts of the real world, frequently imply a relation to objective facts as parts of the encountered world. Whenever an attitude entails or implies a factual statement, it is possible to look and see if the facts are as alleged, and to judge the attitude adequate or inadequate accordingly. Still, again, in many forms of expressive utterance there is a clearly implied system of referential statements which criticism may draw out, state explicitly, and then examine for adequacy. For example, an epic poem may sometimes bear this relation to a metaphysical system. In all these cases we observe the presence of three factors: subjective elements, such as thoughts or attitudes demanding expression; encountered facts; and a process of adequation of thought to things, or of statement to referent. The process of adequation will consist of an analysis of the expressive statements, often taking the form of a paraphrase or translation into verbal prose, and then a look at the pertinent facts.

A final observation about selves and self-articulation is necessary at this point. A self is a value-oriented and value-laden form of reality. In a homely way, this fact is obvious to writers of letters of recommendation. In seeking to describe a person, such letters seek to characterize the values to which he is committed, together with the stability of his commitment to them as integral aspects of his selfhood or personality. To be sure, this aspect of selfhood is always somewhat open and indeterminate and is never completely stable. However, no real characterization of an existent self is at all possible apart from the fundamental values of that self.

This observation is relevant to our problem of the language that articulates or bodies-forth the self, for it suggests correctly that this language is symbolic in character; the basic values of a self—moral, aesthetic, and other—are said or uttered in expressive language. More specifically, as we shall argue in Chapter IX on religious language, these basic values are articulated in a form of religious language called confession or witness.

This view of the value-centric or value-oriented character of the self has at one point been only half understood in some types of analytic or semantic philosophy.[5] Many semantic philosophers are ready enough to concede, and indeed to claim, that there are basic patterns of value in personal utterance which are not derivable as conclusions of rational argument. This is an important factual observation concerning human nature. However, it is obscured by a twofold error. The first error is to deny a priori any possible cognitive significance to direct expression. The second error consists in lumping together all valuations ranging from the preference of tea as against coffee to the decision concerning ultimate values under the single category such as "preference" or "liking." All such judgments, it is often alleged, have the form "I like this" or "I dislike that," or "I value this" or "I disvalue that." Yet upon serious critical inspection, there are significant and irreducible differences between the orders of valuation involved in the preference of coffee or tea, compared to those involved in a serious moral decision or in the judgment of relative significance of two works of art. The task of wise analysis will consist in unpacking this indiscriminately gathered package of preferences or values and carefully inspecting its diverse contents, item by item.

As this inspection takes place we shall also find that while there is a prerational or nonrational element in human valuation, there are frequently also rational elements as well. There is in many different fields of value all the difference in the world between an intelligent, informed liking as against an unintelligent and ill-informed one. For example, taste in the arts, while it has an immediate element, also has a rational and educable element. So, too, in religious experience, which is the field of ultimate valuation, there are wise and foolish faiths.

3. Language and the Objective World

It is important to underscore once more the fact that expression and reference, although distinguishable, are never, in any actual occurrence of language, separable from each other. The self, once more, never occurs cooped up in its subjectivity, but as a unique configuration of responses to the world; and expressive language mirrors this fact. Conversely, there is, in existential fact, always an expressive accompaniment to referential statements, however irrelevant that may be for our understanding of the significance of the latter.

Reference as well as expression has its biological foundation. It lies in the altogether practical uses of animal signals in effectively guiding the behavior of the animal in his environment. In his way the animal is a pragmatist, able and willing to choose and understand his signals in terms of their consequences for him and his kind. In the referential uses of language at the human level of life there is again both continuity and discontinuity. It still has an invaluable and practical significance to guide the course of life, to light man's pathway through the world. But there is another sense in which this language and the knowledge it contains constitutes an end in itself. The world is there to be known in much the same way as the mountain is there to be climbed. There are intrinsic and distinctive fulfillments in both cases. Moreover, human knowledge will be pragmatically effective in the long run only if it is pursued as an end in itself.

Modern linguistic philosophy has been largely and even exclusively concerned with the referential uses of language, often going so far as to define meaning and truth exclusively in terms drawn from the kind of referential language that is found in the natural sciences.[6] Logical positivism, for example, sought to limit meaningful statements to two kinds, namely, empirical statements capable of verification by reference to some sense datum, and logical statements which consist of the ground rules for making and organizing empirical statements. It also held that statements that are not reducible to either of these two kinds are meaningless, nonsensical, or merely subjective.[7]

Essential to this case is the verification principle which defines the meaning of a proposition in terms of the procedures necessary to verify or test it.[8] This principle is clearly an extrapolation from a well-known and highly successful feature of natural science and its distinctive method of knowing. Yet as a general definition of meaning, it is equally clearly unsatisfactory. For one thing, unless we have, prior to verification, some apprehension of the meaning of a statement, we will clearly not know how to set about the detailed business of verifying it. True, verification is often an important aspect of meaning, but it is certainly never the whole of it.

Positivism of any sort, logical or otherwise, confronts another formidable obstacle in its idea of the object of referential saying and knowing. A pure phenomenalism seeks necessarily to define this object as a closed system consisting of a finite number of sense data. Such a definition greatly simplifies the task of confirming or infirming a statement. But neat and simple as it is, it runs headlong into the brute fact that our actual human experience of physical objects does not conform to this description. Actual physical objects present themselves to us as more or less open systems. They have an inexhaustible character in the sense that any given list of sense data appears as a demonstrably incomplete description of any actual object.[9] If, as J. S. Mill wrote, an object is a permanent possibility of sensation, we must add that it is always a more or less open and indeterminate possibility. To this extent the phenomenalist or positivist viewpoint must be judged inadequate to our human experience of physical objects.

A related and equally thorny issue has to do with the question of whether or not a sense datum is a necessary feature of the perceptual act that confirms or infirms a statement. Admittedly such sense data are invariably and centrally involved in physical objects, but the question is whether physical objects are all the objects there are, or whether, on the other hand, there are nonphysical objects that present themselves to us through data that are non-sensory in character. The question is the momentous one of whether the realm of reliable knowledge is limited to that which can be tested by reference to sense data, or whether, plainly stated, it is possible to know nonphysical aspects of the world. If we take the latter alternative, as here proposed, we have on our hands the difficult problems of stating what these data are and how they occur to us.

In this connection we may also observe a certain ambiguity on the part of those who take the first alternative. In arguing critically against competing knowledge claims, they often press a rigorously empirical test, defining empiricism in terms of sense data; but when they turn to working out their own views they speak more adequately but more ambiguously of "publicly verifiable experience" without explicit reference to its sensory or nonsensory character.[10] Clearly this is living by a double epistemological standard! In this study we shall plainly take the alternative assumption that there are publicly verifiable experiences that have no sensory basis, undertaking the responsibility of pointing out what they are and how such verification takes place.

The positivist view of language, asserting two and only two forms of genuine meaning, is so inadequate to the facts of actual linguistic experience that it has led in the course of time to the development of nonpositivist or post-positivist philosophies of language. This movement of semantic or analytic philosophy from a positivist to a post-positivist outlook, while more discernible in contemporary British philosophy than in American philosophy, has some notable examples in the latter. Perhaps the most distinguished and influential philosopher to move in this direction is the late Ludwig Wittgenstein. His earlier *Tractatus Logico-Philosophicus* sought to limit intelligible language to the world of scientific fact, and concluded with the somewhat cryptic and oracular assertion, "Whereof one cannot speak, thereof one must be silent."[11] Did he mean that men must keep a Trappist vow of silence on all philosophic discussion involving human valuation? Wittgenstein's later *Philosophical Investigations* takes a sharply different view of the possibilities of speech.[12] Men are involved, he argues, in a great many different language games, each with its own rules and activities. In each case it is important for the players to know the rules, to play according to them, and to see what this language game, as compared with others, is good for. The metaphor of a game also suggests the author's concern for the problems of how a particular language comes to be and of the purposes it may serve. These views of Wittgenstein mark a radical break with the positivist view of language, and an assertion that there are many forms and possible forms of meaningful speech. Wittgenstein is, in other words, one of the main sources of the assumption that guides our present study, namely, that there are many different and distinctive uses of language. If one takes this view, then the questions that he puts to any particular instance of language are these: What use or function is this? What are its conditions and implications? How is it similar and different from other uses?

A similar proposal is Friedrich Waismann's suggestion of a many-leveled system of languages, made in his notable essay entitled "Language Strata."[13] Waismann begins with discussion of several kinds of variant word usage ranging from puns through different types of extended or metaphorical usage to the deliberate and controlled ambiguity that frequently characterizes the symbolic words of a poem. Particularly ambiguous, according to Waismann, are such words as "true" and "false," "meaningful" and "meaningless," which upon examination do not designate a single meaning but a whole cluster of meanings. Waismann's clue for isolating and identifying different meanings of these and other words is that significantly different uses often belong to different language strata or levels.[14] A particular language stratum is characterized by its own logic or rules of inference, as well as its own logical style and its own use of key words. On the same level, use remains uniform. By contrast, use or meaning changes as we move from level to level. Such ambiguities in fact define the fracture lines that separate strata from each other.[15] Each stratum, moreover, can be studied from within, micrologically, or from without, macrologically.

Waismann illustrates his idea of a many-leveled structure of language by such strata as those sense-data statements, of material-object statements, statements of half-faded memory images (where the law of the excluded middle does not hold), aphorisms (where linguistic meaning is very peculiar, each aphorism resembling a picture with its own frame around it, thus setting it off from others), or the level of poems, or of mysticism.[16] In this connection, he also suggests that behavioristic psychology errs in its attempts to reduce all language about the self to the single level of sense-data language.[17]

Such a multi-leveled view of language is surely not without its perils and problems. How, for example, do we avoid multiplying levels beyond necessity? One suspects that Waismann himself falls into this difficulty in his essay! How indeed do we distinguish a real or genuine level from spurious or imaginary levels which conceivably might be multiplied until every statement of every speaker would occupy its own self-enclosed level? Obviously we cannot here undertake full answers to these questions, but we can indicate a line of thought that will help to discriminate what is valid in Waismann's contentions. Perhaps the best way to ascertain whether one is dealing with a real or genuine level is to try it out in the actual business of human communication, noting whether semantical and logical rules remain fixed and continuous over the whole level and then shift as we move to another level, and also noting whether some significant kind of human communication does in fact take place. A language level is essentially the same thing as what we have been calling a language use or language function.

4. *Two Classifications of Language*

Discussion of language strata or language uses leads us to the more general question of the classification of languages. I shall sketch briefly two such classifications, noting some of the implications of each as well as some relations of each to the other. The two classifications are (*a*) natural and artificial, and (*b*) primary and derived; and, let it be added, it is as important to keep these classifications distinct from each other as it is easy to confuse them. As we shall see, in actual fact the two distinctions often coincide; natural languages are often also primary, and artificial languages are often also derivative. However, as we shall soon see, the meaning or the intension of the two classifications differs fundamentally, the first having to do with processes of origin, and the second with the field or domain in which the language is applied and interpreted.

A natural language is one that has come into being through the processes of custom and historical accident without any large or significant action or human contrivance or construction. By contrast, an artificial language is one that has been deliberately made or constructed. The term "artificial" in this respect is descriptive, and not pejorative; it means "a product of human artifice." If we look for illustrations of natural and artificial languages, all the several hundred known human languages ranging from Ugaritic to Latin, from Chinese to English, are natural languages. While they exhibit in varying ways different kinds of order in their syntax, there is no evidence that any human group ever assembled and said, "Let us construct a language." There is also relatively little evidence of any truly effective remaking or reformulation of linguistic order and rules. Rather, such natural languages are vast structures of custom reflecting the mingled order and disorder of the daily life of the cultures of the world.

By contrast to such natural languages, the propositions of *Principia Mathematica* or the language proposals of Carnap and his fellow semanticists are artificial. These clearly are made or constructed languages. While Esperanto falls short of one hundred percent making, it has large elements of fabrication in it, though its raw materials come from existing languages. We can also point to varying elements of making or contrivance in still other fields of linguistic experience. For example, many of the sciences take verbal prose and by redefining terms and creating new ones, by changing some rules and making new ones, create special languages appropriate to their special needs and tasks.

If we may regard mathematics as a language, we may also ask how much of nature and of artifice is to be found in it. Simple numeration of some sort goes back to a prehistoric past; clearly it is natural rather than artificial. Other natural elements in mathematics might also be pointed out. But on such natural foundations vast and impressive constructions have been erected, particularly in the modern development of mathematics. What is true of mathematics is true of other languages. So then, looking over the varieties of linguistic experience, the general picture ranges from purely natural languages through languages with varying degrees of artifice to the semantic and logical possibility of a completely made or constructed language.

The second classification of language is that of primary and derivative; and it refers not to the processes by which a language comes into being but to the fields or domains of experience in which it is deployed or to which it is applied. The concept of application or interpretation here involved is similar to the same idea in mathematics; pure mathematical symbols are interpreted or applied to aspects of the real world, thus becoming applied mathematics.[18] A primary language is one whose field of application or interpretation is the whole common daily experience of a community of men. Thus it is a fact that most natural languages are also primary. A derivative language is one whose domain or field of application is some particular and limited aspect of the whole field of human experience for which this language or symbol system has particular fitness or competence. What constitutes fitness or competence cannot be stated in general, for it varies according to the distinctive requirements of each specific kind of human experience and the communication of this form of experience.

Since the relation between primary and derivative languages is a matter of considerable importance to the thesis of the succeeding chapters, its implications must be traced further. The verbal prose of daily life is primary language for most men. As I shall presently argue, such ordinary or common language has in it poetic, scientific, moral, religious, philosophic aspects, and many more besides. Indeed, these and other similar human concerns are first known to us as aspects of common human experience and the language that expresses or articulates this experience. In subsequent chapters I shall endeavor to show that, beginning with common experience and its language as a base of operations, these various human concerns may be regarded as the construction or derivation of languages uniquely appropriate to particular areas of experience and the peculiar qualities involved. Thus, for example, both science and art may be regarded as such derivative languages. Both are based upon identifiable aspects of common human experience and common language; but both of these cases present the development of a derivative language or symbol system peculiarly appropriate to the kinds or qualities of experience with which science and art are respectively concerned. For example, the scientist and artist looking at the same object or situation will be attracted to sharply different aspects of it, and their respective languages are derived with a view to stating and communicating these respective aspects of experience.

Some such derived languages are largely or entirely verbal. For example, literature is an art constructed of words. But other such derived languages, such as painting, music, or the mathematical language of physical science, are nonverbal. The nonverbal systems of signs or symbols may still be termed languages precisely in the measure that they are systems or signs or symbols used for some sort of human communication. A language, once more, is a vehicle of human communication.

For the life of the human mind that creates and uses

these systems of signs and symbols, the relation between primary and derivative languages may be compared to the work of the explorer who sets up a base on known and inhabited land, and from there fares forth into new and unknown land, seeking understanding of the new, and bringing back reports to his base. From his base in common experience and its language, the artist or the scientist sets out; to it he returns for reorientation, redirection, as well as interpretation and appraisal of his findings. His work, like that of the explorer, is one of pushing into new areas to see what of human significance lies there. His art or his science is his statement of what he finds. Thus it is that the language in which he expresses and communicates his findings is proportioned to those findings; but it is also his attempt to make them known to his fellowmen who presumably have not yet ventured into the new and unknown land.

For readers who dislike allegory let me try to state briefly and nonfiguratively some elements of this relationship between primary and derivative languages. As the explorer moves from known to unknown land, so the mind moves from primary language and its terms and the forms of experience which they express to derivative language with its categories and the domains of experience to which they apply. So far as definition is concerned, this is an asymmetric relation. Also, as I shall argue in subsequent chapters, each of these derivative languages has distinctive capacities for articulating aspects of experience which are peculiarly significant within its domain. For example, it is possible to say things in music or painting that may only partially and imperfectly be translated into the verbal prose of primary language. So it is that a pianist, once asked what his selection meant, replied by playing it over again. Just these categories of communication and no others are necessary to bring us what he has to say.

The hypothesis that I shall attempt to develop and defend is that art, science, philosophy, and religion (and very possibly many other human concerns as well) may fruitfully be approached as such derivative languages, each having a basis in common experience and common language, but developing its own distinctive categories for the statement and communication of those particular aspects of human experience with which it is distinctively concerned.

This hypothesis involves many formidable problems that I shall attempt to face as discussion proceeds; but one such problem may appropriately be stated and met at this point. It is often claimed that the idea of derivative language stretches the word "language" beyond its elastic limits. In opposition to the view that I have taken, the claim is made that we should, in all logical and linguistic propriety, limit the term "language" to the primary and natural language of verbal prose. Only this activity is language in any literal or real sense. Thus, for example, Edward Sapir's excellent definitional essay on language in the *Encyclopedia of Social Sciences* covers this and only this activity.[19] What I have here termed derivative language is from this other viewpoint regarded as language only in a metaphorical sense, and the metaphor is regarded as dubious. For example, Susanne Langer seeks to limit the term "language" to systems of signs or symbols that exhibit the traits of definite intension or dictionary meaning, translatability, syntax, and grammar.[20]

Clearly, a strong case can be made for this narrower use of the word. Yet I think it is possible to point to enough situations where the term "language" is unquestionably appropriate but which lack one or more of Sapir's or Langer's essential traits. And it is also possible to point to situations of derived languages that possess a significant number of these traits. For example, consider the absence of the normal physical features of oral or written language in the case of Helen Keller or Laura Bridgman. Yet are we to say that these remarkable people lack language? Again, in the case of some primitive and Oriental languages, Mrs. Langer's list of essential traits is only very imperfectly fulfilled. For instance, many Oriental languages lack stable parts of speech. On the other hand, in the case of the formal structure of music, painting, and other nonverbal arts, there are impressive analogies to the rules of grammar, syntax, and logic. Just how many of the essential features are necessary, and just what degree of similarity in these features is necessary, to justify the use of the word "language" for a system of signs or symbols used for some purpose of communication? Frankly no clearcut answers —and surely no generally agreed upon answers—seem possible. In view of such issues I have found it more adequate to this whole area of experience to take the broader definition of language, and then to distinguish among the various kinds and levels of language, noting differences between natural and artificial languages and between primary and derivative languages.

5. *Common and Uncommon Languages*

Among the most popular and suggestive proposals of current semantic philosophy is that which is often termed "ordinary" or "common" language. This is, in a word, a proposal that philosophers speak the language of intelligent nonphilosophic men, or at least that philosophers should test their philosophic formulations by reducing or translating them into such ordinary or common language.

This view of the philosophic task owes its origin to the thought of Professor G. E. Moore and has been widely popularized in the writings of his students and disciples.[21] In the proposal to speak ordinary or common language, several distinguishable claims are implicit. Let us turn this analytic method upon itself by asking what some of these claims are; for behind the facade of somewhat disingenuous simplicity, many important and arguable issues may be observed.

a. Perhaps the clearest claim of this approach to philosophy may be described as a protest against philosophic alteration, sometimes unconscious and thus uncritical, and sometimes deliberate, of terms drawn from ordinary nonphilosophic discourse. It is misleading—such is the contention—for philosophers to pick up terms and alter their meaning without plainly telling us what they are doing. This claim may surely be amply substantiated from the writings of recent and current philosophy. One might perhaps add as a further illustration of this phenomenon the use of the term "nonsense" in the writings of many of the semantic analysts.

b. A further claim clearly implicit in the common language proposal is a tacit assertion concerning the nature of philosophy. It may be put both negatively and affirmatively. Negatively stated, the claim is that philosophic reasoning is not an esoteric method for laying hold of areas of supposed reality beyond the reach of ordinary nonphilosophic thinking and experience. Philosophy—so it is assumed—has no special or secret access to reality not open to the common man. Furthermore, its proper domain is not some distant realm beyond the reach of common sense and science, but rather common human experience. Again, it is possible to see in such claims a valid criticism of much speculative philosophy that has misconstrued its task by just such extrapolations from experience.

Affirmatively stated, this method of philosophy is the rigorous and comprehensive analysis of the common experience of men. In this respect the method of philosophic thinking differs from that of ordinary nonphilosophic reasoning only in its rigor and comprehensiveness. Its domain differs from that of other forms of thinking mainly in its deliberate expansion to include all of human experience of the world. In this connection I shall argue in Chapter VIII that one significant distinguishing trait of philosophic statements is the presence of a completely unrestricted use of the term "all."

c. Still a further implication has to do with the meaning of the word "common." In the common language philosophy it does not always appear to refer to the language of nontechnical daily experience. It can, for example, refer to established usage in such highly technical fields as physical science. Here again the critical contention appears to have both a negative and an affirmative aspect. On the negative side, the claim seems to be that it is no part of the philosopher's proper task to tell the scientist his business. Yet, it *is* distinctly the philosopher's business to note what the scientist believes, practices, and says, and to relate those to other generic human concerns within the inclusive totality of being or reality.

Still a further implication lies hidden in the history and sociology of the word "common." The community in which this form of communication is applied and used might be described as the Anglo-Saxon culture or society of late nineteenth and early twentieth century. It might even be said to be further limited to the academic sub-community of this culture. One observer has even suggested that common language is the language of the common room of the English universities.

If we look at this domain with the help of social science and its emphasis on cultural relativism, we will see a great number of other common languages in human history at different times and places, which show both similarities to, and differences from, this particular "common language" of current philosophic theory. The significant point for us is that if we accede to the term "common language" in this usage we find ourselves with an exceedingly provincial, ethnocentric view of both language and philosophy. It has the force of elevating the preconceptions and prejudices of a small group of British and American philosophers into a normative statement of what philosophy is and ought to be. In sharpest contrast, we must insist that there are as many common languages as there are historical communities of human culture. Similarly there are as many views of philosophy. Bertrand Russell is said to have remarked that Moore's common language philosophy expressed the metaphysics of stone age man.

d. Finally, concerning the term "common" or "ordinary" language, let us note that few attempts have so far been made to explore its value-oriented aspects. Rather, the insistence is upon commonly acknowledged fact conceived as objectively, impersonally, and value-neutrally as possible. Against ambiguity and obscurantism, this insistence has an obvious and significant force. Yet the primary and natural languages of men also show in their various expressive or symbolic aspects the many common value orientations of men and cultures. Michael Foster's essay *"We" in Modern Philosophy* constitutes a significant beginning in pointing out the normative significance of what are ostensively indicative statements.[22] How often valuations hide behind purely declarative statements of facts, or masquerade behind them! Thus Foster asserts that when Moore and others write "we teach" or "we hold," they are not asserting facts but engaging in confession in a manner similar to the words of the Chalcedonian creed, which also begins its overtly normative statements with the words "we teach . . ."

Taken more broadly, there is at least a clear possibility that such generic human concerns as art, morality, and religion, to mention only a few of the many forms of human valuations, will find significant and distinctive expression in the common or ordinary languages of the various human cultures. Thus we ought least to be open to the possibility of acknowledging and studying these aspects of men's linguistic structures as a part of any common language philosophy, in the literal sense of these words. For example, what religious valuations get expressed or uttered in the common language of our time? Men often confess and witness to their faith, not in the special language of particular religions, but in common or ordinary languages. Sometimes, too, they do so without knowing that they do so.

These considerations lead us back again to a main thesis or hypothesis of this book. This hypothesis, which we will elaborate and test over several chapters, is that, embodied and articulated in various primary and natural languages of men are at least the sources of such concerns as science, philosophy, art, and religion. Beginning as aspects of common experience and common language, these activities may be regarded and studied as the development of derivative languages suited to the articulation of these respective forms and aspects of man's experience of the world. We have compared them to explorers who set out from bases on known, inhabited land, to which periodically they return for supplies, reorientation, and reappraisal. However, their distinctive work consists of exploration of new and unknown lands and the reporting of their findings.

The metaphor of the explorer raises the question of whether many human concerns (among them both the practice and the study of religion) do not require uncommon languages. Surely the explorer in reporting his findings is involved with both common and uncommon language. He must, to be sure, make himself intelligible to the men back home. Yet often he seeks to tell them about new lands and new realities, and for this purpose his language must frequently have uncommon or extraordinary qualities.

Many of the human concerns with which this book deals —art, philosophy, religion, and in its way, natural science too—all are involved with both common and uncommon language. To cite just one illustration among innumerable possibilities, the language of the Judeo-Christian or Biblical tradition was at many points radically discontinuous with the religious language of the Hellenistic world in which Christianity got its start. From the elemental term "God," which had sharply different meanings for Biblical monotheism and for Hellenistic polytheism, onward through the whole vocabulary of faith and theology, the fathers of the Christian church wrestled with the problem of common and uncommon language. How could they be intelligible to their contemporaries without distorting their new religious ideas?[23] Christianity and other religions as well have continued to face this issue wherever they have confronted new cultures and new languages, and indeed new linguistic situations. So, too, have philosophy and the arts and natural science. Perhaps we may generalize by saying that the common language viewpoint is, among other things, a proposal of conservatism, with both the strength and the weakness of this attitude, while the alternative proposal of uncommon language entails in its way the opposite proposal of historical or social change with all its characteristic perils and opportunities.

III Images and Imagination

❖ ❖

1. *Definition of Terms*

What precisely is an image? What is imagination, and how is it related to other aspects of the mind's life? How are images and imagination involved in the human activities of thinking and saying which we seek to study? With questions of this sort we will be concerned in the present chapter. By adding image and imagination to language, signal, sign, and symbol we complete the list of basic terms and ideas necessary for the study of religious language that follows in the rest of the book.

Images and imagination have been staple subjects of philosophic reflection and writing from earliest Greek days to the present, Plato,[1] Spinoza,[2] and Hegel[3]—to cite significant names from different centuries—are only a few of the major philosophers deeply concerned with this subject. For many philosophers, including the three just mentioned, a basic and deeply rooted preference for rational order, coherence, and system has led to a largely negative valuation of images and imagination. Such philosophers observe that images do not seem to conform to certain basic logical rules, and thus they conclude images to be of a "lower" order of being, less "real," and less "rational" than ideas and rational statements. For such views, imagination is often regarded as a kind of miasmal swamp in which the basic patterns and rules of order give way to chaos. Yet despite these prejudices, images and imagination continue to interest philosophers.

In the present age they also constitute objects of study for an extremely wide and varied group of inquirers, ranging from artists and art critics to psychoanalysts, social psychologists, advertisers, and propagandists. It should be clear too that students of religion also have an important stake in this study.

Obviously these issues are large, complex, and difficult. Hence it would be presumptuous to claim anything like a solution or an answer. We can, however, aim at initial clarification of a kind such that we will be able to use the words "image" and "imagination" without serious misunderstanding or distortion, and with at least a beginning of understanding. We seek also to relate these terms to the other basic terms of our discourse and to the main goals of our inquiry.

Let us then begin with a provisional definition of an image as any immediate datum of human awareness. Immediacy denotes a mode of apprehension in the mind's life, contrasted with the mediated mode of apprehension that is characteristic of ideas. Images are data—literally things given. As we sometimes say, they strike us or occur to us—metaphors that point to immediacy of apprehension. Images are thus pictures flashed upon the screen of the mind. The simplest and most familiar forms of images for philosophically minded readers are sense-data images such as colors and sounds; but as we shall soon see, they are by no means the only kinds of images. Symbols too occur in the mode of "presentational immediacy," as Whitehead reminds us.[4] They too are "presentational forms," as Mrs. Langer persuasively argues.[5] It is pertinent to add that in their actual occurrence, most, if not all, images come to us loaded with an affective or emotive charge, which is a significant aspect of the datum.

Attention must be called to a widespread ambiguity in the use of the term "image." As here defined, it is an aspect of the mind's life, or in more traditional terms, a peculiar content of consciousness. However, the term is also used in an apparently widely different way to designate a peculiar kind of term in human statement or discourse. For example, writers and literary critics speak of images as the basic terms of literary discourse. Thus they speak of the images and imagery of a poem or a novel. Similar usage can also be found in the case of other arts, such as painting or music, where again image means a basic term in artistic discourse or experience.

Actually this second use turns out to be a harmless ellipsis. The primary reference of the term is to a peculiar aspect of the mind's life. Using it in a secondary and derivative sense to designate a term in various kinds of human discourse, what we mean is a term that is capable of eliciting the appropriate and distinctive kind of image in the mind of the reader or beholder. Thus, for example, a poetic image is a configuration of words which is capable of eliciting a very special kind of image in the reader's mind. The nature and significance of artistic images is a matter that we shall consider in some detail in Chapter VII. Here we simply note that the two uses are actually one. Meticulous readers are invited to fill out the ellipsis, reading for the second use of image "a term in discourse capable of eliciting an image in the primary sense."

Imagination may be defined in Augustine's phrase as the

place of images; or more prosaically, it is the human mind's peculiar capacity for images.[6] It is particularly important not to prejudge the nature of this capacity in the light of any epistemological theory or bias, but rather first to attempt to look at the human imagination factually and descriptively as it actually occurs. We should, in other words, seek a phenomenology of the imagination, in the sense of a detailed description of the immediately given aspects and qualities of the experience. In the historic literature of this subject, some remarkable paragraphs from Book X of Augustine's *Confessions*[7] occupy so unique a place that I shall quote them in detail. Augustine speaks of memory, but in context it is soon apparent that memory is really imagination in its temporal reference to the past, and that his words constitute a phenomenological description of human imagination. The reader will also note Augustine's foreshadowing of modern psychoanalytic understanding of imagination.

"And I enter the fields and spacious halls of memory, where are stored as treasures the countless images that have been brought into them from all manner of things by the senses. There, in the memory, is likewise stored what we cogitate, either by enlarging or reducing our perceptions, or by altering one way or another those things which the senses have made contact with; and everything else that has been entrusted to it and stored up in it, which oblivion has not yet swallowed up and buried.

"When I go into this storehouse, I ask that what I want should be brought forth. Some things appear immediately, but others require to be searched for longer, and then dragged out, as it were, from some hidden recess. Other things hurry forth in crowds, on the other hand, and while something else is sought and inquired for, they leap into

view as if to say, 'Is it not we, perhaps?' These I brush
away with the hand of my heart from the face of my
memory, until finally the thing I want makes its appearance out of its secret cell. Some things suggest themselves
without effort, and in continuous order, just as they are
called for—the things that come first give place to those
that follow, and in so doing are treasured up again to be
forthcoming when I want them. All of this happens when
I repeat a thing from memory.

"All these things, each one of which came into memory
in its own particular way, are stored up separately and
under the general categories of understanding. For example, light and all colors and forms of bodies came in
through the eyes; sounds of all kinds by the ears; all smells
by the passages of the nostrils; all flavors by the gate of the
mouth; by the sensation of the whole body, there is
brought in what is hard or soft, hot or cold, smooth or
rough, heavy or light, whether external or internal to the
body. The vast cave of memory, with its numerous and
mysterious recesses, receives all these things and stores
them up, to be recalled and brought forth when required.
Each experience enters by its own door, and is stored up in
the memory. And yet the things themselves do not enter it,
but only the images of the things perceived are there for
thought to remember. And who can tell how these images
are formed, even if it is evident which of the senses
brought which perception in and stored it up? For even
when I am in darkness and silence I can bring out colors
in my memory if I wish, and discern between black and
white and the other shades as I wish; and at the same time,
sounds do not break in and disturb what is drawn in by
my eyes, and which I am considering, because the sounds
which are also there are stored up, as it were, apart. And

these too I can summon if I please and they are immediately present in memory. And though my tongue is at rest and my throat silent, yet I can sing as I will; and those images of color, which are as truly present as before, do not interpose themselves or interrupt while another treasure which had flowed in through the ears is being thought about. Similarly all the other things that were brought in and heaped up by all the other senses, I can recall at my pleasure. And I distinguish the scent of lilies from that of violets while actually smelling nothing; and I prefer honey to mead, a smooth thing to a rough, even though I am neither tasting nor handling them, but only remembering them.

"All this I do within myself, in that huge hall of my memory. For in it, heaven, earth, and sea are present to me, and whatever I can cogitate about them—except what I have forgotten. There also I meet myself and recall myself—what, when, or where I did a thing, and how I felt when I did it. There are all the things that I remember, either having experienced them myself or been told about them by others. Out of the same storehouse, with these past impressions, I can construct now this, now that, image of things that I either have experienced or have believed on the basis of experience—and from these I can further construct future actions, events, and hopes; and I can meditate on all these things as if they were present. 'I will do this or that'—I say to myself in that vast recess of my mind, with its full store of so many and such great images —'and this or that will follow upon it.' 'O that this or that could happen!' 'God prevent this or that.' I speak to myself in this way; and when I speak, the images of what I am speaking about are present out of the same store of memory; and if the images were absent I could say nothing at all about them.

"Great is this power of memory, exceedingly great, O my God—a large and boundless inner hall! Who has plumbed the depths of it? Yet it is a power of my mind, and it belongs to my nature. But I do not myself grasp all that I am. Thus the mind is far too narrow to contain itself. But where can that part of it be which it does not contain? Is it outside and not in itself? How can it be, then, that the mind cannot grasp itself? A great marvel rises in me; astonishment seizes me. Men go forth to marvel at the heights of mountains and the huge waves of the sea, the broad flow of the rivers, the vastness of the ocean, the orbits of the stars, and yet they neglect to marvel at themselves. Nor do they wonder how it is that, when I spoke of all these things, I was not looking at them with my eyes—and yet I could not have spoken about them had it not been that I was actually seeing within, in my memory, those mountains and waves and rivers and stars which I have seen, and that ocean which I believe in —and with the same vast spaces between them as when I saw them outside me. But when I saw them outside me, I did not take them into me by seeing them; and the things themselves are not inside me, but only their images. And yet I knew through which physical sense each experience had made an impression on me.

"And yet this is not all that the unlimited capacity of my memory stores up. In memory, there are also all that one has learned of the liberal sciences, and has not forgotten—removed still further, so to say, into an inner place which is not a place. Of these things it is not the images that are retained, but the things themselves. For what literature and logic are, and what I know about how many different kinds of questions there are—all these are stored in my memory as they are, so that I have not taken in the image and left the thing outside. It is not as though a sound had sounded and passed away like a voice heard by the ear which leaves a trace by which it can be called into memory again, as if it were still sounding in mind while it did so no longer outside. Nor is it the same as an odor which, even after it has passed and vanished into the wind, affects the sense of smell—which then conveys into the memory the *image* of the smell which is what we recall and re-create; or like food which, once in the belly, surely now has no taste and yet does have a kind of taste in the memory; or like anything that is felt by the body through the sense of touch, which still remains as an image in the memory after the external object is removed. For these things themselves are not put into the memory. Only the images of them are gathered with a marvelous quickness and stored, as it were, in the most wonderful filing system, and are thence produced in a marvelous way by the act of remembering."

2. *The Nature and Growth of Imagination*

In the first chapter, transcendence was characterized as the observable trait of the human mind "to go beyond" or "to go across," and was located in that aspect of the mind called the imagination. The implications of these assertions must now be traced out as we turn our attention to the nature and significance of imagination. Such a power is an observable property of images in their actual occurrence in the mind. They are seldom or never fixed, closed, predictable, or tied to a given context of experience. Rather, they exhibit in their actual occurrence and behavior a peculiar kind of spontaneity, unpredictability, and inexhaustibility. Further, seldom are images wholly under human control; rather, they come and go in part at least, independent of our desire and volition. It is to these and similar observable traits of the mind's images that the term "transcendence" primarily refers.

The life of images and imagination also shows a temporal development in individual personality which, if it is baffling in its complexity, is nevertheless extremely important for the whole varied life of the person. It is so both for the person's own self-understanding and for the student of personality working at the problem of the dynamics of personality. If with William James we may postulate for the newborn infant's mind a big, buzzing, booming confusion, we may also suppose that more or less determinate and defined images soon begin to emerge from this original chaos. From the first, some of these images express the newborn human being's insistent needs, together with the resistance or support of the environment to those needs. If Sigmund Freud was at all correct in his observation of the situation, from the traumatic shock of birth onward there are pains and resistances that soon become internalized as frustrations and anxieties, and make war upon such pleasant images as the softness of the mother's touch, the visual image of her face, or the tactile as well as visual images of breast or bottle, the warmth of the crib or the well-being of a full stomach. These indeed are only a few of the full range and variety of images that flash upon the screen of the infant's mind.

Certain recurrent images, especially those of tactile, visual, and auditory sensation soon converge, and together with general relations of support and resistance of the environment to the organism serve to define a world of commonsense things. The idea of resistance offered to the self incidentally appears to be a basic element in the idea of reality; the real is that which resists the self. The images of real things soon come in the child's mind to have a trustworthy representational significance; they stand for things which are "there." This element of experience is undoubtedly facilitated and developed by learning to talk, for words come to stand for or represent these representational images of things. Yet it is equally important to add that other aspects of the child's mind remain unsubdued by such conceptions of commonsense, rational order. Behind and beyond this fixed and objective world, and also deep within the well of the self, persists a world of dream and fantasy, at once terrifying and fascinating.

The main line of development of the human self toward maturity continues in the direction of its own unified relation to the world. Indeed, if Freud's view of the ego is correct, the self or ego *is* just this way of dealing or coping with the world. Yet along with this close embrace with the world, the life of free, inward subjectivity also continues and deepens. In psychoanalytic terms, frustration and repression force the development of a deep, subconscious or subliminal area of selfhood. In other words, those images which for some reason are unacceptable to the ego are forced into an underground prison house, where they live a buried life, anonymous but powerful in the life of personality.

Whatever one's estimate of Freud and of psychoanalysis generally, it is possible to observe here a fundamental aspect of the mind's life. Speaking from the viewpoint of philosophic idealism, Richard Kroner has termed it the subjective imagination.[8] In the subjective imagination, images do not have any immediately or directly representational relation to the objective world. Rather, they are pictures flashed upon the screen of the mind in all sorts of apparently unpredictable and spontaneous ways. They are the dreams, the daydreams, and the images of free association, so troublesome to the neat and tidy minds of philosophic rationalists, yet so important to human activities ranging from art to psychology and psychoanalysis.

To speak of human imagination in Freudian, or more generally in psychoanalytic, terms undoubtedly raises basic questions, such as the whole difficult issue of the justification of the fundamental psychoanalytic categories and their relation to human personality.[9] Here it may only be remarked in passing that despite egregious errors, the results of psychoanalysis constitute an intellectual achievement too massive to be shrugged off by methodological or logical misgivings. Let us then use this new and growing body of knowledge, but let us do so with critical caution.

Another perhaps more pertinent question turns upon the fact that psychoanalysis is centrally an art for healing sick minds. Since this is so, the issue is its relation to such "normal" enterprises of the mind as art, ethics, or religion, not to speak of critical thinking. Can we study the images that form the case history of the neurotic mind or self and draw conclusions about the nature of the artist's imagination? Clearly there is a similarity in the fact that in both cases the mind has to do with expressive images, but equally there is a difference in the kind of expressive meaning to be found in them, and also in the objectivity, or what has been termed the aesthetic distance of the images of artistic imagination. In a way similar to art, so also in the case of religious experience, men have to do with expressive images. Later in this chapter I shall argue that religious experience comes to us through the mediation of authoritative images that are impressed upon the mind. But this raises immediately the question of the relation of this kind of experience to the compulsive images of neurotic experience. Indeed, did not Freud himself consider religion essentially a neurotic illusion?[10] Into these intriguing and significant issues we cannot go beyond the bare remarks that a careful inspection of the images will reveal differences as well as similarities, and that from psychological evidence *alone* it is not possible to draw factual and logical conclusions.

Meanwhile, I do wish to assert as strongly as possible my belief that a critical use of psychoanalytic categories throws significant light upon human imagination and images in all their varied aspects. Freud, to be sure, was not the first man to call attention to the deep well of the self; Plato and Augustine, to mention just two names, had made their descent into the self, seeking in these subconscious depths the meaning of dreams, daydreams, and subjective images. Whether we make this exploration with the guidance of Freud or these others is not so important as that the exploration be made. It is a sound instinct to take knowledge where we find it.

In at least one sense the depth metaphor for this aspect of the imagination is misleading. The psychoanalytic conception of repression asserts that rejected elements of consciousness are forced into the cellar or prison house of the subconscious mind, where they lead a hidden but influential life. Surely there is repression or inhibition in the life of every civilized person, healthy or neurotic; and for the neurotic, undoubtedly repression is an essential cause of his condition. Yet for the healthy person, and with particular reference to what we shall presently term the creative images of his mind's life, certainly a much more apt metaphor for the imagination is that of conscious mind as a bright center of light fading out to darkness in all directions. Out of the darkness and into the light of conscious awareness come the images that are the elements or terms of our conscious, subjective life. Indeed, the conscious life of a human subject consists primarily of just this play of images, to which Kroner has given the term "subjective imagination."

The subjective imagination, while it may be the first word, is happily not the last word concerning this aspect of the mind's life. For the restless urge of imagination "to go beyond" means also the urge to go beyond the self, in other words, to relate self to world, subject to object. In Kroner's view, objective imagination is that power of the mind, and that phase of the mind's life, in which the self or subject is prompted to seek relation to the world of objects, to cross the gulf between subject and object. Specifically it takes the form of the mind's active capacity to seek images adequate to referents in the objective world (the objective world including whatever lies beyond the bounds of one's own self). Again we note a pertinent meaning of the term "transcendence"; for the term "world," as we shall presently see, is no fixed and final concept whose meaning can be settled once for all. Rather, it is a totality concept having an inexhaustibility which in turn impels a lifelong and never-ending search for adequacy on the part of every human mind.

Considered with the seriousness it deserves, objective imagination is one of the most fundamental and difficult problems of all philosophy. We shall return to it for further treatment in Chapter V. Here, having noted that there is in fact a capacity and urge of this sort in the human subject, we must also point out that it is an active power of the mind, a doing and not a passive undergoing. It is a power of the active or engaged mind. Objective imagination, then, in a word, *is* the human mind in its active encounter with the world that lies beyond its own frontiers.

We must at this point also briefly note two further characteristics of human imagination, of considerable theological significance, and of importance to later phases of our study: (*a*) its ambiguous finite-infinite character, and (*b*) its participation in all the corruptions in which human nature is involved. As we have already seen, imagination shows in its spontaneity and inexhaustibility a kind of indeterminate character. It exhibits that tendency to push beyond any fixed or definite limits which makes the term "infinite" appropriate. But now we must observe, on the other hand, that the raw material of this imagination seems invariably to come from the definite, limited experience of a mortal self and its finite relation to reality. The mortal foundation and source of its varied and infinite life is this very limited base of one man's experience of nature and society.

Imagination is thus not only finite and creaturely, but it also participates—one might almost say, willingly, actively, and eagerly—in the corruptions and distortions of the mind's life that are wrought by man's self-interest or egocentricity. There is thus a form of distortion peculiar to subjective imagination, namely, the creation of illusory or delusory images, which distorts man's relation to the world and even cuts him off from it. In psychological terms this is a significant aspect of neurosis; in the theological terms of rabbinical Judaism, it is the "evil imagination of the heart."[11] Which interpretation we accept is less important than to recognize the facts of the case. These observable tendencies of human imagination are significant not only to the psychologist seeking to diagnose and prescribe for neuroses, but, as we shall see, to the philosopher and the theologian as well. Indeed they are important to all who wish to see man and his imagination as they actually exist.

3. *Images and Ideas*

The difference between images and ideas or concepts may be approached, as we have done, through their respective modes of apprehension by the mind. In contrast to the presentational immediacy of images, ideas occur in the mode of intellection or discursive thinking. There is thus a difference in the way images and ideas come into being. Images, as we have said, are simply presented to us. Ideas or concepts are constructed or fabricated by the mind out of the raw materials of images through a process appropriately called "abstraction." An idea or concept consists of an observed similarity of some significant sort in a group of images. To observe this relation in things and their images, to separate these elements from the innumerable particulars of each image cluster, to gather them into a concept and to say it—this is the work of abstraction. The classic description of abstraction was given by Aristotle in his striking metaphor, in the *Posterior Analytics*,[12] of a rout in battle in which one soldier takes a stand and others gather around him, thus restoring order. So out of the chaotic particulars of experience the orderly concept emerges. The issue, incidentally, was needlessly confused when Aristotle termed the process "induction," which in the view of modern logic is a very different kind of psychological and logical process.

The idealist tradition in modern philosophy has emphasized the mind's own activity in the construction of ideas, and the role of imagination in this process. In this respect the epistemological idealism of Kant set the tone and temper of the whole movement. In Kant's system the mind may be likened to a manufacturing plant whose raw materials are impressions and whose finished products are the ideas and judgments of human knowledge. To be sure, the impressions of Kant, as of Hume before him, constitute a narrower category than images as defined for purposes of the present study. Yet if the mind possesses the active powers imputed by Kant, there is no reason why it cannot deal effectively with this wide range of raw material. Once received, the raw material is successively worked up by the transcendental aesthetic, analytic, and dialectic until it emerges as finished knowledge. The point to be noted concerning this whole enormously complicated and often subtle analysis is that the unifying element is the conscious and self-conscious human imagination. One might say that the management of the factory is imagination conceived as a power of the mind.

Once in existence, ideas or concepts function as terms in discursive thinking. Concepts, or the terms that stand for them, are organized into the statements of verbal prose which are formed and tested according to standards of logic, as well as the more particular norms of truth in each particular field of intellectual activity.

It must be also noted in passing that ideas or conceptions of the highest degree of abstraction can at times become images, or at least can function as images. This occurs when they cease to be terms in discursive reasoning and impress themselves on the mind with immediacy. Thus, for example, eternity is a most abstract concept, but Henry Vaughan could write[13]

> I saw Eternity the other night
> Like a great ring of pure and endless light.

and Edna St. Vincent Millay could declare that,[14]

> Euclid alone has looked on Beauty bare.

Once more, the distinguishing feature of an image is its immediacy of apprehension.

Finally, idea and image are contrasted as thought is contrasted to action. We think in terms of ideas; and we act by means of images. The affective quality of living images noted in Chapter II gives them a motive power which in a wide variety of ways makes them incitements to action. It is for this reason that students of human action, ranging from philosophers and psychologists to politicians and advertisers, have concerned themselves with images. Also, if it is true, as I shall presently argue, that the arts deal fundamentally with expressive images, we may begin in these terms to understand the perennial power of art to influence the springs of human action.

4. Metaphor

Aristotle set the dominant tradition of the West when he defined a simile as an expressed comparison, and a metaphor as an implied comparison, between two unlike objects.[15] Obvious as these definitions have become by long tradition and frequent repetition, it is necessary to point out forcibly that they come to us carrying the whole heavy weight of a traditional logical and aesthetic theory. Contemporary students who dissent from this theory have sought to make a fresh start at this point. Such a new beginning in this matter is to be found in many contemporary writers such as Allen Tate[16] and Philip Wheelwright,[17] who suggest that while a concept in any language is a grouping of particulars of experience which is stable, familiar, and widely acceptable (for reasons best known to the community using the language), a metaphor, in sharp contrast, consists of a grouping or organizing of these particulars in a manner that is new, striking, or in some other way noteworthy. What the metaphor calls attention to is precisely this new grouping of particulars. It is as though a sword were run through the stuff of experience, impaling a number of particulars that no one had thought of bringing together before. The vitality of the metaphor also depends upon a tension or contrast between the particulars thus brought together. They are like each other in one respect, but unlike in other respects.

This analysis points out to us the relation of metaphor to the ordinary and familiar concepts of daily speech. At the foundation of many familiar words lies a dead metaphor. In the beginning, in its first usage, the expression was decidedly a living metaphor; but as its grouping of particulars of experience grew more familiar and more generally accepted, a new word found its way into the language. So it is that by metaphor, language lives and grows. The original tension of the metaphor is moderated by habitual usage.

We may see the significance of metaphor by noting its function in the mind's activity of laying hold upon and understanding new objects. Suppose, for the moment, that a completely new and unfamiliar object suddenly appears like a meteor from outer space in one's experience. After the initial impression of bafflement has worn off, one will undoubtedly begin his inspection of it, walking around it, thumping or kicking it, looking at it from one viewpoint and then another. Then perhaps he suggests that it is *like* this or that aspect of his previous experience. Then gradually the expressed comparison becomes an implied comparison. As the new entity is assimilated to experience, an idea or concept is born. Often old words and old ideas are stretched or radically revised to lay hold upon the new object, and the new object, conversely, is thus assimilated to experience. In a precisely similar way attention is sometimes called to new aspects of experience, or to aspects neglected by our common conceptual groupings and which appear as new and fresh when we focus attention upon them. One of the significant functions of art is to point in fresh ways by its own distinctive means of expression to such aspects of experience. Art in its various media is a kind of fresh look at experience, calling attention to significant features which our hackneyed forms of experience and means of expression have passed over. Art accomplishes this objective by means of metaphorical images which are the basic terms of its discourse.

We begin to see metaphor then not simply as a familiar "figure of speech" but as a basic strategy of human mind and tongue in laying hold upon the world in its manifold aspects. It is the way in which the mind lays hold upon new entities, and hence it is a kind of growing point of the mind's life in its responses to the ever-changing and new character of the world. It is also the way in which the mind uses language to lay hold upon that which is radically unique.

We shall have striking illustrations of the uses of metaphor in several of the chapters that follow, notably in art, philosophy, and religion. The capacity of the creative artist to envisage in and through his medium new, striking, and expressive metaphorical images is a fundamental aspect of his work. Also in a derivative way the artistic beholder must be able to reproduce in his own experience from his contemplation of the work of art the expressive meaning and power of these metaphorical images.

In the case of philosophy and religion, there is still a further extension or stretching of the metaphorical image, which is essential to the language of both of these activities. As we shall point out in later chapters, in the case of both philosophy and religion we have to deal with an object that is in some way beyond our common human experience of the world. The problem here for language is acute and radical, namely, how by means of language that has grown up through man's common experience of the world can it be recast to deal with an object that is literally out of this world? As one reflects upon this predicament he sees why some wise and skeptical minds hold that the only appropriate human attitude toward such a transcendent object ("reality" or "being" in the case of philosophy, and "deity" in the case of religion) is silence. In any case, silence as an initial pause and break with the common secular world is a necessary and fitting beginning to whatever may follow. Yet as we shall be led to see, beyond silence it is possible to take expressive metaphors, and by stretching them, use them to point beyond experience to these transcendent referents. So it is that the language of philosophy and religion may be characterized as essentially one of stretched metaphors or analogies. To this important matter we shall return in later chapters.

Yet as soon as we say this, questions and issues begin to rise before us in great profusion. Which metaphors shall we choose? Why this one and not that? What are the rational criteria for the testing of these root metaphors of religious and philosophic discourse? By what alchemy do such root metaphors or root images become rational analogies. How do we know that the transcendent object of such stretched metaphors is not illusory? These issues which constitute basic problems of philosophic and theological thought will concern us in Chapters VIII and IX. It is sufficient at this point to note again the presence of expressive metaphorical images imbedded in the foundation of all language, and in special and distinctive ways, in the languages of philosophy and religion.

5. Expressive Images as Symbols

A great many of the innumerable images that occur to any man during a day's life come and go, occur, pass through the mind and on into oblivion. Yet in this passing parade some images make a claim to significance. As they occur they claim to tell us something interesting or important about ourselves or our world. This claim which initially is perceived as a part of the act of apprehension of the image stands at the center of what is meant by an expressive image. Expressive images are images which, as they occur, make this claim to significance.

To be sure, we need not—indeed, we most definitely ought not—accept the claim uncritically. On the contrary, it is a proper and distinctive critical activity of the mind to test such claims by every available means. We may seek to scrutinize the image again, or to see it in its wider implications, or to discuss it with other human beings, or to examine its logical structure or its context in the mind's life. In these and many other ways men test the claim to significance. Often too, particularly in the case of the arts, the observing mind may attempt to translate the claim of the image into the language of verbal prose so that critical scrutiny may be facilitated.

Expressive images are closely related to symbols as characterized in Chapter I. Symbols, it will be recalled, are terms in human discourse whose significant function is expression, though we were led also to see referential significance for many symbols. By expressing aspects of the life of the actual or engaged self, they tell us something about the world in which that self takes place and to which it is related. It is now possible to identify expressive images, as we are seeking to characterize them in this chapter, with the symbols of Chapter I, characterized with special relation to their mode of occurrence in the minds that create and apprehend them. Conversely, symbols are expressive images of the mind as they find articulation in some significant language.

Another critical question concerning expressive images or symbols arises again naturally at this point. It came up in the first chapter and in one form or another will be with us to the end of our study. It is asked frequently and in a wide variety of ways. Simply stated, that question is this: Does awareness of expressive images ever constitute knowledge? Is the activity of our minds with expressive images or symbols in any significant sense an activity of knowing or cognition, or, on the other hand, is it simply noncognitive experience? The question has extremely important bearings for activities ranging from the arts to religion. For example, it raises such questions as whether a poem or painting is in any significant sense to be regarded as a form of thought or knowledge, or whether the religious person knows God, and if so, what are the criteria for this knowledge.

From preceding paragraphs, it is apparent that many expressive images or symbols do in fact claim cognitive status. The question is whether they can make good the claim in any significant way. The viewpoint to which we shall be led is that no wholesale answer to this question, whether affirmative or negative, seems useful or possible. For one thing, there are a great many kinds of symbols. Hence we shall try to assess specific claims as they come before us, and come to whatever conclusions are warranted by the facts of the case. Obviously too, our answer to this question will be greatly influenced by our prior view of

what cognition or knowledge is. If we limit the term, as
do many contemporary philosophers, to the kind of cognition men achieve in common sense and natural science,
then it follows obviously that symbolic or expressive forms
of mental activity are excluded. However, if we take a
wider view of knowing and knowledge, then it is at least
possible that symbolic forms may fruitfully be regarded as
forms of thinking and knowing.

6. *Imagination as Creativity*

Creativity means literally the capacity to bring some
significant new thing into existence.[18] It is thus a category
of the engaged mind. It is a form of doing or action; indeed, it is that form which may be described as imagination at work. A great many of our doings or actions are
uncreative, producing no new or significant results. But
of others happily the opposite is the case. Hence, now the
process of creation and the role in it of imagination is
before us for study. The capacity for bringing significant
new things into being, as a trait of mind, is often called
"originality"; and genuine originality is widely esteemed
as a valuable quality of human thinking and acting.

The new things that are the result of the creative process
range over an almost infinitely wide field, from new ideas
such as new scientific theories or new poems, new modes of
musical composition, or new philosophies, to new objects
where again the range is from new bridges or machines to
new chemical elements. The actual processes of creation, it
is well to add, are as many and as various as the new things
created.

Here we are concerned with the role of imagination in
the creative process. The heart of the matter is that every
new thing that finds its way into the world is first a new

image in the mind of man. And it is important to add at this point—in the mind of an individual man. The new bridge before it is a new thing or even a new blueprint is a new image in the mind of some engineer. The new poem is a new image before its words spell out a new significant expressive form. The translation of the one into the other, the process by which the new image finds embodiment in words or in the steel of a bridge, is also an equally important aspect of the creative process. The whole integral process of envisagement of a new image and the subsequent embodiment of it in its appropriate form constitutes the creative process. And once more the process may be understood as imagination at work.

In the strictest sense of a much misused word, the creative process is a mystery. It is so in the sense that in this activity the mind operates under no known rules and in a manner under no direct human rational control. A few of the necessary conditions of creativity may be stated, such as acquaintance with the subject matter, openness, or receptiveness, and the like. But the blunt fact is that of the minds that fulfill these conditions, some come up with a significant new idea and some do not. The various attempts at a logic of discovery or creativity thus appear as pretentious nonsense, or, as in the case of J. S. Mill's canons of discovery,[19] rules for testing what is already created.

While the problem of creativity is not essentially different in the arts or in the sciences, it can be more sharply focused in the latter field. Many times in the history of the natural sciences there have been large fields of problematic factual data demanding a new theoretical explanation. Such was the situation in physics before Newton and before Einstein, to cite only two examples. The ability to solve the unsolved problem, to formulate and to answer adequately the question put by the data—this is precisely the mark of genius in science as in other fields of intellectual endeavor.

The creative process exhibits a great many specific differences as we move from science to other forms of human thought, yet some general features persist. In every case there is the unsolved problem, the unanswered question, and the ability, which defies rational control and prediction, to speak the solving word, to give the new answer, to construct the new and illuminating form. Mysterious as it is, creative imagination is wind in the sails of mind, enabling it to sail the seas on voyages of discovery and exploration.

7. *Imagination and Religion*

The creative process, we have said, consists of the occurrence in the human mind of new images out of which emerge in the course of time new ideas and subsequently new things as well. In varying ways this generalization applies to all the various fields of experience in which the mind responds to reality, from physics to poetry. If now we ask what role image and imagination have to play in religion, several new issues open before us. If we limit ourselves to the study of human religious experience as such, it soon becomes clear that this form of experience is articulated and communicated by its own distinctive kind of expressive images or symbols. This assertion is confirmed whether we look at the individual religious person or at the religious community and tradition. Taking the former view, whether informed or guided by the approaches of James, of Freud, or of some other psychologist of religion, we may observe that religious experience is expressed or articulated in terms of symbols. The experience is said in and by means of expressive images. Indeed, the religious experience in one of its important aspects *is* the demand for expressive images or symbols that will body forth or articulate the content of the experience.

A similar conclusion may be reached by a study of the world's primary religious documents. Here surely is an extremely varied literature in which powerful expressive images of many sorts are the predominating feature. Thus, for example, if we analyze a passage of the Bible, of the Bhagavad Gita, of the Vedas, of the Koran, of the Analects of Confucius—or, for that matter, of the Communist Manifesto—the common feature is the presence in all these documents of powerful expressive images which as a matter of historical fact have proven themselves deeply influential in the lives of religious adherents.

Images and imagination can help us in the understanding of still another religious idea, namely, that of revelation. The essential point was expressed by Bernard Shaw in his play *Saint Joan of Arc*. Joan of Arc when questioned regarding her "voices" replies: "I hear voices telling me what to do. They come from God." To the charge that these voices come from her own imagination, Joan answers, "Of course, that is how the messages of God come to us."[20]

Revelation or communication from God to man has been an essential category of many human faiths and theologies, particularly those of the monotheistic sort. The assumption of one God leads in turn to the idea of God's decisive word to humankind. Traditionally, revelation has often been interpreted as the supernatural communication of information from God to man. Thus, for example, what Moses received from God on Mt. Sinai was the series of propositions constituting the Decalogue. From this it was only a step to the idea of the verbal inspiration of a whole book—Bible, Koran, or whatever. It is a well-known fact of history that this idea has created vast difficulties for its adherents in the modern world. It is also a fact, perhaps less widely known, that the contemporary revival of theology in Protestant Christianity has involved an idea of revelation which abandons once and for all the idea of propositional or verbal revelation. So according to these contemporary theologies, God communicates with man, not directly through the propositions of some sacred text, but through what has been termed the divine-human encounter.[21] Yet while this new view of revelation has been welcomed as deliverance from bondage to a text, it has encountered thorny issues and problems of its own. How in detail does God meet or confront man? What precisely takes place in the divine-human encounter?

It is at this point that our study of the images of religious faith can be of great assistance to us. The revelatory process consists not of propositional communication, not of words uttered by deity and heard and recorded by man, but rather of the occurrence of images in the mind of man.[22] These images, luminous, powerful, and sacred, are the medium of God's self-manifestation to man. In the case of a religious founder or innovator, such as Moses or Christ, these will be new images, while in the case of persons within a particular tradition or community, the images and revelation of faith will be mediated through the tradition and community. Radically new images mean, in effect, a new religion.

To the observing mind of the phenomenological student of man's religions all that takes place in the life of the person receiving revelation is the occurrence of images which are reported as luminous and powerful or authoritative. To the recipient of revelation the images claim both light and power in such a way that he must respond in acknowledgment and obedience. To him they claim and receive the full authority of divine self-manifestation and truth.

Which of the many possible interpretations of the images of faith and revelation is correct? Are they authentically the medium of messages from God? If so, what is the process by which the human mind translates from authoritative image to the words of one's own religious confession or witness? Or is the skeptic correct in his assertion that the appearance of objective validity is only a projection of altogether subjective experiences having no relation to any reality? In either case, the adjudication of these claims and counterclaims constitutes important agenda for theological study. But the point to note here is the central role of powerful and luminous images in religious experience, and hence as data for such discussion. Furthermore, by a process of the study of documents and artifacts of men's religions, the historical student of religion can lay bare and understand the images that lie hidden in them. To these issues we shall return in Chapters IX, X, and XI.

IV Religion as Life Orientation

❖ ❖

We have now proceeded far enough to raise the central question of our study: What is the nature of religious language, or more precisely of the religious use (and uses) of language? As the result of the first three chapters we have enough categories at our disposal to attempt at least an initial characterization. For religion does involve language of many kinds—the language of witness and confession, of prayer, worship, scripture, commandment, of creed and theology. Moreover, as we have argued, religion is a form of human experience which as an integral aspect of itself demands its own distinctive kind of expression and communication. We ask then: What are the essential features of this use of language? What goes on or takes place in faith language? The answer to these questions, which is also the thesis of this chapter, is that religion or faith may be understood as total or comprehensive life orientation, and accordingly that religious or faith statements may be interpreted as orientation statements. At this point it is necessary to repeat for emphasis our earlier assertion that this thesis does not prejudge either affirmatively or negatively the question of the validity of religion. From the present viewpoint it may be a message from on high, or it may be a fundamental delusion. In either case, life orientation is its human function. Such is our thesis, and once more it is asserted as a proposition of phenomenology of religion and not of theology.

A major obstacle lying directly across our path is the real vagueness of such terms as "religion," "religious," and "faith." Vague words have fuzzy edges. In the case of religion, ideas, feelings, and practices that one man of undoubted knowledge, goodwill, and perceptiveness includes as significant aspects of religion will be excluded by another man of equal knowledge, goodwill, and sensitivity. Sometimes too these men of different opinions write their views into dictionaries, as may be seen by an inspection of the definitions of religion in some of the standard English dictionaries. In the case of religion, implications drawn out by one man are questioned or denied by another. For example, some contemporary Christian theologies argue that there is a total discontinuity between the divinely given Christian revelation and faith on the one hand, and other human religions on the other. The issue becomes even more complicated if we enlarge our view to take in non-Western cultures and faiths. Here the differences become so great as to raise the question whether the common noun "religion" has any meaning at all. Is there any religion as such, or are there only religions?

In such a situation we can at least begin the task of clarification by working as closely as possible to factual data from various cultures as well as from the results of study of the various intellectual disciplines, in search of a factually adequate definition. Not least of all, we can also keep the issue open for further study. These are the first steps in achieving clear and adequate definitions. Meanwhile, with misgivings, reservations, and qualifications, we must perforce continue to use such words as "religion," "religious," and "faith." It is also a good hunch in such situations that, like the blind men in the Oriental parable, each investigator has hold of a particular and partial aspect of the elephant in terms of which he proceeds to define the whole animal.

Despite their bewildering variations of meanings, terms like "religion" and "religious" do have a persistant recurrence in the lives of both cultures and individual persons. In the case of cultures, it is a widely accepted conclusion of anthropology that every human culture of which there is reliable knowledge has some behavior or practices to which the term "religion" may appropriately be applied, although as we move from culture to culture these practices show a truly baffling variety. With this beginning, our problem is to find in this variety some common core of meaning.

1. *Religious Language: Some Current Views*

In recent years semantic philosophers have displayed an increasing concern for religious language. As already noted, the earlier verificational analysis of logical positivism was content to consign religion and theology along with metaphysics, ethics, and poetry to the limbo of nonsense or purely emotive meaning.[1] Since these forms of utterance were neither analytic nor synthetic, neither logical nor empirical, they must be nonsense! However, as also observed in the post-positivist development of semantic philosophy there has been a growing realization that language has not just two but many distinctive functions.[2] Of these it is at least possible that the religious use is one. Thus there has grown up among semantic philosophers a lively interest in this language. In some cases this interest has sought to discover and define a distinctively religious use of language, while in other cases it has been concerned with the critical analysis of other men's views of this matter. While it is still too early to undertake any definitive evaluation of this movement, nonetheless a few features begin to emerge. Here we shall note briefly a few significant current views and issues.

In a periodical symposium entitled "Theology and Falsification," later published in *New Essays in Philosophical Theology*,[3] Antony Flew expounds a parable taken from John Wisdom's essay "Gods," concerning a plot of wilderness ground that bears equivocal resemblance to a garden in the wilderness. Of this garden plot one observer asserts that it is the work of an invisible gardener, and so the issue is joined. In the ensuing argument the original assertion of the invisible gardener is so modified under the pressure of negative evidence that in the end, as Flew puts it, this "fine brash hypothesis dies the death of a thousand qualifications." Flew's point is that to be meaningful a hypothesis must submit to the criterion of falsifiability. In other words, we must know and state the kind of evidence that would effectively disprove the hypothesis. A hypothesis that is "true no matter what" is in effect meaningless.

Flew's parable makes two assumptions, very possibly unconscious, but nonetheless significant. It identifies (*a*) God statements and religious statements, and also it identifies (*b*) religious statements and theological statements. The latter identification is of widespread occurrence, but we shall find good reasons in Chapter IX for rejecting it as confusing and misleading, and for adopting a clear distinction between religious and theological statements. The first identification, while it has a certain plausibility in the monotheistic religions of the Western world, becomes questionable the moment we look farther afield. In a great many of the Oriental faiths, religious statements are certainly not to be identified with God statements. Even in the West, it is possible to point to much discussion of deity that is quite devoid of religious import as well as much obviously meaningful religious discussion that does not involve the word "God." In other words, these seem to be independent variables; Flew is wrong again.

Yet the most fundamental issue in Flew's parable and its most dubious aspect is its tacit assumption that religious statements are by nature hypotheses that seek to explain problematic factual data. Thus they are not different in form or function from scientific hypotheses, though, as the author contends, they turn out to be "bad" hypotheses because they violate the principle of falsifiability. Yet Flew's brash assumption that religious statements are by nature explanatory hypotheses concerning problematic facts is not without parallels or support from the history of Western theology from Plato[4] and Aristotle[5] to the present. An inspection of Thomas Aquinas' arguments for the existence of God,[6] as well as the tradition that stems from him, shows a view of statements concerning God very similar to that of Flew. In the discussion following Flew's paper, a modified version of this traditional Thomist view is taken by I. M. Crombie for the stated purpose of maintaining the possibility that religious statements may be understood as significantly true or false.

What shall we say to the view of religious statements as explanatory hypotheses? In subsequent chapters, I shall present an alternative view of religious and theological statements that seeks to maintain the rationality of religious utterance without falling into the fatal errors of Flew's views. Here it may be observed that if we adopt Flew's approach, we will presently end by saying with Laplace that we "have no need of this hypothesis." Moreover, it is a view which in effect makes religious statement irrelevant to what takes place in actual religious experience. Whatever the religious experience may turn out to be, it is surely not an experience like that of the scientist or detective seeking to solve a problem or answer a question. Indeed, to force this interpretation upon the experience is violently to distort the experience itself. The religious person confessing his faith is clearly doing something different from the scientist seeking to explain problematic facts.

In the symposium that follows, Flew's parable elicits another parable from R. M. Hare, who tells the story of a university student who has a deep-seated psychoneurotic attitude (called rather preciously a "blik" by Hare) that all dons are out to kill him.[7] As is widely recognized, such psychoneurotic compulsions are not open to rational persuasion or factual evidence. Religion, Hare assures us, is not an insane blik like this; rather it is a sane or right blik, which is to say, a deep-seated subjective attitude, normal rather than neurotic, close to the foundation of personality and indeed constitutive of personality. The reader's first reaction to this suggestion may well be that it is a desperate expedient to protect religion from Flew's kind of skeptical criticism by locating it deep within the subject. Yet if it turns out that expressive language has its appropriate standards of truth and falsehood, then it is at least conceivable that rigorous rational criticism can penetrate to the innermost aspects of subjecthood. This is an issue that will recur throughout our study. Meanwhile, it is pertinent to observe that the peril of Hare's view is that of capricious subjectivity. Nonetheless, stated against that of Flew, this view does have the virtue of calling attention forcibly to the real nature of religious experience and the way in which religion actually functions in human selfhood.

Seeking to preserve the valid points of both Flew and Hare, Basil Mitchell adds to the discussion still a third parable.[8] This one is about an occupied country in time of war, in which a mysterious stranger assures the members of the underground resistance that he is not (as sometimes appears) a member of the opposing general staff, but is actually on the side of the resistance, indeed is in command of it. Members of the resistance debate the truth of this assertion, but some of them continue to trust the stranger despite appearances that conflict with his assurance. The point of this parable is to maintain two essential features of religious utterances: (a) they are expressive statements of faith or trust and not simply detached and objective hypotheses, as Flew's parable implies, and (b) they are nonetheless assertions whose truth or falsehood must be tested by evidence. Here we shall seek a view of religion and religious utterance which conserves both of these essential features; and Mitchell's parable is a welcome item in the search.

Another somewhat more radical suggestion for the nature of religious statement is made by R. B. Braithwaite in his Eddington lecture for 1954, entitled *An Empiricist's View of the Nature of Religious Belief.*[9] Examining and rejecting the position that religious beliefs are of the same sort as scientific beliefs, Braithwaite argues that they are essentially moral in nature, having to do with human action and the accompanying emotion. In effect his conclusion may be regarded as a semantic reformulation of Matthew Arnold's nineteenth-century liberal view that religion is morality touched with emotion.

It is not hard to see significant truth in the position for

which Braithwaite contends. Religious statements do have a significant relation to human action; and in the view of religious statements as orientation statements, to which we shall presently be led, we shall endeavor to keep this relation clearly in mind. But this relation is surely an insufficient basis for Braithwaite's oversimple assertion of the virtual identity of religion and morality.

Among the increasing number of articles and books in this field two contributions especially illustrate the growing maturity of this approach to theological study, namely, John Hick's *Faith and Knowledge*[10] and Frederick Ferré's *Language, Logic and God.*[11] These two writers assume semantic analysis as a viewpoint and as a context in which to work. They also exhibit both interest and competence extending to both the theological and philosophical aspects of their topic. Hick's book is an analysis of the nature of faith and of the ways in which verification of faith is, and is not, possible. Hick's central contention is that faith is the assertion of the total significance of life. "The primary focus of religious significance is the believer's experience as a whole. The basic act of interpretation which reveals to him the religious significance of life is a uniquely 'total interpretation.' "[12] This is a particularly valuable insight to which we shall have repeated occasion to refer as the present discussion proceeds. Specifically, it bears close similarity to the ideas of ultimate concern or ultimate valuation of the next section of this chapter.

Concerning the logical testing or verification of faith, Hick makes a noteworthy suggestion which he calls "eschatological verification."[13] Clearly, not all the evidence for or against faith is available to us at any given present time, nor will it be till the end. Then presumably a decisive judgment will be forthcoming. Yet this suggestion surely raises as many questions as it answers. For example, does Hick mean that the experience of dying will provide the individual person a basis for verifying (or disproving) the Christian doctrine of eternal life? If so, the suggestion has all the theologically and morally questionable qualities of otherworldly or next-worldly types of religion. Surely the evidence available in the present life may well be as decisive as that available in the hereafter. Or does Hick mean to ally himself with the more sophisticated eschatologies of contemporary theology? If so, the problem is how a verification of theism is possible on these terms.

More recently, Frederick Ferré's book, *Language, Logic and God,* has undertaken a critical survey of the burgeoning literature of the field of theological language. Again we note the author's double concern and competence for both theology and philosophy, and his consequent refusal to accept exclusive proposals in either direction. Surely one result of the British development of semantic analysis with which Ferré is chiefly concerned, and which becomes apparent from his treatment, is a resumption on this new basis of the agelong critical discussion between philosophy and theology. This is no small achievement when we observe the way in which other contemporary types of theology and philosophy have permitted this critical discussion to go by default, with both of the participants lapsing into mutual isolation. Ferré's critical exposition of issues and viewpoints is well designed to facilitate this resumption of discussion. Several of his specific contentions will find their way into future pages of the present discussion.

An instructively different view of religious language in the current discussion is that which has been formulated by Willem Zuurdeeg in his volume *An Analytical Philosophy of Religion.*[14] The author's background in contemporary European philosophy and religion, embracing the extremes of logical positivism and existentialism, as well as his role as a minister of the Remonstrant Brotherhood in Holland during the Hitler period, are reflected in his book. These interests are brought together in a view of religious utterance which regards it as a very special, indeed unique, kind of emotive meaning to be taken with existential seriousness and significance, and to be seen amid the clash of faiths, philosophies, and ideologies of the contemporary world. Zuurdeeg's approach continues the radical separation of scientific and religious meaning that characterized logical positivism in its original form. Completely absent from his views are the older traditional forms of rational theology with their attempts to prove the existence of God, or by some process of philosophic speculation to stabilize or defend religious belief. By contrast, he begins with man and his language. In Zuurdeeg's own terms, man is *homo loquens* who in one aspect of his life becomes *homo sapiens* and in another becomes *homo convictus*. *Homo sapiens* brackets his convictions and speaks indicatively and empirically like a good logical positivist, while *homo convictus* spontaneously expresses his existence in symbolic words like a good existentialist.[15] Once this radical start has been made, human reason, even philosophic and theological reason, finds work to do in studying human convictions and relating them to the world views that follow from them. Yet as one looks over Zuurdeeg's whole philosophy of religion, a persistent question is that of the relation of these distinguishable aspects of the mind's life to each other and to the whole, integral human mind. One has the uneasy feeling that Zuurdeeg has converted initial distinctions into separate, watertight compartments.

Especially is this true of the relation of philosophical language to religious language. The logical positivist aspect of his own viewpoint leads him to deny categorically the validity of traditional philosophical theology. Subsequently his analysis leads him tentatively and uneasily to something called world views which seem to be, in essence, philosophical corollaries of conviction systems or religions. However the relation of this type of utterance to conviction statements is not explored, and in the end, for Zuurdeeg religion is deprived of philosophical criticism and appraisal. From this treatment one would not suspect that *homo sapiens* and *homo convictus* are aspects of the integral life of man. Faith and reason are nowhere brought together.

The heart of Zuurdeeg's view of religious language is his assertion that it is convictional language. Rejecting the traditional positivist category of emotive meaning as inadequate, he accepts and adopts what is termed "convictional meaning."[16] Shifting from a positivist to an existentialist outlook, he asserts that such convictions establish a man's existence, and issue in the sense of power which conviction engenders.

Having established this ground on which to stand, Zuurdeeg moves on to a phenomenological description of the conviction situation which begins with what he terms the convictor, namely, the agent in eliciting the attitude of conviction in man. As Zuurdeeg recognizes, the traditional Western religious term for convictor is God.[17] Yet granting the claim of man's religious experience to be under the influence of such a convictor, it is no part of Zuurdeeg's analytic philosophy of religion rationally to analyze and appraise this claim. Rather, from convictor we move successively through such descriptive phases of the experience of conviction as witness, testimony, decision, assent, membership in the confessional group, and even theological reflection; and in every case the author has illuminating comments to make, enabling us to see how these various forms of experience and statement flow from the original experience and statement of conviction.[18] However, it appears to be no part of Zuurdeeg's study to examine, appraise, or criticize the validity of what he describes.

Fundamentally then, religious statements are direct expressions of the experience of conviction which lies at the center of religious experience. One further criticism turns upon the nature of conviction. As Zuurdeeg uses the term, it has strong Biblical and Calvinist coloring, which is natural enough in view of his own religious views. Yet it is somewhat constricting to define all religion in these terms. How in these terms shall we understand religious experience in non-Biblical traditions from Greece to India and China? Their primary utterances express conviction in a key very different from that of Calvinistic Protestantism. Indeed, is it conviction or is it vision which is their most basic category? This is a question to which we shall return in Chapter X. Meanwhile it is fair to observe the suggestion of Calvinist apologetics which has thus crept into this definition.

The views of these and many other students of religious language who might be added to the list constitute an impressive beginning on this new approach to theological study. However, in this situation, as in so many times in the past, philosophic and theological study benefit from periodic scrutiny of pertinent facts. In the present situation this scrutiny will be facilitated by a look at religious experience.

2. A Descriptive Approach

As a beginning let us fix attention upon religious experience in as wide a sense as information and imagination will permit, and ask what traits recur amid all its multiform variety. As has often been pointed out, to say religious experience is to speak subjectively; but when it is pointed out that in actual occurrence such experiences have a clearly objective context, the perils of subjectivism largely disappear. As we look then at religious experience, three main features force themselves upon our attention. Religion is an experience of (a) ultimate concern or valuation, which (b) carries the unique affective accompaniment of the holy or sacred, and (c) seeks and finds expression in powerful and imaginative symbols. Let us consider these features in turn.

a. Paul Tillich has suggested that religious experience is an experience of ultimate concern.[19] The term "concern" serves to locate the experience in what psychology has often called the affective or motor-affective area or aspect of the human self. The traditional Western philosophic and theological terms for this aspect of the self are "will" or "volition." If our characterization of self and will in Chapter I is valid, then we may translate Tillich's ultimate concern as ultimate valuation. Surely in common usage "value" and "concern" are synonyms. Religion, then we may claim, is a form of experience which deals with ultimate values, or more precisely, ultimate valuation.

Tillich's widely quoted "ultimate concern" has been attacked as a form of psychologism and also as a form of reductionism which explains by explaining away. Yet Tillich's own writings provide adequate defense against these charges and dangers. It is the adjective "religious," which is characterized as an experience of ultimate concern; and subsequent exposition relates the adjective successively to such nouns as "religion," "faith," "revelation," and "God." In context, Tillich's ultimate concern is a way of establishing contact with his reader, after which exposition proceeds onward to other facets of the reality under discussion.

Values, as already suggested, are what more traditional Western philosophy termed "goods." Goods are, in general terms, objects of human interest, affection or conation. But what of the term "ultimate"? Tillich has asserted unequivocally that the ultimate or absolute is not a thing or object, but rather primarily a quality or dimension of human concern or valuation.[20] Perhaps the primary meaning of "ultimacy" is not as a substantive but as an adjective or even as an adverb. Attention may be called to the fact that this is often the meaning of the term in ordinary nonphilosophic usage, as when one asserts that a man is absolutely or ultimately committed to this or that object. The term here means unqualifiedly, unreservedly, completely. An ultimate concern or value is thus any concern or value having this unqualified or absolute character. The root meaning of the term is thus again verbal or adverbial rather than substantive.

Using the term in this common, nontechnical sense, I shall quickly state four unequivocal indices of ultimacy. An ultimate concern is, first of all, one that has top priority in the scheme or system of concerns that constitute a personality. It is thus an interest or concern to which "in a pinch" a man would sacrifice every other concern. It is, in other words, that value from which all a man's other values are derived, but which is itself not derived from any other value. Incidentally, etymological propriety ought to lead us to call such values primal rather than ultimate. Whether there are in fact such values is a question that ought not to be settled a priori, but rather by rigorous factual study of the structure of existing human selves. Also, it may be remarked, it is psychologically a quite possible state of affairs for such ultimates to change from time to time. One writer even goes so far as to speak of functional gods and momentary gods![21]

A second index of ultimacy is totality of application. An ultimate concern or value is one that finds deployment or application in the inclusive totality of a man's experience. Nothing that he is or does is alien to it. Such values or concerns are to be contrasted with immediate or proximate values that have a limited application to a defined part of experience, and that exist alongside other values in a relation of mutual accommodation. The most obvious contemporary illustration of this phenomenon is the nature of political allegiance in free, secular societies and in totalitarian societies. For example, the adherent of Communism agrees to guide *all* his activities by the directives of the party. It is precisely the total character of this allegiance which generates its religious quality. The total deployment or application of ultimate concerns is expressed by the completely unrestricted use of the term "all" in religious statements, which will concern us later in our study. In this connection we recall Hick's view of faith as total interpretation.

These two features of ultimate concern, namely, top priority and total deployment, suggest a third, namely, that of the integration or unification of personality. An ultimate concern or value serves as the center about which personality is unified or integrated. Ultimate concerns are thus, as John Herman Randall has suggested, unifying concerns.[22] To be sure, unification or integration is a relative term, but insofar as actual human selves are unified at all, they find unification around such a center. There are, of course, two kinds of integration or unification which must be clearly distinguished. Neurotic or exclusive unification is achieved by shutting out threatening forces, while healthy or creative unification is not exclusive but inclusive in character. Factually, both neurotic and healthy unification may well find illustration in religious experience, though the latter is both possible and desirable, religiously and in other ways.

A fourth and final feature of ultimate concern or valuation is the presence of the unique emotion usually called the holy or sacred. Of this emotive quality let us first note that it is the affective accompaniment of experiences of ultimate concern or valuation. Wherever men commit themselves ultimately or absolutely, this quality emerges. This fact has, accordingly, an importance for the study of religion comparable to the relation of the height of a mercury column to temperature for students of physics. Since such a correlation exists, we have an extremely valuable indicator of ultimate concern. Negatively it may be asserted that where it does not occur we may be certain that ultimate concern or valuation does not exist. To the holy or sacred as a feature of religious experience we must now turn our attention.

b. The holy is first and most basically a unique human emotion or affective quality. It comes to inhabit a wide variety of symbolic objects, but before that it is a quality of human emotion. Moreover, as Rudolf Otto[23] argues, it is a unique emotion, and, like all unique things, it can be indicated or pointed to but not described or classified. It is this uniqueness of the emotion which leads Eliade[24] to avoid definition, simply drawing a line that separates the sacred from the secular or profane areas of human experience. By way of description, one may point to the holy, saying with Otto that it is like fear, wonder, awe, and that it is a *mysterium tremendum et fascinans.*

Yet perhaps the most illuminating way to locate this quality of religious experience is to indicate its relation to human concern or valuation. As we have argued, the holy is the emotive accompaniment of ultimate concern or valuation. This relation has led John Oman to distinguish between the holy as an emotion and the sacred as a value.[25] Oman regards the holy as precisely the kind of emotion that has been described in preceding paragraphs. However, the term "value" has to do not with feeling or emotion but with volition or will. The sacred, he writes persuasively, is the holy held as a supreme value. Sacred value may thus for Oman be said to consist precisely of ultimate value together with an accompaniment of holy feeling.

Now if there is any feature altogether and inclusively common to all the bewildering variety of religious attitudes and phenomena, it is the holy and the sacred. Moreover, the holy, while first a quality of human emotion, gets itself expressed symbolically and thus comes to inhabit symbolic objects. Such holy things or objects exist in incredible variety. Religion, then, may be defined as that human concern which deals with the holy and the sacred. From the viewpoint of factual description or phenomenology of religion this is clearly the best, most adequate definition available to us.

c. Religion, as we have previously argued, involves expressive words and nonverbal symbolism of many sorts. As Cassirer[26] has argued, it is one of the symbolic forms. If we exclude the language employed by the professional theologian (an exception to be defended and argued in Chapter IX), one common feature of religious language is precisely its expressive or symbolic character in the sense described in the first three chapters. The language in which religious experience seeks and finds utterance is thus a language of expressive images. The particular images vary widely from religion to religion, but expressive images there always are.

There is nothing particularly novel or surprising in this observation. Almost fifty years ago Santayana[27] characterized poetry as myth in which we no longer believe; and a few decades later Reinhold Niebuhr[28] replied that myth is poetry in which we do believe. In either formulation the relation is a close and significant one. Moreover, religious experience has equally close and significant relations to other arts as well. Hence it is again an altogether general characteristic of religious experience to seek and to find symbolic expression. Yet the symbols of religion, similar as they are to other symbol systems, differ precisely in the fact that they have the quality of the holy or sacred.

If it be asked what is the content of religious experience that gets expressed in the verbal symbols of religion, one useful answer is that it is ultimate concern or ultimate valuation. Or with equal validity, it could be replied that it is the holy and sacred which gets expressed in these many and varied forms. Yet if one persists in questions of this sort, there is another and in many ways a more illuminating answer which may be given, to which we must now turn.

3. *Life Orientation*

We come now to the heart of this chapter's thesis, namely, to the contention that religion may be understood as total or comprehensive life orientation and that accordingly religious statements are orientation statements.

Of the system of expressive forms or symbols that constitute religion we have asked: What goes on here? What do
these forms do? Religion is a persistent and recurrent fact
in man's life, of which one asks, What is its function? The
answer to be given here is that it affords total or comprehensive life orientation. However, this answer is likely to
evoke the reply: But what on earth is *that?* What under
heaven is total life orientation?

The approach we shall take in answering this last question will be to describe as clearly and adequately as possible the situation in which this human need arises. To this
end, let us begin with the life of an organism in its environment. The term "life" in this context has a clearly
biological meaning; the life process at this level is completely and adequately described in terms provided by
biological science. Animals seek ends or goals often guided
by instinct or inherited or unlearned responses, and
prompted by such basic needs as those of respiration, activity, food, sex, and the like. Granted the realization of these
ends or goals, the animal has, or appears to have, a good
life. For the organism the satisfaction of these needs or
goals defines adjustment to its environment.

With man the situation is radically different. In the first
place, he seems to be completely lacking in instincts (defined rigorously as unlearned behavior patterns). At least
no such patterns have been established to date. Furthermore, as to natural needs, man seems able always to raise
the question, Ought I to satisfy this need? It is at least
formally possible that the answer which man gives is "no";
and the incidence of such phenomena as asceticism and
suicide shows clearly that the formal possibility is by no
means empty. If the answer is "yes," the significant question follows, How ought I to satisfy it? At that point
emerges the whole "secondary environment of culture" by

whose complicated system of instrumentalities the primary biological needs of man are met.[29]

It is as a consequence of human freedom that there opens before man an enormously wider field of possibilities than appears to be the case for the animals. The taproot of all these complications of life at the emergent human level appears to be the freedom of self-transcendence which transforms the organism in an environment into a self over against the world—a self who ponders such questions as: Who am I? Why am I here? Man's active life is in a functional sense his answer to these questions.

One significant corollary of these propositions concerning the nature of the human self is that life at the human level has an indefeasibly and inescapably value-oriented character. As we have noted previously, at the human level, animal needs and drives become human values, and as long as man remains man he cannot evade or elude this aspect of his life. The acid test of this assertion is the desire or proposal of some men to live "on an animal level." But in that case certain biological goods become life values and are somewhat dubiously affirmed as such. The term "life" at the human level seems inevitably to have the meaning "the good life." It is a value-oriented term which elicits the question, What kind of life? and demands an answer. It is in this unavoidably, indefeasibly human situation that the question of life orientation arises. How shall man guide the course of his life? His animal relatives apparently do not have to raise this question. Man does. In him the life impulse becomes self-conscious, open and free, and hence must be defined in terms of the conscious or intentional goals or ends which are sought. It is in this situation that the need for life orientation arises. This, in fact, is what life orientation means.

Two possible answers to the question of life orientation are widely suggested in current social thought, namely, intelligence and culture. It is frequently asserted that man may not possess instincts to guide his actions, but he has something better in his creative intelligence. Furthermore, an individual may question the immediate satisfactions of natural need, but his culture, consisting as it does of vast reservoirs of social experience, can provide functioning answers to these questions, channeling and guiding his individual behavior.

There is truth in both of these contentions, and I have no wish to deprecate in any way the guidance or orientation given to the individual human being by intelligence and culture. Yet a single question can be put to both. Though they are extremely valuable for provisional guidance, do they offer ultimate or final guidance? Intelligence is like a guide we hire to help us find our way through the woods. If we tell him where we want to go, he will help us to arrive there. But he cannot tell us what our destination is. Intelligence cannot, without being viciously circular, derive from its own resources a set of ultimate values that will provide us with a final goal for living. Philosophies of creative intelligence invariably beg the question of ultimate goal or destination, sometimes in ways quite unconscious and uncritical of the problems involved.[30] Sometimes they simply deny that the term "ultimate value" has meaning.

Similarly, culture is invaluable for the transmission to each individual of values and skills indispensable for human life. Often a culture transmits values which it has received from beyond itself. The only circumstance in which a culture is the sole source or originator of ultimate values is the dubious situation when it is given an absolute primacy to its own values, a situation appropriately called "ethnocentrism." Furthermore, it is formally possible for the individual to question or reject any given value of his culture. That this is no empty formality is underscored by the fact that some of the most creative consciences of human history have done just this, and in doing so have wrought significant human improvement. Concerning both intelligence and culture, we must say again that while they afford excellent provisional guidance, they cannot provide total or comprehensive life orientation. In this respect they both stand in precisely the same situation as the individual human being—needing it and not having it.

Our search takes us then to other possible sources, and thence to religion. We recall what was said earlier about the nature of religious language as consisting of luminous and powerful images or symbols. My thesis in this chapter is that these luminous and powerful images do provide precisely the total life orientation that man needs. He needs a convincing and authoritative statement of who he is and what he is living for. It is an answer to precisely these questions that comes to man through these images. That, in short, is their function in relation to human life. They provide to individuals and communities to whom they are convincing what C. W. Morris has called a "path of life."[31] Translated into less metaphorical language, what comes to a man through these images is a set of life values that provide him with the goals which engage and fulfill his human powers. That different religions have different images, and therefore different sets of life values and thus constitute differing paths of life, does indeed accentuate the problem of choice or decision as well as the diversity of human religious behavior; but it confirms and does not disprove the view of religion as a scheme of total life orientation.

The thesis I have been advancing might alternatively have been asserted in terms of the will to live. The term "will to live," or "life impulse," is widely suspected at the present time by both scientists and philosophers. The former suspect a vitalism that multiplies entities beyond scientific necessity by adding to biological processes a special vital impulse. The latter challenge the same life impulse as being metaphysical in the bad sense of the word. However, both of these issues can be met by the clear definition of the life impulse, or will to live, as the observable tendency of living systems to go on living and to resist forces that threaten their life. So defined, these terms ought not to be offensive to the strictest positivist in our midst. They are shorthand expressions for observable facts of experience.

At the animal level the will to live may be understood largely or entirely in terms of the instinct and needs of organic life. But at the human threshold, as Bergson has pointed out, the life impulse faces a crucial fork in the road.[32] It may find expression in the closed society of the anthill or beehive, or it may become open and free. Life can, in the latter case, mean aspiration and freedom. The point of these reflections on the will to live is simply to assert that at the emergent human level of life, religion is an expression of the will to live. It is so in and through the luminous and powerful symbols we have found central to religious experience.

Nowhere is this understanding of religion more pertinent than in prehistoric and primitive religion. As we contemplate the situation of our prehistoric ancestor, the wonder is that, surrounded by other more powerful species, amid a nature always precarious and often hostile, he survived at all. In such an extreme situation his religion expressed for him the life impulse set against all the threatening forces and steeling him for the desperate encounter. So he appeased the hostile forces of nature, and he celebrated the friendly forces.[33] Furthermore, our prehistoric ancestor could survive at all only with the assistance of nature and by the cooperation of his fellows. So his first gods were more or less personified aspects of nature and tribe. There was a genuine realism in all this. The meaning of his life did, in fact, consist in these processes. Thus, in these terms he expressed his faith in the living reality of which he was a part.

For our first ancestor as for his descendants the final problem was death, which seemed to cancel out the meaning of life. A very great deal of prehistoric and primitive religion thus consists in an affirmation of life against the great negation of death.[34] Many funerary customs and beliefs demand to be understood in these terms. Here, as elsewhere, primitive man's religion may be interpreted as an expression in the imaginative language of myth and rite of his will to live.

If this is true of prehistoric and primitive religion, it is also equally true of the different religions of civilized humanity. Each of these religions may fruitfully be regarded as a path of life, which by means of its expressive images or symbols provides answers for its adherents to the questions: Whence? Whither? Why? In Chapters X and XI this analysis of religions as paths of life or systems of total life orientation will be pushed further. Here we may conclude by noting again in summary that at the emergent human level, life requires total orientation or guidance, and that to meet this need is the function of the lively images of faith. Conversely, faith and its symbolic expressions may be regarded as expressions of the human will to live.

V Varieties of Cognitive Experience

✦ ✦

1. *The Problem Stated*

At several points in previous discussion the question of the cognitive significance of various kinds of utterance, particularly symbolic or expressive utterance, has arisen. Does this or that form of statement constitute a valid instance of knowing? Are the categories of truth and falsehood applicable, and if so, how? Or, on the other hand, is that statement in question simply an aspect of noncognitive experience, having no genuine noetic significance? Since these large and difficult questions lie directly across our path, we must now attempt to face them and deal with them.

If we look to the tradition of modern Western philosophy, some clear answers are forthcoming. Speaking generally, the main line of this philosophic tradition has limited the area of knowledge or cognition to what may be termed propositional knowledge expressible in verbal prose, and clearly subject to the various norms of logic and epistemology. Thus, we must be aware that any attempt to broaden the denotation of the term "knowledge" goes against this long and impressive tradition of critical philosophy. In recent times some philosophies have restricted the field of knowledge even more radically. Positivism has limited bona fide knowledge to that which is definable and testable in terms of natural science. This limitation must literally be regarded as suicidal, for if positivism be defined as a form of philosophy whose statements are not within any of the sciences, but are philosophic statements about science, then clearly positivism cuts the ground from under itself. Many forms of naturalism are only slightly less restrictive. The naturalism of John Dewey and his many followers emphasizes the instrumental function of knowing, and somewhat equivocally includes philosophy along with science as species of knowledge. However, in all these types of philosophy, such enterprises as art and religion, while considered as instances of experience, are not to be accorded cognitive or noetic significance![1]

It is difficult to see precisely how much of these contentions is a factual claim about the nature of human knowing, and how much on the other hand is an a priori stipulation about the use of the terms "knowing" and "knowledge." If they are the latter, it is sufficient to indicate their prescriptive and persuasive character. On the other hand, if the claims are intended to be factual, argument is called for. The argument of this chapter will take the form of pointing to other types of cognitive activity inescapably given as data in human experience and yet excluded by these philosophic theories.

We begin by recalling Waismann's remark, quoted in Chapter II, that terms such as "meaning" and "truth" do not have a single meaning but a whole cluster of meanings, each of which corresponds to a particular language stratum. Confusion results when a particular meaning is shifted from one context or stratum to another. Rather, as the mind moves from one language stratum to another, it must be prepared for new definitions of these basic terms as well as new logical norms peculiar to the new stratum. Thus, for example, the terms "true" and "false" may have one meaning in physical science and another one in ethics and legal theory, and still another in poetry. The hypothesis to be elaborated and tested in this chapter is that Waismann's view of language strata may be fruitfully applied to the problem of knowledge, enabling us to see the varieties of cognitive experience in which our human minds are engaged.

Consider first, then, some of the many meanings attached in daily nonphilosophic discussion to such words as "truth," "falsehood," "meaning," "thinking," "knowing," and the like. Men speak of statements as true or false, but they also speak of friends as being true or false. Again, they ask, for example, if this object is a true chair or table; or, if discussion is extended to the Gospel of John, the term "truth" acquires still different meanings, enabling Pilate to ask his cynical question, What is truth? and Christ in reply to discourse concerning mystical truth. Analogously, the terms "false," "falsify," and "falsehood" range through varieties of meaning from logical negation at one end of the spectrum to varieties of personal deception and infidelity on the other end. A similar spectrum of meaning might readily be constructed for the terms "meaningful" and "meaningless," ranging from linguistic meaning of a relatively impersonal sort (dictionary meaning) through a wide range of expressive meaning to the kind of existential meaning illustrated by the oft-repeated "the meaning of life." In the writings of Reinhold Niebuhr, "the meaningful character of existence" frequently assumes the role of a major premise. According to this view, all functioning faiths (and philosophies as well) assume the meaningful character of existence as a postulate, and then proceed to interpret and elaborate it in their own distinctive terms. These faiths and philosophies may then be compared in terms of the kinds of meaning they ascribe to existence. What is significant here is Niebuhr's particular use of the term "meaning." Clearly it is a profoundly different meaning of "meaning" from that of the semantic philosophers. Perhaps Niebuhr's might be characterized as "existential meaning,"[2] i.e., personal meaning for actual, engaged human beings. If we further assume, as Niebuhr does, a Kierkegaardian view of man's anxiety and despair, then existential meaning might be characterized as that which enables a man to cope with these threats to his being. It might even be defined negatively as the alternative to suicide.

We shall achieve a certain initial clarification if we note a prevalent custom of projecting or transferring meaning from terms or statements to their referents in the objective situation. So, for example, instead of speaking of the truth of a statement referring to situation X, we speak rather of the truth of situation X. Analogously, we speak of the meaning of the situation, or perhaps of a meaningless situation. Also, in similar ways we speak of a coherent or consistent person, or of a coherent or consistent situation. In such usages, once we become aware of what has taken place, the projection assumes the significance of a harmless ellipsis; it is then easy enough to return the terms "true" and "meaningful" from the referent to their original locus in the statement, if one wishes to do so.

This linguistic practice also serves to raise the extremely important ontological question of the relation of language to referent. It is a fact familiar to students of semantic philosophy that many current semantic philosophies, inhibited by antimetaphysical attitudes, seek to deny or avoid a consideration of this relation. Here we shall take an opposite view. As Paul Tillich[3] has asserted, no semantic philosophy can permanently avoid the question of the relation of language to referent; and once this issue is raised, we are plunged into the midst of issues which are both epistemological and ontological. Later in the present chapter, I shall argue that we forcibly encounter this referent as we turn from theory to action.

In the whole cluster of words that designate the mind's characteristic activity, if we move from "meaningful" and "true" to the closely related words "thinking" and "knowing," and their respective substantives as well as their numerous synonyms, we confront an even more luxuriant and bewildering variety of uses and meanings in common language. As already observed, in one well-defined and generally recognized sense, thinking is the cognitive activity that produces propositions and undertakes to test their truth and falsehood. Thinking, in this sense, takes place in language, which while not identical with thinking, is its necessary vehicle. Knowing, in a closely related sense, is a synonymous but perhaps stronger term, meaning the successful cognitive activity of creating, testing, and certifying propositions; and knowledge, the product of this activity, is gathered in bodies of statements tested by competent minds and certified as well-founded both by the general rules of logic and by the more restricted rules of each intellectual discipline. Let us call this propositional or intellectual thinking and knowledge.

Yet, the verbs "to think" and "to know" exhibit many other meanings as well. For example, I speak of knowing my friend, or, with Socrates, of knowing myself. Indeed, in French and German, there are two verbs for knowing, as personal acquaintance and as propositional knowing. Gilbert Ryle, among many other philosophers, has pointed

to another recognized use of this word as know-how or
practical technique.[4] Let us expand upon Ryle and assert
that men may know (a) that, (b) whom, or (c) how. Each of
these three main types has its appropriate and recognized
features; and each of the three exhibits a significant variety
of subdivisions.

Take first the matter of "knowing that," or propositional knowledge, which embraces such commonplace cog-
nitions as that I am seated at a desk writing, or, as Professor G. E. Moore likes to insist, that this is a hand, indeed
that it is my hand—my right hand. Or consider such cog-
nitions as that last summer I journeyed to New England,
or that yesterday a merchant shortchanged me. From such
commonplace items, "knowing that" extends to knowing
that the Declaration of Independence was signed in 1776,
that living forms evolve in a manner set forth by Charles
Darwin, that the symphony now being received by the
radio is Beethoven's Seventh and is a profoundly significant work of art, or that physical bodies behave according
to the law of gravitation. All of these and many more illustrate varieties of the species, propositional knowledge.

Turning from propositional knowledge or acquaintance
knowledge, we find a similar variety ranging from the immediate intuition of sense data (for which Bertrand Russell coined the phrase "acquaintance knowledge"[5]) through
my perceptual recognition of the quality of the music to
which I am now listening, to my self-knowledge, or to the
knowledge of my friend, or to that peculiar sort of knowledge of a student which I seek to communicate in the letter of recommendation that I write a prospective employer.
Truly, acquaintance knowledge is a larger and more varied
type than Russell recognized.

A further study of the words for knowing, thinking, and
the like, in various natural languages verifies and rein-

forces this impression of wide and irreducible variety. For example, the Greek language is characteristically rich in such words, ranging from the know-how of the capable craftsman to the intellectual vision of the philosopher. The latter Greek word, *nous,* embodying the highest intellectual aspiration of the ancient Greek tradition, expresses an aesthetic, contemplative viewpoint in which the mind assumes the role of an observer viewing the world.[6] A similar perspective is apparent in the Sanskrit term for "knowledge," *jñāna.* Both of these are views of knowledge very different from that of the modern West with its emphasis on natural science. Chinese has several terms for different kinds of knowing and knowledge. Still another sharply contrasting viewpoint is expressed in the Hebrew word *yada',* which is fundamentally personal and active in its meaning. Indeed, the highly personal character of knowing in Hebrew provides a clue for the Biblical use of this verb for sexual intercourse as the most intimately personal kind of knowing of another self, which in turn tells us a great deal not only about ancient Hebrew linguistics but about their whole life outlook. Many students have pointed to the active, volitional context of this same verb. For the Biblical Hebrews, knowing is a special continuation of doing.[7]

As we survey this wide, varied, and complex field of human thought and knowledge, we think nostalgically, perhaps, to the simplicity of the behavioristic view of signals and anticipatory responses as discussed in Chapter I. Yet, if human cognition or noesis is variegated and complex, it is so for the good reason that the world which confronts the human mind exhibits this same characteristic; and successful cognitive activity must be proportioned to its object. Hamlet's well-known observation is pertinent at this point:

There are more things in heaven and earth, Horatio,
Than are dreamt of in your philosophy.

A full recognition of this fact will lead us to avoid the
folly so prevalent in much contemporary philosophy of
narrowing the field of things to be known in order to fit
a preconceived view of knowing and knowledge. Surely
this is a procrustean epistemology which excludes by a
priori stipulation much of the significant data to be
studied. In opposition, a truly factual study of human
knowledge will want to begin with the actual and significant meanings of the verb "to know," and other closely
related terms, as they occur in actually functioning human
languages and cultures.

From this point onward the problem will then be to
see what varieties of actually significant cognitive activity
we can lay bare and describe, and how these kinds compare
and contrast with each other. The real task of epistemology, in other words, is to explore the varieties of cognitive
experience as they actually occur in human experience.

2. *Propositional Meaning, Truth, and Knowledge*

In so confused and complex a field of experience, there
is some point in beginning in an area where issues are
relatively clear, and where at least minimal consensus and
agreement exist. From this area it will then be possible to
work outward into other regions where clarity and agreement give way to confusion and controversy. We begin
then with the idea of propositional knowing and knowledge as generally depicted by modern critical philosophy.
Since this form of knowledge lives, moves, and has its being
in true propositions, attention may well be focused upon
truth and falsehood as identifiable properties of entities
called "statements" or "propositions." There is a wide and

growing consensus among contemporary philosophers that the primary locus of truth and falsehood is statements or propositions, or, conversely, that whatever other or whatever more meanings the terms "true" and "false" may have, they denote, first of all, identifiable properties of propositions.[8]

Yet this minimal position is not without formidable issues. For example, a distinction is frequently made between statements and propositions, the latter being defined as the meaning of the former. Thus, if a sentence is translated from one language to another, we get two statements, but the proposition remains the same. Must we then, as some critical realist philosophers have argued, posit a realm of meaning independent of the linguistic forms and of human experience? An even more formidable as well as a more pertinent question lies in this area. Are propositions to be limited to those declarative statements whose meaning and truth can be established and tested by clearly known and accepted activities of the mind?[9] Thus, expressions like "Hurrah," "Phooey," or "Ugh" are usually excluded, since there is alleged to be no generally known and accepted way of establishing and testing their meaning and truth. A similar exclusion is often applied to poetry and to such other forms of expressive statement as moral commandments or religious confessions. The real issue is just how wide a definition of truth and falsehood can be given without stretching these words beyond their elastic limits. In this connection let it be added that if one is inclined to a broad definition, he is under clear obligation to distinguish carefully among the significant varieties embraced by his definition.

As there is a wide consensus in modern Western philosophic study concerning the nature of propositions, so also there is a similar consensus concerning the rules by which truth and falsity can be tested and established. Some of these rules are very old, going back to Aristotle's *Logic* and to the philosophic tradition that lay behind it; others are newer, dating from Hume and the modern tradition of scientific empiricism which found expression in his writings; still others are even more recent, reflecting the influence of nineteenth- and twentieth-century mathematics and logic. The contemporary Western student of these issues thinks and writes, to his great advantage (and equally to his great responsibility), with these men of the past looking over his shoulder. Here we shall attempt a kind of quick summary statement of some of the main rules for the establishment of the truth or falsity of statements that would be widely accepted among contemporary Western philosophers—though it is important to add that different individuals and schools of thought will have their own particular dissents, reformulations, and additions to this summary.

a. The rule of consistency or noncontradiction makes the assertion that a proposition or group of propositions must not include contradictions (not both A and non-A); and it may be said to stipulate the willingness of reasonable men to abandon or revise propositions that may be shown to involve a contradiction. Traditional logic claimed this rule as one of three of the laws of thought, and gave it ontological expression, asserting, "A thing cannot both be and not be."[10] Contemporary logicians tend to assert it as a rule for propositions. Thus, in a famous essay, Nagel reformulates traditional logic to read, "A statement cannot be both true and false."[11] In either interpretation we note consistency as the first rule, necessary but not sufficient for the establishment of the truth of propositions. Propositions, thus, cannot be valid if they contain logically incompatible elements.

This raises the issue, pertinent to both philosophic and religious statements, of paradox, which might be characterized as an apparent contradiction. It is a statement that contains elements which seem to have the relation of logical opposition. Thus it poses a fundamental problem for the mind to whom the statement is addressed, for if the paradox or apparent contradiction turns out to be a real contradiction, acceptance of the statement will stultify any rational mind accepting it and attempting to use it as a rule of discourse. The rule of consistency appears, then, to involve the assumption that true statements (as well as the minds that utter them and the referents to which they point) are free of inconsistency. So it is that paradox turns out to be apparent contradiction used to point up or indicate some notable feature of the subject matter under discussion. Further implications of paradox for religious discourse will be developed in more detail in Chapter XI.

The other two traditional laws of thought, namely, identity (A implies A), and excluded middle (A or not –A), may be regarded as essential features of consistent discourse which recognizes two and only two truth values, namely, truth and falsehood. It is to be noted, however, that in many modern systems of logic they appear as theorems rather than as postulates or axioms. Further, modern logical theory tends to regard them together as necessary but by no means sufficient conditions of rational discourse.

b. The second rule, namely, that of coherence, may be said to presuppose consistency or noncontradiction, and further to assert of any valid proposition or group of propositions an inner harmony of meaning. Taken rigorously, coherence is a much harder trait to identify and define than is consistency. The harmonious relation of the propositions within the group or of the elements within the proposition may be expressed in terms of any one of a variety of logical relations. Of the various possibilities here, perhaps the closest to common sense is that of implication, the logical relation verbalized by such words as "since," "because," or "if . . . then," or "it follows that . . ." We cannot enter here the technical questions discussed among logicians as to the nature of this relation, except to remark that it seems to be the relation between the postulates and theorems of any valid logical system, and that the activity of valid discursive thinking may be said to consist of the process of drawing out or tracing relations of implication. Thus, a body of statements or propositions may be said to be coherent if it is netted together by relations of implication. A single statement is sometimes said to be coherent if a similar relation obtains between its constituent parts, or if the statement has this relation to statements expressing the rest of the speaker's beliefs. In the latter case, one might speak of a coherent mind or a coherent personality. The opposites of coherence are either irrelevance or contradiction. The rule of coherence bids rational men to seek inclusive logical unity among the propositions which express the life of their minds.

Both of these rules may be termed internal to a proposition or group or system of propositions or to the mind that expresses them, in the precise sense that one need not look outside the system of propositions or outside the mind to their objects or referents in order to apply these rules. The two rules of consistency and coherence taken together may, in one legitimate sense of a multivalued term, define the idea of meaning. Thus a term, a statement, or a body of statements is meaningful if it satisfies these two criteria of consistency and coherence. In a quite literal sense, a system of pure or uninterpreted logical or mathematical statements might be said to be meaningful. By contrast, when they are applied to aspects of the real world, the terms "true" and "false" become relevant. This distinction between meaning and truth has several important implications. I shall presently seek to apply it to certain types of expressive statement. Here it may be asserted that meaning may in this sense be characterized as "possible truth." It indicates the free play of possibility, as well as the limits of possibility without any reference to actuality, reality, or existence. Thus, meaningful utterances become candidates for truth or falsehood, a candidacy which is tested as the further criterion of adequacy is applied to them.

c. The rule of adequacy may be characterized as an external rule, for it establishes a relation of mind to objects, of statement to referent. In general, the relation of adequacy places upon statements the twofold requirement of avoiding discrepancy with factual evidence and the satisfaction of all pertinent factual evidence. Thus, a statement is inadequate if it conflicts with factual evidence; and it is also inadequate if it leaves any datum or group of data unilluminated or unexplained. As indicated previously a fact may be most readily characterized as something the mind finds and does not make in its encounter with reality. The idea of adequacy also extends to the requirement of seeking out and getting new factual evidence to test statements, and of which statements must take account. Hence the rule of adequacy does not have a fixed but rather an ever-expanding domain. At this point, surely logic and epistemology must be said to touch the metaphysical idea of totality. In a profound sense the life of reason may be characterized as a lifelong, never-ending, and unrestricted quest for adequacy. It is a quest in which no finite mind ever arrives at the final goal. Yet the goal is necessary to measure and to motivate progress toward it. Chapter III characterized this quest as a function of that aspect of the mind called "objective imagination."

It may be noted in passing that the ideas of discrepancy with factual evidence, and satisfaction of such evidence once they have been stated, may be defined in terms of the consistency and coherence of the resultant body of propositions. Yet the mind, in the midst of actual questions and issues related to its encounter with reality, finds such data not internal but external to its previously existing system of propositions. Like meteors from outer space, new facts move into our consistent and coherent systems, forcing us to take account of them. What is really involved here is not so much the difference between two traditional types of epistemology, idealist and realist, as it is the difference between two views of the mind's characteristic activity of thinking which might be likened respectively to a still picture and a motion picture. The former is the body of consistent and coherent propositions affirmed by a rational human being at any given moment, and the latter is the mind in action, confronting new facts, reorganizing previous systems, reaching out for new facts which in turn must be systematically organized and ever reorganized.

These three rules of consistency, coherence, and adequacy, while variously interpreted and understood by different philosophers and philosophies, would, I believe, with appropriate variations and qualifications gain wide acceptance as basic working norms for critical thinking. Thinking and knowing in one fundamental sense are defined and guided by these rules. However, taken singly or together, they do not constitute a complete or sufficient set of ground rules for intellectual activity. Other guiding principles seem also to be involved. Four such principles, or, as we shall call them, maxims, demand recognition, namely, (a) sufficient reason, (b) economy or parsimony, (c) factuality or empiricism, and finally (d) critical rigor. Obviously all four are variously understood and applied by different men and different movements of thought. Yet let us attempt a rough and brief sketch of them as they function in the process of critical thinking.

The rule of sufficient reason postulates that for every event there is a cause or reason why, and it is a necessary assumption for minds dedicated to ferreting out the reasons or causes for particular situations. Its necessity may be perceived by contemplating its negation. Obviously if one assumed that some events have no reason or no cause, then the pursuit of causes would be a futile game indeed. Yet in applying this maxim, caution must be exercised to interpret it flexibly in different areas or fields. Causes or reasons why, in the natural sciences, may differ profoundly in meaning and significance from those of history or psychology.

The rule of parsimony or economy asserts in the classic words of Occam's razor that "entities must not be multiplied beyond necessity." Other things being equal, "reality" seems to be biased on the side of the logically simpler explanations, namely, those with the smaller number of independent logical elements. So it is that critical intellects are invariably critical of explanations that do appear to multiply entities beyond necessity, whatever the logical unity or power of such explanations or theories. This principle, with its preference for unity and simplicity, may be regarded as one of the formative maxims of the modern critical intellectual tradition. Yet here again a caution is necessary. It is possible to cut one's throat with Occam's razor. The rule of parsimony indiscriminately applied yields not critical intelligence but the manifold fallacies of reductionism.

The maxim of factuality or empiricism, while difficult to state in any adequate, explicit form, may surely be observed in operation as a part of the modern critical philosophic tradition. While it is of wider meaning than the philosophy of empiricism, yet surely the latter is one of its formative influences. Empiricism, in its classical representatives from Locke and Hume through Bentham and Mill to the present, may be regarded basically as a critical philosophy which bids men to test all claims to factual knowledge by the evidence of the senses, and to erect our edifice of factual knowledge on this foundation alone. This philosophy and its critical viewpoint owe much to the success of the natural sciences. Surely too, no group of men has been more influential than natural scientists in inculcating respect for careful, factual knowledge clearly based upon human experience, and always open to further question and testing. Yet as we have previously argued, the issue here is whether the empirical test is to be understood as conformity to sense evidence, or more broadly to experiential evidence. It is this wider meaning of factuality or of the empirical spirit as it operates throughout the modern intellectual tradition that is here called the maxim of factuality or empiricism.

Closely related to factuality or empiricism is a final principle which may be termed the maxim of critical rigor. Perhaps it may be formulated as the duty of intellect not to be fooled. If at times this maxim appears ruthless and negative in its impact upon cherished human values, we must recall that this attitude derives from a single-minded devotion to truth and a corresponding antipathy for falsehood and sham. Furthermore, the alternative to rigorous critical pursuit of truth is a complacent contentment with half-truth and falsehood. Thus its negative appearance has an altogether affirmative foundation.

Undoubtedly there are other significant principles or maxims that might be observed as operating ground rules of the modern critical intellectual tradition. Yet it is safe to say that, taken together, those outlined here will afford some notion of the nature of this tradition. What is particularly pertinent to our concern in this book is that these principles and maxims taken together may be said to constitute a kind of basic morality of intellectual or propositional knowledge. To these general principles of intellectual morality must, of course, be added the working rules of particular fields or disciplines.

3. *Expressive Meaning, Truth, and Knowledge*

To what extent can the ideas of truth and knowledge, developed in the fields of propositional and referential knowledge, be extended to the various fields of expressive statement? These fields include, as we have seen, such human concerns as the arts, religion, and, at least in some current interpretations, traditional speculative or metaphysical philosophy. Many of the issues involved in these fields will be developed further in subsequent chapters of this book. Here, however, we must at least begin the task of analogical or metaphorical extension of the ideas of meaning and truth into these other regions of human experience. This extension is proposed and attempted frankly in the spirit of experiment and exploration, and not with any dogmatic preconception as to results. And it must be added in all candor that experiment always holds the possibility of a negative result. Exploration always holds the possibility that one may find nothing significant. But nothing ventured, nothing learned; therefore let us try. We do so on the initial presumption that these areas of experience in the West and in other human cultures have often been deemed significant areas of the mind's cognitive life and activity. Yet, as previously pointed out, we do so in the face of the negative judgment of much modern critical philosophy which has assumed or asserted that the field of genuine cognition or knowledge is limited to propositional knowledge of common sense and natural science. The rest of human experience, however significant and poignant it may be as experience, is not to be regarded as knowledge. It is a significant form of experience, of doing, and undergoing, even perhaps of insight, but not of knowing. To call it a knowing is, according to this view, to force a good word to carry a cargo which it is ill designed to carry.

The first issue in our experiment concerns the proper denotation of the terms "language" and "statement." Of the arts, literature in its various forms consists of configurations of expressive words, and therefore quite literally it consists of statements. Thus, the issue here is whether or in what sense these distinctive statements are meaningful or true in a sense continuous with ordinary language. However, the other arts—music, painting, sculpture, architecture, and the dance—have other nonverbal media of expression, ranging from musical notes to bodily movements. The question in these areas is whether such organized media can in any serious and fruitful sense be likened to language or statement. Perhaps the first step in answering this question is to ask whether through these various media there is an intention of the artist to communicate. If so, there is some presumption that the art as a functioning system of communication constitutes a language. Are these arts in some way systems of communication? Are they ways of saying? If so, the unit of communication or language may, I think, appropriately be termed a statement. My own answer to these questions concerning the arts is affirmative; and I shall defend it in more detail in Chapter VII.

To the intent to communicate we may add, for both the verbal and nonverbal arts, the presence of bodies of rules or norms in some way similar to syntax and grammar. Also there exist units of the medium similar in some sense to the terms of verbal language (in many arts these terms are customarily called "images") together with the organization of these terms into significant structures through which communication takes place. Such structures are as true of music, architecture, and the dance as of literature; and in each case there is genuine analogy to the organization of words into sentences or statements by means of the rules of grammar and syntax.

In addition to syntax and grammar, there are analogies to the logical categories of consistency and coherence. Indeed, it is an observable fact that these terms do find their way into the discussion of the arts. Consistency and its opposite, contradiction, denote ways in which the terms of artistic discourse are combined in internally compatible or incompatible ways. Coherence, applied to the arts, means a unified and harmonious system of meaning. Categories of this order seem not only permissible but indispensable elements of artistic communication, though it must immediately be added that they can be given specific meaning or interpretation only within the context of a given art and of its criticism.

As argued in the previous section, consistency and coherence are internal tests for any body of statements; and they do not involve any external relation of statement to referent. Now let us extend this distinction to the expressive statements of the arts.[12] In the case of some of the arts, these rules of consistency and coherence are as far as they go. There is no assertion of a referent. Such artistic statements are thus analogous to statements in pure logic and mathematics, internally consistent and coherent, but not applied or referred to any aspect of the real world. Accordingly they must be judged or appraised by these standards. Far from being statements about aspects of the real or existential world, they constitute the statement of pure possibility, the play of pure essence or meaning, unrelated to any real or existent entity. This at least is a possible or conceivable way of understanding many of the arts. Music as well as extensive areas of painting and sculpture offer numerous illustrations of such an understanding. Incidentally, we must be careful not to limit such interpretation to abstract or nonrepresentational works of art. Its application is conceivably much wider.

Other arts and works of art claim, however, to make statements that are not only meaningful but true. Again, we must guard against identifying the idea of truth too simply with the representational as against the abstract arts as such, for we are dealing here not with the category of subject matter but of expressed content, or what the artist says about his subject matter. Despite the fact that literature is a representational art, some poems are in their expressed content as abstract as a Bach fugue, and must be judged or appraised by appropriate criteria. However, other works of literature and music, as well as other arts, clearly claim as an aspect of their expressed content to tell us something about ourselves or the world in which we live. Insofar as any work of art makes this claim it must be judged by the standard of adequacy or truth. Accordingly, we must put the question: Are its statements true or false?

The answer to this question will be in terms of some application of the idea of adequacy. For truth, we have argued, consists of the adequacy of thought to things, of statement to referent. But how, then, is adequacy to be applied to artistic statement? The answer is that no wholesale or blanket application is either possible or desirable. Rather, the application must be undertaken by responsible critical judgment on the basis of evidence internal to the various arts, and indeed to each work of art. In each case such judgment must say whether or not the idea of truth is relevant, and if it is, to proceed specifically with the task of adequation. This task of digging out what it is that the artist is saying, and of assessing its truth or falsehood, must be judged as a fundamental aspect of criticism. It will vary from art to art, but it will always consist of a critical judgment of whether the artist's statement conflicts with factual evidence, and of whether it satisfies all the relevant factual evidence.

While I have illustrated the idea of expressive meaning and truth by the arts, there are equally possible and pertinent applications in ethics, religion, philosophy, and other fields. However, it is well to add that each of these many fields has its own peculiar rules of speaking and thinking in addition to the general rules sketched here; and thinking in each field consists of finding and using the appropriate rules in such ways that one makes sense to himself and others.

4. *The Existentialist Perspective*

The intellectual community of the Western world has in recent decades become familiar in varying degrees with the

movement called "existentialism." Extending from literature and the other arts to philosophy and theology, the
existentialist movement has exhibited both the unity of
certain significant common features and also a puzzling diversity of outlook. The latter trait makes the task of precise
definition difficult to the point of impossibility. There is
clearly no easy or final way of saying who is and who is not
an existentialist.

Yet now that the faddish novelty of existentialism has
worn off sufficiently to begin the task of critical appraisal,
it becomes increasingly possible to locate it in relation to
other intellectual tendencies, and also to see the historical
lineage of its main tenets. In this section, we shall sketch a
few significant features of the existential perspective; and
in the next, undertake a constructive statement of an existentialist approach to meaning, truth, and knowledge,
also noting a few implications of existentialism for language and symbolism.

It is, of course, important to note that the adjectives
"expressive" and "existential" are independent variables.
True, existentialists have frequently employed expressive
forms of statement, and conversely expressive communication in the various arts often has existential meaning or
significance. Nevertheless, the two terms and their referents are clearly distinguishable and separable.

The central and controlling element of the existentialist
perspective may accurately be characterized as a radical
concern for the human self as an actual, existing entity
prior to all theories about it. The existence referred to in
existentialism is the existence of real, actual human selves.
Man, declares Sartre, is the being in whom "existence
precedes essence."[13] Thus it is that the dog does not seem
to be concerned about his caninity, which is his essence,

nor does the cow seem to be concerned about her bovinity; but men of all faiths and philosophies put to themselves in one form or another the searching question, What must I do and be to be genuinely human? Man's humanity, which is his essence, is a poignantly serious problem to him. As an existing being, man seeks his essence. Thus existentialism puts the question, What is man?, or rather more personally, Who am I?, at the center of human thought. It is this common question, What is man?, asked with poignancy and urgency and given a central place in a total system of thought, which draws together the diverse men and works to whom the term "existentialism" is applied. It might also be added that all men act out in deed and life their answers to this question.

Beyond this existential question, existentialists exhibit also certain further common features in their systems of thought. Most prominent is a fundamental concern with human freedom. According to existentialists, whatever else and whatever more man may be, he is fated to be free.[14] The burden of freedom is not only the key to human fulfillment; it is also the source of the alienation or dehumanization which, under various names and in various interpretations, has been a common concern of existentialists. Because man is radically free, he is free either to fulfill his humanity or to dehumanize himself.

The essence of man, which defines his humanity or humanness, thus appears in existentialism as a radical question which each man puts to himself, to which he must find an answer that is then lived out in his existence. In other words, man's essence lies in the radical freedom which empowers him to put this question. The answers that existentialists of the past and present have given to the existential question have exhibited the widest diversity, ranging from the Christian faith of Kierkegaard to the anti-Christian creative freedom of Nietzsche, or from the lonely and tragic freedom of Camus to the I-Thou relation of Buber. Yet in each case, the common feature is that it is a functioning answer to man's question, Who am I?

As the existentialist approaches problems of meaning and truth, he is acutely aware of the polar relation of the terms "essence" and "existence." Like north and south, up and down, neither essence nor existence has meaning apart from the other. Essence and existence are polar or correlative aspects of the wider term "being." Existentialist views of meaning, truth, and knowledge may thus be understood as signifying truth and knowledge for an engaged, existent self, in contrast to essentialist views of these matters which endeavor to be as impersonal and objective as humanly possible. In a word, essentialism seeks to abstract from actual human existence. The existentialist viewpoint is that of the engaged, active self; the essentialist viewpoint is that of the observing self. To cite a single clear and radical illustration of this difference, Kierkegaard in his monumental *Concluding Unscientific Postscript* defines the truth as "objective uncertainty held with the most passionate inwardness," deliberately attempting to move away from Hegelian rationalism and commonsense objectivity in the direction of a radical subjectivity.[15] It is pertinent to observe that common language confirms Kierkegaard's meaning when it speaks of being a "true man" or "true friend." Personal authenticity is apparently one facet of the many-faceted term "truth."

Historically, existentialism looks back to a long tradition. In ancient Greece, Plato drew a clear distinction between essence (or idea) and appearance. He also regarded the former as true being and the latter as a realm of shadows or illusory half-realities. For example, the metaphor of the cave in Book VII of the *Republic* locates true being in the bright sunlight of the realm of Ideas, and understands the realm of common daily existence as a place of images, shadows, and darkness. Plato, in short, is the arch-essentialist of Western philosophy.

If we turn from Plato and his world of ideas and his allegory of the cave to the Bible, we are immediately aware of a radically different view of the world. The famous verse Ex. 3:14 is doubtless erroneously translated as "I am that I am," and the mistake is compounded in the traditional Western philosophic understanding of deity as absolute and self-subsistent Being, yet no critical student of the Bible doubts that the Biblical Hebrews regarded deity as in some sense the supreme existent. Furthermore, there is in the Bible not a trace of the Platonic duality of essence and appearance. Rather, in sharpest contrast, the human mind and self are, in the Biblical view, totally immersed in existence, which conversely is conceived as the reality man confronts in daily life and action. Furthermore, the Biblical Hebrews never doubted the freedom and responsibility of man (along with his finitude or creatureliness) as he lives and acts in this world.

When this Hebraic or Biblical perspective came into relation with the Platonic Greek mind, as it did in the patristic period of early Christianity, radically new intellectual results were to be expected. This is precisely what took place. The significantly new view of man and the world, to be seen in such documents as Augustine's *Confessions,* exhibits many of the characteristic features of existentialism. For example, in Augustine's writing one sees the freedom and depth of the human self and mind, as well as the deep alienation of human sin. The new view is to be understood historically in terms drawn from both Greece and Israel.

The Scholastic thought of the Middle Ages first formally

stated and philosophically elaborated the difference between essence and existence, thus testifying to a double inheritance from Greece and Israel.[16] It is important, however, to add that while the distinction was stated, it was certainly not developed in its full implication by Scholastic thought.[17] In most of its significant features, Scholastic philosophy and theology can hardly be characterized as other than essentialist.

A similar essentialism appears in the definition of the self as thinking substance (*res cogitans*) by Descartes, who is often termed the founder of modern Western philosophy.[18] Yet behind the facade of Descartes's mathematical rationalism and subjectivism lurk other differing suggestions which later took definite shape in existentialist philosophy. Behind the assertion, "I think, therefore I am," lay the question, What am I?, or better, Who am I? It remained for future thinkers to separate question from answer, and to press the question in radical fashion. Similarly, behind Descartes's confident and somewhat artificial invocation of the ontological argument for a good God lurked the grinning face of the demon who would deceive man with false ideas. Who can deny that as the modern age has developed, the face of the good God has dimmed, while the visage of the demon has grown clearer?

These philosophic reflections have, in the nineteenth and twentieth centuries, been reinforced by deep misgivings about the actual fate of the human self in the storms of these turbulent times. Is the self being lost or obliterated by menacing forces? Is man being dehumanized or depersonalized? Out of such broodings have come the somber views of man of such writers as Dostoevsky, Kierkegaard, Marx, Nietzsche, and others. Sometimes called "the nineteenth-century underground," these men have in common a mordant, sometimes tragic realism concerning the nature and prospects of man. It remained for thinkers and writers in the twentieth century to take these historical elements in varying combinations and to construct out of them systems of philosophy called "existentialist."[19] Now we must turn attention to the bearing of existentialist philosophy upon human knowing and speaking.

5. *An Existentialist View of Meaning and Truth*

If the reader has reflected, as these historical elements of existentialism were sketched, that much of this viewpoint has found its way into the viewpoint that informs and guides these pages, he is entirely correct. Let us call attention to a few specific illustrations. In Chapter II, the essentialist prejudices of much contemporary semantic philosophy were indicated, and a new beginning was attempted in the idea of language and symbolism as features of the lives of human persons and communities of persons. In Chapter I, intension and extension were identified as essential and existential aspects of the meaning situation: the engaged or participant self and mind have been contrasted with the observing or contemplating self; and the priority of the former has been asserted. Some of the implications of such an existentialist approach for the problems of language and symbolism have also been pointed out. Here we must seek to fill a few of the gaping holes in this line of philosophic argument, and in particular to sketch the nature (or meaning), truth, and knowledge as seen from this viewpoint.

First let us focus attention upon the persistent duality of elements, subject and object, intension and extension, essence and existence, contemplation and action, theory and practice, and then let us try to draw them together and see them *sub specie existentiae,* under the aspect of existence. It is man's root freedom, the freedom of self-transcendence, which enables him to look upon himself, his world and the world of pure possibility or essence, clearly envisaging the distinction between existence and essence. Once this distinction has been established, the fundamental duality denoted by all these pairs of opposites comes into being. Most fundamentally with respect to man's own nature, it is the duality of the life of idea and the life of action.

The question arises whether man's life, riven by these dualities, can ever find or restore its lost unity, healing the breach between essence and existence, bridging the chasm between subject and object, actuality and possibility. The answer I wish to propose is that we do precisely this in action. In the life of action, essence and existence, subject and object, self and world, are brought together. As these elements are separated by theory or contemplation, they are brought together again in action.

There is a deceptive simplicity, perhaps even the appearance of triviality, about this assertion. But as we dig into its implications we shall find how false this appearance is. For one thing, the idea of action, of doing, must, I think, stand as a logically primitive or undefined term.[20] As John Locke proposed to reply to anyone who wanted a definition of solidity by putting a football between his hands and asking him to bring them together, so if anyone wishes to know what the terms "action" or "doing" mean, let him turn upon himself as he sets about to do something or to act in some particular way, and let him attend carefully what takes place. As he says to himself, "I do this," let him pay careful attention to the referent of his words.

If he looks carefully, he will note that there is no sense

datum corresponding to action. This is what makes action so troublesome an idea to positivists and empiricists, despite the fact that these philosophers are actually deeply dependent upon the idea of action. Nor may action be equated with physical displacement or overt organic behavior, though both of these facts are involved in action, for there are types of action (such as mental action) in which neither physical displacement nor overt organic behavior are involved. In short, all that we can fairly and factually say of human actions is that we *do* them.[21] Doing is thus a logically primitive idea.

So conceived, action is the widest category of human selfhood. The duality of contemplation (or theory) and action is overcome when we recall that human contemplating, theorizing, and thinking are among the things that men *do*. It is to be noted that the converse of this statement is clearly false; while thinking is one of the things we do, it is not true to assert that doing is a form of thinking. So we conclude, not that *esse est percipi*, but, as Austin Farrer has asserted, *esse est operari*.[22] To be is to act. Such at least is the case for a human self. It will not be false to take this statement as an assertion of the primacy of volition or will in human selfhood, and to associate it with the voluntarist tradition stemming from Augustine and, before him, from the Bible.

From this viewpoint, now let us look at the traditional ideas of meaning, truth, and knowledge. Truth has been defined as adequacy of statement to referent, and meaning as possible truth, or, in a word, the candidacy of an essence or meaning for the test of adequacy to the referent. Putting these ideas together with what has been said about the existentialist perspective, existential truth may be defined as the adequacy of essence to existence; and existential meaning may be defined as possible existential truth. To such meanings or essences the tests of consistency and coherence still apply. In the case of truth, the further test of adequacy to the facts of existence is the crucial test. Furthermore, all these ideas are asserted from the viewpoint of an engaged, active self, that is to say, a self in active encounter with reality, as it were, on the playing field, and not in the grandstand. Indeed, it is precisely this claim for the primacy of the active self—that the self is on the playing field engaged in the game of mortal human existence—that provides the definition of the term "existentialist" as here used.

Over wide fields of the mind's cognitive activities, these views of meaning and truth will coincide with those of commonsense realism, empiricism, and pragmatism that are common in contemporary American philosophy. In such areas the terms "experience" and "existence" will be virtually synonymous, since they both designate the same elements of the interaction of self and world. In other regions this coincidence of views will no longer occur. So, for example, when the human self is included in the area to be understood, the relation of essence to existence takes on a peculiar significance and urgency. For truth here means the essence which I take as adequate to my existence, and which in a sense I *become* or I *am*. Here too, it is not only the essence I take as adequate but also the way or manner in which I take it. In short, I must do it in freedom and responsibility. Thus the concept of personal authenticity assumes particular significance for the existentialist viewpoint. It indeed is this whole subjective area of meaning and truth to which existentialist philosophy has devoted so much attention.

Often this preoccupation has led existentialists from

Kierkegaard onward to emphasize the subjective aspects of truth to the exclusion of objective aspects. For Kierkegaard, apparently any "truth" appropriated with wholehearted passion has authenticity. But in all candor there seems no reason why an emphasis on these aspects of truth must necessarily lead to a neglect or exclusion of the objective aspects. Both are aspects of the total conception of adequacy. Indeed, neglect or denial of any aspect is to that extent an inadequate view of the situation as a whole.

One further issue must be briefly treated. We have frequently alluded to facts and to reality; and now both words must be drawn into the philosophic viewpoint of this chapter. The term "fact," as here used, may be characterized in a variety of ways. Logically, it might be described as any value of the existential propositional function which will yield a true proposition. Psychologically it may be described as something which the mind finds and does not make, discovers and does not invent in its encounter with the world. In this characterization it is important to note that such finding or discovery takes place as an aspect of the mind's active encounter with the world. Facts are then data for the active self. Metaphysically a fact might be characterized as a piece of reality; and reality, conversely, as the total structure of facts. As Wittgenstein wrote in the *Tractatus,* "The world is the totality of facts."[23] However, the view here outlined differs from Wittgenstein's in at least one respect. He sought to limit the realm of facts to the value-neutral facts of natural science, values having only a nonfactual, subjective nature. On the other hand, I assert an objective "structure of requiredness" in all serious human valuation.[24] Values, in other words, have their own distinctively factual aspect.

A psychological aspect of fact and reality to which attention was called in Chapter III may be characterized as resistance to the self in action. Both fact and reality are action-oriented words. It is characteristic of the factual and the real that it resists me, enforcing its reality upon me as I encounter it in action. Facts are simply units or items of reality; and, conversely, reality is the total structure of facts.

In summary, then, existentialism bids us see these issues from the viewpoint of free, active, engaged selves or minds confronting reality. In this encounter, truth is the adequacy of essence or meaning to existence, and meaning is possible truth or candidacy for truth or adequacy. Reality is what we find and do not make, discover and do not invent, in the encounter of mind or self with what lies beyond its own frontiers; and facts are pieces of reality. The heart of an existentialist philosophy will then consist of the expression and adjudication of the various claims to meaning and truth which occur in this encounter of self or mind with world.

To return, in closing, to the question with which this chapter began, we ask what distinctive kind of knowledge is obtainable from the existentialist viewpoint. What, if anything, is distinctive about this language stratum and knowledge stratum? Surely this viewpoint has no monopoly on the kind of objective factual knowledge of common sense and natural science, though existentialist interpretations of natural science such as Polanyi's *Personal Knowledge* have achieved impressive results.[25] Rather, the kind of cognition distinctive to this viewpoint will be an insight into the ends or goals of human life as envisaged by the engaged active human mind or self. Since this envisagement is reflected back into the whole body of human experience, and indeed plays a very important part in that experience, here is a viewpoint of fundamental and distinctive importance. Men of different faiths and philosophies will not always agree in what they see or say or know from this viewpoint, and sometimes their disagreements will be wide and deep; but it is an aspect of the mind's life too large and too important to be overlooked by any philosophy worthy of the name.

VI   Science as Language

❖ ❖

In Chapter II the hypothesis was advanced that science, art, philosophy, and conceivably many other human concerns as well, might be construed and studied as derivative languages. In each case we find a basis for the form of activity in common experience and common language, but as each of these human enterprises develops it creates its own distinctive language through which it is articulated and communicated. Thus, conversely, the enterprise may be approached and studied fruitfully through its language. Such at least is the hypothesis; and the next three chapters will be concerned to apply and test it in the three fields of science, art, and philosophy.

These three human concerns are selected for consideration because of their relations to our main object of study, namely, religion and religious language. These relations are very different for each of the three. In the case of science we will be led to see that the relation is almost entirely one of difference and contrast; but it is important to delineate this difference, for the good reason that science and religion historically have often been confused with each other—to the great misfortune of each. Art and philosophy, in their respective ways, have closer and more affirmative relations to religion. Indeed, at some points there is, in both cases, an overlapping relation. But in all three cases we shall gain a clearer idea of religious language by a look at each of these other three forms of language.

1. *Science and Common Experience*

In his essay "Magic, Science and Religion,"[1] Malinowski characterizes science as the body of tested common knowledge, possessed and passed on in any culture, which serves to guide the important common techniques and activities of the culture. In the case of Malinowski's Trobriand Islanders, such science includes knowledge of boatbuilding and navigation, yam cultivation, and many of the other processes of the nature upon which these people are dependent. While this science does not exclude attempts at pure explanation, its main purpose is thoroughly practical, namely, to guide common social practice. It has to do particularly with prediction and control. It is also wholly secular, having no trace of the holy or sacred about it. Its limits, according to Malinowski, are the limits of man's prediction and control of his environment. When men face the unknown and uncontrollable, they drop the scientific attitude and resort to magic or religion or both.

In this definition of the term "science" as tested and reliable knowledge about common processes of nature or the world, it is clearly a recurrent aspect of the common life of men and cultures. It is that aspect of common human experience which enables men to discriminate facts, to understand or explain them and to use them for purposes of prediction and control. In this sense of the word, not only does every culture have its science but also every man is his own scientist, for the good reason that science is a basic aspect of human experience.

It may also be noted that this is the aspect of common human experience which serves as the foundation upon which modern natural science has erected its unique and imposing edifice. The term "natural science" has acquired, during the past three or four centuries of Western culture, a different and special meaning. Indeed, it is not common but a most uncommon kind of knowledge. While it clearly has a foundation in common human experience, the edifice it has erected upon this foundation is an altogether distinctive kind of knowledge. This construction must also be regarded as a uniquely great historical and spiritual achievement. To modern natural science and the language in which it is articulated we must now turn our attention.

2. *Some Traits of the Language of Science*

Looking more closely at the modern natural scientific movement, we see that it is, among other things, men talking and writing in highly distinctive ways. Natural science has many other aspects as well, but in one of its aspects it is a body of specialized language. It is the research papers in which new knowledge is embodied, together with the criticism of these papers. It is the language of the lecture room, of laboratory manual and report. It is the conversation of professor and student, of master and apprentice. It is the journals and the statements of scientific societies. Modern natural science is all these and many more kinds of language, together with the community of men that utters these words. It may well prove to be illuminating to approach science through the distinctive kinds of language in which it is articulated and embodied.

In all of this it is well to recall our previously expressed caution concerning the relation of speech to thought, of saying to thinking. Clearly, scientific language is the nec-

essary vehicle of scientific thought; and without its distinctive forms of language, scientific thinking would be
impossible. Yet equally we must avoid any complete identification of scientific thought and language. Science is,
first of all, a highly distinctive way of thinking that has
been fruitful in creating many new ways of language to
meet its continually new and changing needs and problems. Here, as in other areas, language is the necessary
vehicle of thought.

What, now, are some of the significant traits of scientific
statements and language? One extremely important feature, namely, that they are created, sustained, and used not
by solitary thinkers but by a particular community and
tradition of men, will be discussed in the next section.
Looking now directly at some of the various kinds of statements scientists make, we shall list eight significant features of scientific utterance.

a. The feature of scientific language most immediate to
our study of language is its systematic avoidance of expression or symbolism in the sense in which these terms were
defined in Chapter I. The terms of scientific discourse are
uniformly and deliberately signs and not symbols; and the
function of the language is accordingly one of reference
and not expression. If expression or symbolism occurs, it
is wholly irrelevant to the scientific use of language, for
science is an enterprise which seeks impersonal, referential
understanding. Science, in other words, is not poetry.

b. A second feature is science's peculiar quality of precision. To be sure, poetry is precise in its own way, but it
is a very different way. Scientific terms are often artificially
constructed in order to avoid the vagueness and ambiguity
of natural language and to guarantee precision. In some
sciences, Greek or Latin terms are used for this purpose.

In other situations new words are coined; and in still other situations, words are given a precise mathematical meaning, as for instance such words as "distance," "time," "mass," "force," or other basic terms of physics.

c. The last illustration leads us to the mathematical character of the language of physical science and of some aspects of other sciences. Mathematics is frequently spoken of as the language of the physical sciences; or, conversely, physical science is defined as applied mathematics. Natural science is, in this view, pure mathematics interpreted or applied to significant aspects of the physical world. The problem of application or interpretation is so large and complex that we cannot here enter it beyond the observation that a great many contemporary mathematicians profess to be pragmatists at this point. That is to say, they use whatever mathematical systems are most useful for their purpose of understanding specified aspects of the world; and they apply their mathematical systems in any way that will work. If one system of mathematics is not useful, it is dropped in favor of one that gives more promise of successful performance.

Some qualifying comments are important for the view of mathematics as the language of physical science. First, physical science seems never to be reducible completely and without remainder to mathematical statements. Some nonmathematical terms and statements, if only those guiding or directing the application or interpretation, persist. Second, mathematics is the language of physical science only if we include in our understanding of the term "language" what is often called a calculus, namely, a system of signs by means of which calculations or deductive operations may take place. Verbal prose is indeed often used for this purpose in daily life, so there is some justification for stretching the idea of language to include this function. However, it must also be added that for many good reasons physical scientists prefer to perform their deductive operations in mathematical language if it is possible to do so.

These three foregoing traits of scientific utterance go far in making clear what is often called the technical language of science, so baffling to the layman, so intriguing to science-fiction writers, and so essential to the scientist. It is, we repeat, a derivative and largely artificial language constructed by the scientific community for the purpose of eliminating irrelevant considerations and focusing attention on scientifically relevant issues.

If now we turn attention to the different kinds of statements, we find in the whole body of scientific writings that a threefold classification suggests itself. The next three features, which follow here, will consist, in order, of these three types of scientific statements which, incidentally, taken together comprise the essentials of scientific method.

d. One significant kind of scientific statement consists of the questions scientists ask of nature, or the problems they formulate for solution. It may perhaps be queried whether questions may in any strict and proper sense be statements or propositions. In the present case, scientific questions as here characterized might be put into the form of declarative sentences expressing the problems to which other scientific statements are the solutions. At least, then, scientific questions may be said to imply statements.

Several features of scientific questions or problems demand our comment. One essential feature is that these questions invariably extend over a limited domain. That is to say, they are not questions about the universe as a whole or any other completely unrestricted totality.[2] Indeed, such total questions would be scientifically meaningless. The word "all" in scientific statements invariably involves either explicit or implied delimitation of one sort or another. This constitutes a clear distinction between scientific statement, on the one hand, and philosophic and religious statement on the other; for, as we shall presently see, these two types of utterance do involve completely unrestricted uses of "all" in their inclusive totality statements.

The fact that scientific problems have a carefully delimited domain or extension is altogether essential to science. By fencing off a particular area, science is able to deal decisively with it—to solve one problem and then move on to another. Thus emerges the progressive or cumulative character of scientific knowledge, in contrast to the noncumulative or nonprogressive character of many other forms of knowledge. In passing, let it also be noted that this process of marking off or delimiting the domain of his problems properly commits the scientist to a strict agnosticism regarding the rest of reality. Concerning aspects and areas of reality beyond the boundaries of his problem or his science, he literally does not know and does not need, as a scientist, to commit himself. Thus the practice of some scientists of offering presumably authoritative pronouncements on all things in heaven and earth must be regarded as clearly unscientific. A scientist's authority is limited to his scientific domain.

A final observation concerning the statements that formulate scientific questions or problems is that to produce them is an act of genuine intellectual creativity as mysterious as any other form of creativity. Granted essential knowledge of the field, it is simply a fact that some minds come up with fruitful questions and others do not. The alchemy by which felt difficulties in a situation become significant questions is a process beyond human knowledge or control. Yet the art of spotting significant problems, of formulating fruitful questions, is surely the beginning of scientific thinking. It is to be understood as a function of the creative imagination discussed in Chapter III.

e. If some of the statements of science can be classified as questions, others may be regarded as answers or solutions. To be sure, the question-answer dialogue between mind and world is by no means limited to science; rather, it extends to the whole field of significant human thought. Explanation in all its varied forms may be described as an answer to a question. In terms of formal logic, the explanatory statement stands in the relation of implication to the statement of the problem. This means that if the explanatory statement is true, the statement of problematic data follows logically from it and is also true. The perception of this relation is what is often meant by the metaphor of illumination in reference to explanation; we find explanations illuminating precisely because we see or directly perceive this relation of implication between premise and conclusion.

Like scientific problems, a scientific explanation has a delimited, defined character. It must be of sufficiently definite nature that its formal implications can be developed by specifiable operations of thought and that it can be tested for truth or falsehood. This means that we must be able to envisage its falsifiability.[3] An explanation true under all circumstances, or true no matter what, is scientifically meaningless. Scientific answers as well as questions appear to have a definite, limited extension.

Also like the statement of problems, that of explanation is an act of originality or creativity. The ability to give answers, like that of asking fruitful questions, is a mysterious human capacity concerning which no rules have been successfully formulated. As previously observed, logics of discovery are either, like J. S. Mill's so-called canons of discovery, ways of testing explanations already in existence, or they are useless nonsense.[4] In either case, they fall short of what they claim to be, namely, a logical instrument of creativity.

Scientific explanations are of a wide variety of kinds. The terms "law," "hypothesis," and "theory" come to mind as a rough classification or set of pigeonholes. A law explains by stating an orderly relation among the problematic data. In some views of science, such as that of Karl Pearson,[5] law is regarded as the whole of explanation. In some scientific situations this appears actually to be the case, but in other situations, law raises the further question, Why? It thus leads on to hypothesis or theory. These two latter terms denote statements of determinate relations or events of such a sort that problematic data may be derived or deduced from them. Roughly speaking, a hypothesis or theory is a story that scientists tell, of such a sort that if one grants the truth of this story, the problematic factual data are thereby explained. A hypothesis is a relatively unproved or untested theory whose field or domain is less extensive than that of a theory; and, conversely, a theory is a factually well established hypothesis, and also one that extends over a wide field. Good hypotheses or theories prove their worth not only by organizing and unifying previous knowledge in a given field, but also by suggesting new questions to be put to nature. It is essential to scientific method that hypotheses or theories are never regarded as demonstratively true, but forever subject to further empirical, experimental tests.

f. A further type of scientific statement is accordingly

that which states the empirical test to which all theories must be put, as well as the results of such tests. The heart of this test is a perceptual act carried out in the context of theory and, if possible, in the controlled situation of a laboratory. Hence the statement of this perceptual act will invariably be some sort of specific factual statement which either verifies or disproves the theory.

Of the many observations that might be made concerning verification, I limit myself to three that are particularly pertinent to our present subject. First, verification illustrates again the delimited, determinate character of scientific thinking and speaking. Surely scientific verification clearly presupposes a delimited extension—literally, a field with a fence around it. If the field of verification were infinitely or indefinitely large, men might conceivably look forever without finding the facts that would enable us to decide for or against a hypothesis. Thus, verification is a scientifically meaningful concept only to the degree that we have a delimited field in which it is to be applied.

Second, the reference to altogether particular facts and particular structures of facts involved in scientific verification is a distinctive trait of scientific thinking, especially when it is compared to systems of thought in philosophy and religion, which, once they take off into the upper air of speculative ideas, seem never again to come back to earth. In sharpest contrast, scientific thinking makes periodic landings on the earth of altogether particular human experience. Such periodic landings are essential to science.

Third, the activity of verification always has the character of a journey of exploration in which the results are never clearly known before the fact. This open character of verification is persuasively argued in Waismann's essay on "Verifiability."[6] In this respect scientists might be compared to hunters who are trained and equipped with powerful weapons, and then issued hunting licenses. However, as they fare forth into the woods, whether they will bring back game and what kind of game they will bag remain open questions.

Once a scientific theory or hypothesis has been put to experimental test a never-ending game of leapfrog begins. It is a game of leapfrog between theory and fact, and of this game the ongoing life of science consists. Theoretical statements are tested factually, and thereby confirmed or infirmed. In the latter case, they are either rejected or revised in the light of new facts. Then they are tested anew, and so on without end, as long as science goes on. From this characteristic of the scientific process follow two further traits of scientific statement that must be briefly noted.

g. All the statements of science without exception are conceived to have relative and not absolute truth. They are truths and not Truth. There are, in short, no absolutely final, closed, or certain results in science. This assertion is not a reluctant concession to skepticism, but is an essential and affirmative feature of scientific knowing and saying. In virtue of this attitude, science takes on the character of cumulative or progressive knowledge. Indeed, natural science is the clearest and best example of progress in all human experience, as well as being the historical source of this idea.

h. As a consequence of these features, science faces an open future. It is a future that will remain open as long as men seek to push back the frontier of human knowledge. Science, as it faces the open future, is always an open system of knowledge, never a closed or final system; thus the body of statements that embody science at any given moment is always in process of being revised and remade.

3. Science and Scientists

Now we must turn from the objectivity and impersonality that characterize the statements of science to the more personal and subjective issues of the tradition and community of men who produce these statements, whose work consists of this distinctive form of thinking and talking. While many of a scientist's personal attitudes or valuations are systematically excluded from his scientific thinking and speaking, it is equally clear that his science is conditioned and affected in many ways by these human attitudes. There are, in short, such things as scientific attitudes and values.

In any human group it is allegiance to a common set of values which constitutes the group as a community; and it is the communication of these values to each new individual and to each succeeding generation which constitutes a tradition. These facts are illustrated by the community and tradition of men over the past three or four centuries who have created and sustain modern natural science. To be sure, scientific values form no part of the explicit content of the various natural sciences. Nor do scientists customarily make formal professions of faith in their values or preach sermons to their colleagues and students proclaiming these values. Rather, the process of value creation and value communication takes place here by personal example, or, as it were, by the contagion of life. But these values do exist, and they play an indispensable role in creating and defining the community and tradition in which science and scientific statements have their existence. They will continue to be important as long as scientists are men.

If we ask what are the values that thus underlie and sustain science, the indispensable minimum will include an allegiance to freedom and to the pursuit of knowledge. The root meaning of freedom for the scientist is the freedom to decide scientific issues on the basis of scientific evidence, unimpeded by outside forces whether religious, political, or of any other sort. Freedom also means the freedom of publication and of communication with other scientists. Yet here as elsewhere the other side of freedom is responsibility. This means the making of decisions or choices in devotion to the aims or goals of science. So, for example, the editor of the scientific journal must accept this paper and reject that one, the committee must approve this candidate or that proposal and reject others, if science is to go on.[7] Such free and responsible decisions are essential aspects of the scientific movement.

The other main value of the scientist is devotion to the scientific knowledge or truth that he pursues. As we have noted, scientists seldom explicitly or verbally pledge their allegiance or engage in overt acts of devotion to truth; yet this value lies at the foundation of their activities. If they place other values, whether the pursuit of money or allegiance to a political party or a religious creed, above their allegiance to scientific truth, they are very likely to become bad scientists however great their talents. In a real sense this value is the ultimate concern of the scientist.

If we ask whether there are other essential values of the scientific community, no uniform answer is forthcoming. Value patterns are as various as individual men and their motivations. Yet in all of this variety two general types of motivation and valuation seem to show themselves in the scientific community. Let us call them "truth for truth's sake" and "truth for life's sake." As we observe different scientists and different regions of the broad field of science, we see many combinations and permutations of these two patterns of motivation and valuation.

Issues of value and valuation are important to science not only in relation to motivation but also in relation to human and social situations where science is applied and used. However, here we must recall and underscore the rigorously value-neutral character of scientific knowledge and statement. At a minimum this means that in the body of statements that constitute a natural science, value judgments have no place. Readers who disagree are invited to produce a single statement of human value that is a functioning part of any existing natural science. What this means, in turn, for the application of science to human life is that sciences, unlike some other kinds of instruments, do not come nicely packed with directions for their human use. Rather, they are in this respect entirely dependent upon the moral valuations of the men who use them. In themselves they are morally neutral instruments of great power. This relation between science and man defines some of the most urgent and poignant problems of our time.

4. *What Science Is Not*

Having described some aspects of the nature and uses of science, we must now point as well to what science is not, and to some of its misuses. For the great success of the scientific method has led to uncritical adulation and to many attempts to make this great intellectual instrument do things it was never designed to do. To come directly to the point, science is excellent as science; but it is not art, philosophy, or religion and it comes off badly when it is used as such. The proper use of science is the discrimination and explanation of determinate, delimited bodies of objective facts. In a word, science is factual understanding of a highly impersonal, determinate, and objective sort. Scientific method devoted to this end has produced an intellectual movement uniquely successful and fruitful in human history. Philosophy and religion have other, different functions; that of religion, as we have seen, being ultimate valuation, and that of philosophy, as we shall see in Chapter VIII, being that of synoptic understanding or of understanding within the widest possible context. Whenever science is asked to function, not as science, but as philosophy or religion confusion results for all parties concerned. The confusion is compounded when the men who perpetrate it are blissfully unconscious of what they are doing.

"Scientific philosophy," as it has often been called, usually consists of taking the method or results of modern natural science and generalizing and expanding them into a total view of knowledge and the world. Granting the success and prestige of science in the modern world, it is probably inevitable that such extension should take place. Yet it is scientifically an illustration of that very dubious process called "extrapolation," namely, the extension of an idea beyond its evidence. Indeed, once this particular extrapolation has taken place and we have on our hands the idea of an inclusive totality of all things, do we not have an idea which scientific methods are peculiarly unsuited to handle? And is not this idea scientifically meaningless for the good reason that it is not susceptible of genuine verification? In Carnap's terms, propositions employing this idea are in the "material mode,"[8] with all its deceptive appearances. In other words, they appear to be empirical, but turn out to be metaphysical in nature once we try to test them.

This violent stretching of science to an all-inclusive totality has taken place at different times alternatively in terms of the method or of particular results of science. The first way consists of an assertion, conscious or unconscious, of the omnicompetence of the scientific method of knowing. It is asserted that science and science alone can validate the claim to be reliable knowledge. Such a claim may be regarded as the formative impulse of positivist philosophy, whether in its nineteenth- or twentieth-century forms. The assertion that science alone is reliable knowledge immediately raises insoluble questions, since this statement is not itself an utterance within any science but is, rather, a philosophic observation about science. Hence, in its own terms, it is unreliable.

The subject matter of scientific knowing is frequently given the overall name "nature" (with or without a capital *N*). The philosophy of naturalism may be said to derive from the root assertion that nature is the whole of reality. The naturalist's claim is that nature is all there is. There isn't anything more, he asserts, or, in other words, there isn't any supernature. It is not easy to give unambiguous meaning to this assertion; but we shall not be unfair to this philosophy to assert that the philosophical idea of nature consists in stretching the subject matter of science into an all-inclusive totality concept.[9] Where the positivist makes a total claim for the method of science, the naturalist makes a similar claim for the subject matter. In either case, the process is suspect for many reasons. Psychologically it is so often unconscious and uncritical. Logically it is difficult to give it self-consistent statement. Substantively it is simply not possible to give scientific evidence for it. Again, science does not ask or demand this interpretation of itself; those who believe that it does are invited to submit the scientific evidence for their belief.

Philosophy can assuredly learn from natural science its critical spirit. It must also take full account of scientific results in its view of reality. But if the term "scientific philosophy" is interpreted to mean more than this, the results will be unhappy to all concerned. For properly and critically considered, science and philosophy are clearly distinguishable ways of thinking and speaking. It is unfortunately not a simple tautology to assert that science is science, and philosophy is philosophy.

If we turn to the ways in which science has been converted into a religion or religious substitute, we observe here also results that are equally unhappy. This violent shift of function consists of seeking in science a system of ultimate valuation or of total life orientation. It occurs in a variety of ways extending from vague phrases like "the scientific way of life" through the various ways of treating scientific theories as religious myths on to the popular messianism of science.

Some examples will make clear the nature of this illicit transformation of science into religion. The scientific theory of evolution has a recognized scientific meaning and significance, but in the century since Darwin there has been a persistent tendency to tear it out of this scientific context, to spell it with a capital *E,* and to use it as a religion or religious substitute. The scientific use consists of explanation of problematic factual data, while the religious use has been a source or justification for cherished values. The latter use of a scientific theory is particularly ironical when we consider the value-neutral character of all genuine scientific utterance.

The shift from science to religion is usually made in two steps.[10] In the first step, the clear and sharp boundaries of the scientific concept are blurred; its definite denotation is eliminated. Evolution ceases to be a definite and recognizable scientific idea, and becomes something large and cosmic, having no clear limits or boundaries. It becomes what no self-respecting scientific concept can ever become, namely, an all-inclusive totality concept. Thus we see why "all" in an unrestricted sense is such an important linguistic symptom; it is here a clue to the illicit transformation from science to religion. A particularly interesting illustration of the difference between scientific terms, on the one hand, and philosophic and religious terms, on the other, is the different meanings given to the word "universe" in these two contexts. Physicists, astronomers, and other scientists use the term "universe" with a characteristically definite extension; philosophers and theologians use it in a very different way as an all-inclusive totality concept.

The second step in the illicit transformation is to forget the value-neutral character of all scientific ideas and to infuse with value the concept in question. Since this process is unconscious, it is also uncritical. At this point evolution becomes Evolution, and Evolution becomes all one with Progress, which may then be used as a scheme of justification or origin for cherished human values of many sorts. One of the most interesting aspects of this whole dubious process is the wide and conflicting variety of values that men have sought to justify by reference to Evolution. Herbert Spencer and other social Darwinists found here a cosmic justification for laissez-faire capitalism, while Marx and Engels found in the same Evolution the source of socialism. Liberal Christians found here a justification for human brotherhood, while Nietzsche found in the same source a justification for the opposite values of Overman.

While the religious role of the idea of evolution has been for the most part hopeful and optimistic, social pessimists have frequently laid hold of another scientific concept, entropy, and have used it for their purposes. Despite differing scientific views concerning the nature and significance of this idea, scientific laymen from Henry Adams to the present have not hesitated to pick it up, expand its meaning to cosmic significance, invest it with desired values, and find it an eschatology, a story of the end, or of last things.

In every one of these and other similar cases we shall not be wrong in seeing the root error as one of confusing the scientific and religious uses of language. This same error has been amply illustrated by both sides in the ludicrous and vexatious Genesis versus Evolution debate, from Huxley and Wilberforce to Darrow and Bryan. On the one hand, many religious people have insisted upon treating the Biblical creation story as a scientific hypothesis—with baleful results. Incidentally, what has gone largely unnoticed is that this interpretation involves a violent misunderstanding of religion as well as an interference with science. But on the other hand, many (though by no means all) evolutionists take the statements of evolution not as statements of scientific theory but as a religious mythology, a mistake in its way as egregious as that of their opponents. Such ideas as those of absolute Beginning and End, while essential to religion and myth, are invariably extrascientific in character. Indeed, are they not clearly scientifically meaningless? One might conclude that the ability to distinguish a religious statement from a scientific statement is, like the fear of the Lord, the beginning of wisdom, and that the corresponding inability is the beginning of folly for both religion and science.

This same inability continues in all the various appeals to scientific ideas and indeed to Science (as to God) for life orientation or life valuation. One such appeal was expressed in the book entitled *Can Science Save Us?*[11] to which the author gave an enthusiastically and uncritically affirmative answer. The messianism of science, so pervasive an element in modern Western thought, assumes a wide variety of forms; but in all of them the basic confusion, once more, is between what takes place in two different forms of experience and in the respective kinds of utterance that express and communicate them. We misunderstand and misuse both science and religion when we force either to perform the function of the other.

5. *Science—Limits and Possibilities*

Our discussion has led us to see both the limits and possibilities of natural science. Its limits are those of impersonal, objective explanation of carefully defined and delimited bodies of fact. Expressive statements of human values, whether aesthetic, moral, or any other sort, are well outside these limits. Furthermore, as we have seen, science functions ill as a system of value creation or value justification. On the other hand, once a value or a value system is in existence, science has important critical work to do. This task is the critical appraisal of all value systems in the light of its own criteria of rational coherence and factuality. Thus science takes a hostile view toward all value systems that involve either inner contradiction or conflict with known fact. For example, it has been unsparing in its criticism of racist philosophies or faiths which conflict with known facts of genetics.

More generally, the main significance of science with respect to fundamental human values lies in the areas of criticism and implementation. Such criticisms must not be interpreted necessarily as hostile attack, but rather as rigorous analysis and appraisal in the light of scientific knowledge. The implementation and facilitation of basic human values is also a significant task of science. Once any fundamental value or value system is in existence, science in its varied aspects can be of enormous help in the concrete application and realization of these values.

Discussion of the relation of science to human values leads us necessarily to cross the boundary that separates the natural from the social sciences. Factual observation of this boundary line will show both continuities and discontinuities. In this connection, it is too bad that so many social scientists waste valuable time trying to prove that they are just as scientific as the natural sciences, rather than getting on with the proper business of understanding their own distinctive subject matters and acquiring such knowledge as they are capable of.

If one examines the statements of the social sciences, many differences from those of the natural sciences immediately become apparent. They seem less detached and objective—in a word, less scientific. They are less value-neutral, and this in two ways. First, insofar as they describe the human situation as a whole, in contrast to specific and limited structures (as, for example, the human nervous system or digestive system) they tend inevitably to include man's goods or goals as a part of their subject matter. As we have previously noted, the term "life," referred to man, has a persistent way of becoming the good life by its inclusion of values basic to man. Also, in the second place, many of the social sciences contain either explicit or implicit normative statements in which values or value systems are stated or recommended by the author to his readers.

If we examine the statements of the social sciences, we will want to locate them in the spectrum of significant human knowledge in the large middle area between the natural sciences and the humanities. For they still preserve many of the aims and traits of natural science. Among other features, like the natural sciences their main ideas are usually given a quite definite and delimited extension. The social sciences are not about the human situation as a whole, but about carefully delimited aspects of human life, such as man's politics, economics, etc. The humanities, on the other hand, with their frankly expressive and intuitive forms of thought, more frequently move toward the synoptic envisagement of wholes or totalities, extending at times to total views of man and the world. Exceptions to these generalizations will come to mind readily enough; but applied generally to these three regions of knowledge, I believe that they will help us to distinguish the kinds of thinking and saying that are encountered in the natural sciences, the social sciences, and the humanities.

VII
Art
as
Language

❖ ❖

1. *Art and Common Experience*

We shall continue in this chapter the project begun in the last one of looking at the languages through which certain basic human concerns find expression. However, it must be pointed out that this chapter's application of the hypothesis involves a hazard not present in the last. No one doubts that science is, in one of its essential aspects, a highly distinctive use of language, but whether this is the case with the arts is a matter of much controversy. Some competent inquirers say yes; others equally competent say no. The position we shall attempt to develop here is a guarded yes.

We begin again with common experience and common language, seeking here for the roots of artistic experience. What human being has not been moved or enlightened by a striking figure of speech, a powerful phrase, or a cadence or rhythm as they sometimes occur in ordinary language? Nor are these responses limited to linguistic experience. Bodily gestures, sounds, colors, the sight or sound of striking forms—all these and many more elicit responses of poignancy, or clarity, or unique fulfillment of some other sort. As such, these experiences demand our attention, claiming significance for themselves and challenging our analysis and understanding. They constitute the human raw materials out of which in the long course of human history the arts have been constructed. Furthermore, it is to such elemental experiences as these which men must recur to take their bearings in exploring new and unfamiliar forms of art.

In the course of time these primary human materials of sight and sound, of shape and form, have been worked up into the media of the various arts.[1] This working up consists of the organization of these experiences according to certain basic rules or patterns of organization. Thus, for example, sounds are organized into the notes of the musical scale, words are ordered by basic patterns of rhyme and rhythm; and the rules of perspective find their way into painting. These preliminary forms of order or organization vary widely with different arts and different cultural traditions, but in general they constitute the first step in the emergence of the arts as explicit human activities.

Along with these rules and forms emerges the professional artist, and with him conscious, deliberate works of art. Yet here a caution is necessary. The relation between the expert and the common man is different in the arts from this relation in science; and it is still different in other forms of experience. While many great works of art have been created deliberately as such, this is by no means always the case. Particularly in literature and painting, it has sometimes been true that works subsequently recognized as great art were not deliberately created as such. In this and other respects, the relation of art to common life never ceases to constitute a significant problem.

2. *Three Ways of Understanding Art*

If now we turn our attention to activities and works of human art commonly or widely recognized as such, we find ourselves in the presence of a large recurrent and persistent aspect of man's existence in every known human culture. Taking literature, music, painting, sculpture, architecture, and dance as the major arts, we find significant activities in some or all of them in every human culture of which there is reliable knowledge. In many cases, these activities afford valuable clues as to the nature of the culture. In many cases, too, these major arts are related to and continuous with minor arts such as pottery-making, jewelry-making, weaving, and the like. Also, in many instances there is no clear distinction between the fine arts and the useful arts. The useful arts are fine in the sense of affording intrinsic satisfaction; and, conversely, many fine arts are deemed by the culture to be useful to man.

This large and significant segment of human activity which is art sheds light on the nature of man. The fact that cries, sights, sounds, shapes, and patterns of many sorts are transmuted into objects of intrinsic delight and meaning sheds light on the creature who makes and enjoys these objects and activities. It is in consequence of the self-conscious and self-transcendent quality of his awareness that man is able to take certain of the immediacies of experience, and, as it were, hold them off at a distance, divorcing them from their original practical or instrumental function, and enjoying them for their own sake, seeing in them intrinsic and unique meanings. Thus, when man became man he sang a song, he danced a dance, he began to paint and sculpt and design; and he has been busy at these activities ever since.

Yet there remains here a large, baffling, and philosophical question. It is this: In what terms shall we understand
the arts? Persistent and recurrent as they are, they seem in
many situations utterly useless and sometimes even dan-
gerously aberrent activities. At best, art bakes no bread; at
worst, the artist and his followers appear as social deviants
and subversives. How shall we understand the fact that
there have been men and cultures who have deprived themselves of bread in order to sing songs, or mime, or dance?
How shall we understand the tenacious hold that art has
on human interest? Just what goes on here? The questions
are both fair and significant; moreover, they lie directly
across our path.

There has been no lack of reflection on these problems
throughout the centuries of Western history. Artists themselves have often sought self-understanding. Students of
the arts, and critics both sympathetic and hostile, have
addressed themselves to these questions. In very general
terms, three kinds of answers have been given. First, artistic experience has been explained as a form of making
or construction. Second, it has been characterized in terms
of the pleasure, satisfaction, or joy it has afforded. Third
is the answer that will be developed briefly here, namely,
that art is a distinctive form of saying or communication.
All these explanations involve what may be termed the
expansion of a metaphor. Making or constructing, pleasure, and communication or saying are all identifiable,
recognizable human experiences. Each of these approaches
takes one of these experiences as a basis for interpreting
and understanding artistic experience. In each case, we
shall find important truth as well as inherent limitations.

In the case of the first—namely, the approach to art as
a form of making or constructing—we must note that there

is a significant literal truth here.[2] Whether in baking a cake, building a bridge, painting a picture, or writing a poem, one takes certain raw materials and works them up according to certain rules and plans toward an end or goal. In some cases, the goals or products of these activities are distinguishable by their instrumental utility, while in other cases they are simply intrinsically satisfying. Thus arises the distinction between the useful and fine arts, the art of baking bread and the art of painting pictures. But in both cases, materials are worked up to some desired and satisfying conclusion.

From ancient Greece to the present, it is not too much to say that this had been the majority view in the West for understanding the arts. It has many clear advantages. For one thing, it emphasizes the continuity of useful and fine arts. It calls attention to the processes of conscious and controlled making involved in artistic activity and experience, as well as the perception of form, structure, or organization so important to both the artist and his audience.

Yet this classic view, as we may call it, leaves other important questions unanswered. Why this particular organization of materials and not the innumerable others that are possible or imaginable? Why is it that just this form elicits a significant response, while other forms do not? One answer is that this is an expressive form, that is to say, a form which expresses or says something significant. Again, how do we understand the fact that some forms are in fact expressive or significant, while others seem to signify nothing? What also of the experience of unique pleasure, satisfaction, or joy which is the accompaniment of artistic creation and beholding?

This last question points to the defining aspect of artistic experience according to the second main approach. For this view the crucial aspect of art is the pleasure it affords. Among adherents of this view, Santayana is preeminent for his genuine interest in and sensitivity to the arts.[3] Yet concerning him and other adherents of this view, I for one am driven to the conclusion that their practice is better than their theory. Surely pleasure of a unique sort is a significant accompaniment of artistic experience. But this is at best not a very illuminating statement to make, and at worst it is seriously misleading. For it characterizes the experience in terms of its emotive accompaniment, and in typically hedonistic fashion it often assumes the commensurability of pleasures. Thus, in effect, it makes the pleasure of drinking a Coca-Cola commensurable, in appropriate Benthamite fashion, with that of listening to a Bach fugue. It is sufficient here to assert that this is not self-evidently the case. If the adjective "unique" is appended to the term "pleasure," the commensurability is negated, and with it goes the explanatory value of the hedonistic theory.

There is, on the contrary, good ground in experience for the view that many human pleasures are altogether incommensurable with each other. Each is what it qualitatively and uniquely is. This criticism may well go on the offensive and invite the hedonist to state clearly and fully the basis of commensurability. To such questions no very satisfactory answers have as yet been forthcoming. Moreover, the term "pleasure," in any ordinary usage, seems inadequate to the kind of satisfaction which, in fact, accompanies artistic experience. To be sure, there is nothing wrong with pleasure (and much that is right with it), but it is too small a word and too closely related to specific nerve endings to be adequately descriptive of artistic experience. There are, for example, pleasures of taste, touch, audition, vision, and other senses; and while specific nerve endings invariably form a part of artistic experience, I do not believe that artistic experience can be explained without reference to the whole person involved. Thus, it is not simply my eye that sees or my ear that hears, it is *I* who see and hear—and enjoy.

Many writers, perceiving this defect of hedonism, speak more adequately but more ambiguously of the satisfaction rather than the pleasure of art. Personally I prefer an even simpler word, namely, "joy." It is frequently a paradoxical joy when one considers the pain and frustration involved in much artistic creation, as well as the ugliness and tragedy that are depicted in art. Artistic satisfaction is the joy that accompanies any significant, intrinsic form of human fulfillment or realization. But these assertions also raise a further question. Why the joy in artistic creation and beholding? How is it that the arts function as human fulfillments?

These questions lead to the third way of understanding artistic experience, namely, as a distinctive form of human expression or communication.[4] This way of interpretation is even more plainly and frankly metaphorical than the first two ways. It claims that artistic experience is comparable to human speaking or saying. While art always entails formal organization as well as accompanying satisfaction, nevertheless it is here asserted that in essence artistic creation is a form of saying or communication, and also that the form of re-creation which the artistic beholder must undertake is like hearing or listening to what the artist has to say. In this whole process of expression we find an intrinsic and altogether distinctive fulfillment or realization of man's humanity which affords great joy, but it is to be understood as the satisfaction which accompanies successful expression or communication.

It may be useful to note some of the sources of this view of artistic experience. The philosophy of semantic analysis has not been more than peripherally concerned with aesthetic issues, being principally a philosophy of science. Nonetheless, other semantically oriented philosophers, such as Cassirer and Langer, have been deeply involved with the aesthetic implications and applications of their ideas. At this point, they have made common cause with workers in the arts and art criticism who have found language and expression indispensable categories. There has also been in recent years a notable rise of theologically oriented study of literature and other arts which has likewise taken expression or communication as a basic postulate or assumption.

To the explication of this category we must now turn. I shall attempt this task by unfolding the metaphor of saying or expression in ways that illuminate artistic experience.

3. Unfolding a Metaphor

In previous chapters we have forged many of the categories essential to the task of construing the arts as language. The ideas of symbol, expression, and image were delineated with this end clearly in view. Similarly, the distinction of primary and derivative languages was made in order to distinguish between artistic aspects of ordinary language, on the one hand, and, on the other, those derivative languages which are the arts. In this connection, it is also not without interest to ask whether the arts are natural or artificial languages. Recalling the distinction as one between systems of communication which have simply happened in the course of history, and those which are deliberately constructed, we may perhaps conclude that artists who are content to use the traditional, received rules of their arts without intentional change are probably working with a natural language; but those who undertake fundamental changes in the rules of their medium seem to be constructing artificial languages. Schoenberg's attempts to construct a new musical scale, the lifelong efforts of Picasso to formulate new conventions of perspective and form in painting, or James Joyce's verbalization of stream of consciousness come to mind as illustrations of the latter attitude of attempting to construct new artistic languages.

Chapter III pushed the analogy of language and art several steps farther. Artistic images were related to the terms of expression or statement. It may be added here that the task of defining a term is one that must be done by students of each art on the basis of pertinent evidence from within the art. To attempt to do it from the outside or for all the arts would constitute a kind of philosophic imperialism. What combination of sounds or words constitutes an image for a particular poem must be decided by competent critics and only on inspection of the particular poem. Similar judgments hold for the study of expressive images in music, painting, and other arts.

As words are organized into sentences or statements, so images are organized into unified configurations or *Gestalten*. Again, the question can be asked as to the size or extent of such a configuration; and again I must answer that no reply can be given apart from inspection of particular works of art. It might be that the whole work is the minimum unit, but in other cases specific unit statements may clearly be discriminated out of the whole. In either case this determination is an aspect of the analysis and appraisal of particular arts and works of art.

Chapter V also suggested that the basic rules of each of the arts might be compared to the grammar and syntax of a language, inasmuch as they are the basic rules for sentence formation. Furthermore, beyond grammar and syntax lies logic; and Chapter V also defined meaning in terms of consistency and coherence of terms, and truth as the adequacy of statement to referent, suggesting the possible extension of these ideas to the various forms of expressive statement. This is a matter to which we shall return in the next section of this chapter, since it has particular pertinence to the task of criticism there discussed.

We must raise still a further question relating to the content of what is said in the arts. In the case of representational arts, such as extensive areas of painting, sculpture, and literature where a part of the artist's task is to depict a subject matter, it is particularly easy to confuse subject matter with expressed content. But to note this distinction between subject matter and expressed content will put us on guard against the confusion, and will also help us to identify the latter concept. Broadly speaking, subject matter is what is talked about, while expressed content is what is said or asserted about the subject matter. Thus, for example, a painter may use a religious subject matter such as the Madonna, but what he says may have little or no religious meaning. The religious paintings of many late Renaissance figures such as Titian and Veronese are cases in point. The expressed content of what the artist says may well be altogether secular in its significance. Conversely, he may take a conventionally nonreligious subject matter and in these terms say something religious. In this sense Rouault's clowns have been termed more religious than his paintings of Christ. Expressed content, once more, consists of what the artist says in and through his medium.

The idea of expressed content must be carefully guarded against several misinterpretations. In the first place, it must be asserted with all possible vigor that expressed content is, first of all, an aesthetic category and not primarily or initially at least, religious, political, moral—or of any other kind of experience than art. This assertion is necessary to avoid the idea of propaganda art or other forms of "message art." Art, as we must insist, is a distinctive and autonomous form of experience, having its own conditions and its own distinctive satisfactions. We do violence to it if, like Tolstoi,[5] we conceive it simply as a vehicle for moral and religious messages, or if, like Russian socialist realism, we think of it as a vehicle for political propaganda. Rather, it is here asserted as a factual observation that significant human art has its own existence and that it varies independently with other kinds and forms of experience.

After we have asserted the autonomy of art, and only then, can we go on and point to the role of the artist as commentator upon the human situation in many significant ways—political, religious, philosophical, and the like. It is necessary to make this assertion in order to avoid the position of the aesthete who seeks to "purify" his art by separating it from all other human concerns. In so doing he renders it effete and trivial. Vigorous and vital art, once it is established as art, will seek and maintain all sorts of relations to other activities of human culture, but it will do so freely, in its own way, and on its own terms. It functions as the artist's comments on all these aspects of the human situation which interest him as a man.

But granting that expressed content is an aesthetic concept, we still have the question of just what the expressed content of any particular work of art or kind of art may be, and how we shall go about determining what it is. The answer, once more, is that no overall rule is possible. Certainly no outside or external judgment is possible, whether by the philosopher, the theologian, or anyone else. Rather, what is the expressed content of a particular work of art is a fact to be established as the conclusion of competent critical study of it, and only thus.

All that can possibly be said in general is that different arts present differing distinctive possibilities and limitations for expressed content.[6] Thus, for example, music offers unique possibilities for the expression of inner life, though let it be added immediately that there are obvious pitfalls of sentimentality and subjectivism here. Landscape painting offers likelier possibilities than music for the expression of man's responses to nature, though again musical compositions like Debussy's tone poems bid us hedge any such generalizations with qualifications.

One objection to the view of art as communication or saying which I am attempting to develop here takes the form of asking to whom the artist is talking or seeking to communicate in his art. The question is entirely fair, but again no overall answer can be given. In some works of art a definite audience is clearly envisaged and must be held in mind if the work is to be understood. In other cases, the artist may be addressing mankind, or posterity, or God. He may be speaking, as the expression goes, for the record. All kinds of possibilities exist, and may be illustrated in specific works of art. He may even be talking to himself, a form of cognitive activity not always silly, and in many cases profoundly significant. In such a case, the beholder, reader, or listener is, as it were, invited to overhear the artist's soliloquy.

The relation of dialogue or conversation opens up genuine possibilities for the understanding of artistic experience in its various forms. Martin Buber has written widely of the life of dialogue based upon I-Thou relations, or person-person relations.[7] By this he means that human selves occur only in community with other selves, that indeed it is the relation to another person which constitutes any man as a person. "I become I in relation to Thou." Buber's writing constitutes a sensitive, probing, and yet remarkably objective account of the nature of human selfhood in these terms. While he by no means ignores the arts, the main development of his thought lies in the direction of ethics and religion. The reason for alluding here to Buber's I-Thou relation is to suggest that this fruitful idea might offer as much illumination to the arts as it has to many other fields of human experience. Consider, for example, its application to stage and audience in the drama.

Its extension to the field of art might begin with the understanding of the artist, who in this view is a person seeking communication through his medium with other persons. To be sure, it is possible by overemphasis of such personal factors to underestimate such other elements as the artist's mastery of his medium, but there is no necessity to do so. The various rules and requirements of his art are of basic importance as the grammar and syntax of his speaking. To neglect them is to fall into incoherence. But behind the formal features of every art stands a person. It is essential in this view of art that to understand the work of art we must understand the artist and his intention, including his intention to communicate. There can be no adequate understanding of the work apart from this. For art is a very personal kind of communication, concerning which we must ask who is the speaker and what is he seeking or intending to say and to whom is he addressing himself.

It also follows from such a "dialogical" view of art,[8] that we may come to understand a work of art by placing it within a community and a tradition. The terms "community" and "tradition" have recurred throughout our study. Here we mean a community and tradition of culture. Thus we understand a particular artist's work by placing it within such a community, which is to say a group of people gathered together by common valuations, and also by locating it historically in the development of a particular tradition, relating it to what came before and what came afterward. To locate a work of art in this manner within such a community and tradition, and, if possible, within the personal development of the artist, is the first step in critical understanding.

These categories, so essential for the understanding of works of art, are essentially personal in nature, and thus they may be understood as an extension of Buber's personalism. Once more, we must not apply them to the exclusion of other aspects. Formal structure or organization is an indispensable category. So is aesthetic quality in its full presentational immediacy. So, too, is the human fulfillment which is the consequence of art. Yet all these and other aspects of art might be interpreted as aspects of a highly distinctive form of person-to-person communication between artist and those to whom he addresses himself.

4. *Everyman His Own Critic*

There is a real sense in which any artistic perception is final and decisive. We look at a picture, listen to a sonata, read a poem, and ask if we have perceived anything of significance. If not, we answer no, and turn to something else. Like all forms of perception, artistic perception involves two elements, one of pure immediacy and another of mediated, rational structure. The metaphor of seeing stands for the intuitive or immediate aspect of artistic apprehension. As previously noted, artistic apprehension takes place through sense organs of the human body, usually those of sight or sound, assisted and accompanied by kinesthetic sensations of a subtle sort. Yet, as already noted, in artistic perception it is not simply my eye that sees or my ear that hears, but *I* who see through my eyes and hear through my ears. Artistic perception is an activity of the whole unified person; and as such it is agenda for rational analysis. It has its own distinctive rational structure, and shows itself to be an activity of human thinking or reasoning which takes place through expressive images. Artistic perception might in this sense be characterized as image thinking. As a form of thinking it is subject to analysis and appraisal in these terms.

One way of getting at the second or nonimmediate aspect of artistic perception is to point to its educability. I look at a picture or listen to a musical selection and either respond or not. However, then I begin a study of this work of art, analyzing it, relating it to other works, asking what in the light of these factors I see in it, or what it says to me. After this study I look again, and in many cases as a result of my study of a work of art I see depths of meaning previously hidden to me; or, conversely, a work that initially seemed meaningful is now, upon study or critical analysis, rendered trivial or meaningless. In other words, artistic perception, like any other significant activity of the mind, is educable.

The word "taste" is often used as a term for rational and civilized standards of artistic perception. The maxim that "concerning taste there is no disputing" refers to the immediate, intuitive aspect of perception. However, if we look to the other, rational aspect of perception, it soon becomes apparent that concerning taste there is very much disputing. We study the personal and social context of a perception, we analyze rationally the elements in a given form or structure. Then once more we return to immediate, direct perception which now in judgments of taste is seen to be informed and guided by rational criteria.

The task of art criticism consists of precisely this kind of analysis of a work of art and our perception of it. The critical process begins and ends with just such acts of direct perception, of looking or listening. But between the two acts it involves hard study, analysis, and reflection upon any and all aspects of the work of art and our human relation to it. One essential feature of criticism consists in the attempt to discover or lay bare the expressed content and then to translate it into verbal prose. After study, one concludes that just this or that is what I see, or what the work of art says to me. The deliberate effort to put this into verbal prose lies at the center of the criticism of any art. Yet always such ideas must be put to the test by actual looking or listening, or, in other words, by direct perceptual experience.

Often the term "art criticism" refers to the activities of men who engage professionally in this form of thinking and writing. But there is a more fundamental sense in which each beholder of art is his own critic. He must look and study and look again. Frequently he resorts for help to the professional critic, but the professional is at best a guide over a mountain path that each person must walk for himself. Each man must in the end be his own critic. His own considered and deliberate experience of art *is* his criticism, and vice versa.

We have developed the idea of artistic perception at some length with reference to the artistic beholder. But there is a sense in which everything that has been said applies a fortiori to the process of artistic creation, for, after all, beholding is a derivative form of creation. It is literally re-creation. Thus, the same dual elements of intuitive apprehension and hard study, analysis and reflection, apply to the process by which the work of art comes into being. Such processes vary widely with different men, but it is safe to say that both the elements of intuition and rigorous criticism are invariably involved in the creative process.

The processes of artistic creation and criticism are highly individual matters, yet some canons or rules of judgment seem to govern both of them. However, their application to any particular art or work of art is again a special and individual matter. Three such rules or canons of artistic thinking or judgment may be stated in terms of the analogy between art and language.[9] They are, in effect, rules for the saying and thinking that take place in and through an artistic medium. These three rules are those of meaning, truth, and greatness.

The rule of meaning applied to art consists of the absence of incompatible or contradictory elements, together with the harmony of images or other elements in the unified whole which is the work of art. To the extent that these conditions are met, the work of art is meaningful; to the extent that these conditions are not met, it is meaningless. Meaninglessness may take the form of contradiction, incoherence, or the inchoate state which might be characterized as not yet meaningful. To be sure, much contemporary art appears to be deliberately incoherent or disharmonious. Yet it must be asserted that some kind of coherence or harmony of meaning is still present. The incoherence is never total. In many instances such deliberate forms of incoherence may be regarded as protests against superficial or sentimental coherence. In other situations they bear a close relation to paradox or apparent contradiction in theology.

As argued in Chapter V, in many artistic situations the play of pure essence unrelated to existence (or, in other words, statements of meaning without reference to truth or falsehood) constitutes the whole significance of the work. The art constitutes a form of expression or saying which is self-contained and harmonious but has no cognitive reference to any objective reality. Like the statements of logic or pure mathematics, such works of art are meaningful but not materially true or false. In other situations there is an equally clear reference to existence, and thus a claim to truth is expressed or implied in the artistic statement of judgment. Such claims must be appraised according to the rule of adequacy, which means, as stated in Chapter V, both the absence of conflict with fact and the satisfaction of all factual evidence. What is the referent of artistic statement, and what constitutes factual evidence which confirms or infirms artistic judgment rendering it adequate or inadequate, is a question that must be settled in relation to each particular work of art. In many cases the determination of adequacy or inadequacy is the heart of the critical process.

A third canon of critical judgment in art is that of greatness. It presupposes the canons of meaning and truth, and goes on to raise the question of the human magnitude and significance of the expressed content. Statements that are meaningful and true may still assert large or significant human values or issues or, on the other hand, smaller or less significant issues. The human magnitude of the issues or values is the measure of artistic greatness. Thus, *King Lear* is a greater work of art than *Lucy Gray* or even Keats's *Ode on a Grecian Urn*. Once more, granting meaning and truth, artistic greatness consists in the magnitude of the human values or insights that constitute the expressed content of the work of art. Humanism in art consists of the expression of truth of significant magnitude about man and his world.

6. *Art and Religion*

Many of the categories as well as many of the conclusions of our analysis have led us to the relation of art to religion. Historically it is an obviously factual assertion that in most human cultures the arts are religious in their inception and significance, and that, conversely, religion finds expression in significant artistic forms. So, for example, literature in many cultures is sacred myth, recital is drama, and dance is sacred ritual. Painting, sculpture, and architecture through most of human history live, move, and have their being in a world of sacred realities. Illustrations will come readily to minds familiar with the pertinent historical and cultural data. To be sure, whether the relation is one of historical accident or whether it is a relation of meaning or essence is a matter to be determined by critical analysis. Also, it is fair to add the qualification that in most cultures in human history at least some artistic activity has been, in any commonsense definition of terms, secular in character. Conversely, too, it might be noted, as we shall presently see, in the most secular of human cultures some arts will be religious in their fundamental significance.

These observations necessitate a definition of sacral and secular cultures. In general, a sacral culture is one in which the religious center of human and cultural life is obvious, clear, and explicitly present, and consequently one in which sacred realities are visible and generally acceptable to all. If we may employ a metaphor from physical science, a sacral culture is one in which the resultant of cultural forces is a line extending centripetally inward toward the religious center of life. On the other hand, a secular culture is one where the religious center is more or less invisible, and where consequently the resultant direction of cultural forces is outward toward the circumference which represents immediate or proximate interests or concerns. The terms "secular" and "sacral" describe dominant tendencies of cultures, and of personalities as well. In relatively secular cultures men live and act for the most part in terms of immediate or proximate concerns, with little relation to ultimacy and sacredness. In sacral cultures the opposite is true. Obviously this distinction is susceptible of a continuous gradation of degrees, ranging from the most sacral to the most secular of cultures.[10]

Illustrations of these differing attitudes will come readily to mind. For example, the classical culture of China was undoubtedly more secular and less sacral than that of India. The culture of Greece at the time of the great tragedians was less sacral and more secular than it was at the time of either Homer or Hesiod. European culture moved far in the general direction of secularization between, say, the thirteenth and eighteenth centuries, or indeed even between the twelfth and thirteen centuries. A similar movement may be discerned in America between 1650 and 1850, or indeed again between 1850 and 1950.

Perhaps the clearest example of a massive movement of secularization in all human history is to be found in the post-Renaissance West. In the development of this culture, almost all the major human concerns—politics, economics, art, and science—have one by one moved away from the household of the faith, setting up housekeeping on their own. Thus, men have worked and ruled and painted and sung, not to the glory of God, but for the advantage of their nation or to their own self-interest, or as ends in themselves. All of this is to be acknowledged as one of the facts of life in this culture. It is easy to see both gains and losses in the new situation. Surely one of the great gains to be reckoned in the new situation is the great increase in intellectual and cultural freedom or autonomy for the human individual.

This new situation of a secular culture in the modern West has raised new issues of greatest importance for art and religion and their mutual relations. Many of them, incidentally, are rooted in the unprecedented degree of freedom for the individual in this largely secular society. If these observations are combined with the distinction made in the previous section between the subject matter and expressed content, we have a situation in the relation of religion to art in which the artist may work with either a religious or nonreligious subject matter and also a religious or nonreligious expressed content. He may talk about religious or nonreligious subjects, and what he says may or may not be a statement of religious significance. Combining these terms of analysis, we get four possibilities which may be represented schematically as follows:

a. Religious subject matter; religious expressed content.

b. Religious subject matter; nonreligious expressed content.

c. Nonreligious subject matter; religious expressed content.

d. Nonreligious subject matter; nonreligious expressed content.

This scheme is useful for representing the possibilities present in modern and contemporary Western culture. It is possible in traditional fashion for an artist to take a religious subject matter and to treat it religiously, as such paintings as Rouault's *Christ Mocked by Soldiers* or his *Miserere* illustrate. It is possible, however, to take a traditional religious subject matter and treat it nonreligiously, as a great many officially religious paintings assuredly do. The artist may be uninterested in this aspect of the subject matter and interested in any one of the many other aspects of artistic creation. He may, in short, say something nonreligious in a traditionally religious subject matter. As already indicated, many of the later Renaissance paintings of such men as Titian and Veronese were of Biblical themes, yet it is apparent that the artists were often enormously more interested in colors, textures, formal structure or some other secular aspect of art than in religious meaning as an aspect of expressed content. Similar comments may also be made of such painters as Rubens or Poussin.

On the other hand, an artist may take a conventionally nonreligious theme, such as Picasso did in *Guernica,* and say something of profoundly religious import. In this connection it is only fair to point out that the word "religion" is here used in the wider meaning of ultimate concern symbolically expressed. Such expressions may be in traditional terms or they may be quite untraditional. In either case, the heart of religious experience is the symbolic or expressive presentation of ultimate concern or ultimate valuation. Contemporary art in all the various media abounds in illustrations of works that are nonreligious in subject matter but religious in expressed content.

Whether the fourth possibility of art, which is nonreligious in both subject matter and expressed content, exists as anything more than a limiting possibility is a matter on which happily we need not make a decision. Certainly it is entirely possible for an artist to immerse himself in other aspects of the artistic experience, such as formal structure, the immediacies of perception, the nature of his medium, to the exclusion partially (and perhaps wholly) of expressing ultimate concern. Again, illustrations will come readily to mind from significant works in all the arts. Whether this viewpoint may be consistently maintained over a lifetime is another question which here may be left as an open question.

I have used illustrations of these relations from painting, but I believe that they are susceptible of completely general statement in respect to culture, to art, and to religion. In other words they are applicable to any art, any religion, and any culture. Taken in this sense, there is good basis in the nature of art, of religion, and of culture, as well as in actual historic experience, for the view that the arts more often than not say something religious, that religion finds expression in the arts, and that the resultant works are among the great achievements of human culture.

VIII Philosophy as Language

✧ ✧

In this chapter we continue the experiment of looking at various forms of cognitive experience through the distinctive languages in which they are articulated, here the application being to philosophy. The hypothesis to be stated and elaborated is that philosophy may fruitfully be construed as a type of language whose function is the expression or articulation of the widest, most inclusive totality of experience of which the human mind is capable. Hence the significance of the unqualified "all" in philosophic statements. In other words philosophic statements are statements of the most comprehensive unification of experience which is possible to man.

In order to guard this hypothesis and to give it more detailed formulation several other subsidiary assumptions are also necessary. Thus, for example, we shall argue that the method by which the human mind lays hold of this subject matter is a special kind of metaphorical or analogical thinking and speaking. Again, we shall argue that philosophic language has both a referential or objective aspect and an expressive or subjective aspect, or, in other words, that the major terms of philosophic discourse function both as signs and as symbols.

Some readers will undoubtedly regard these as outrageous hypotheses; yet these readers may be reminded of the value of outrageous hypotheses. Others may regard them as trivial, or as the author's personal crotchets. In any case, the proposal is to test these hypotheses on the primary factual data of Western philosophy, namely, the body of writings that constitute the Western philosophic tradition. Such names as Plato and Aristotle, Augustine and Aquinas, Kant, Hegel, Dewey, and Whitehead come readily to mind in this connection. Whatever else and whatever more philosophy may be, it is these men and their writings, and the great tradition embodied in this succession. To be sure, the tradition still continues in contemporary books, papers, and conversations. Students of Western philosophy need also to remind themselves that philosophy extends to analogous processes of thinking and speaking in the non-Western world.

In this wide field there is both a great deal of variety and also of conflict in the understanding of what philosophy is. In the West, the variety of meanings range from the ancient Greek lover of wisdom who originated the term "philosophy," through the medieval doctor writing his *summa,* to the natural philosopher of the seventeenth century, or the *philosophes* of the French Enlightenment, or the system builders of nineteenth-century Germany. In the contemporary situation, perhaps the most notable feature is the wide variety of conflicting schools. For example, the term "philosophy" means different things to existentialists and logical positivists. There are also practitioners who, as Whitehead once remarked, have made a career in philosophy out of denying the possibility of philosophy.

The present chapter may be located in the contemporary

situation as one suggestion among many others for the resumption of traditional speculative or metaphysical thinking, though with the lessons learned from contemporary criticism. Much recent and contemporary philosophy has been harshly antimetaphysical in outlook. Semantic analysis, for example, began with a proposal for the complete elimination of metaphysics as a kind of nonsense. Yet as this movement has developed from verificational analysis to functional analysis, there has been a cautious reappraisal of metaphysics. Perhaps such discourse does have some significant and identifiable human function, after all—such is the present mood. The proposals of this chapter are modest suggestions for what this function is and how the business of metaphysical thinking and speaking may be carried on.

It is worth noting that I am using the words "philosophic" and "metaphysical" interchangeably. The usage is deliberate. True, there are different and distinguishable aspects of the philosophic task ranging from metaphysics to epistemology and ethics. Yet my assumption is that these aspects of the work of philosophy are different aspects of a unity. Thus it is possible to begin with metaphysics and to make one's way within a particular viewpoint or system to epistemology, or vice versa. Such at least is my assumption. I further assume that for any particular viewpoint or system, the depiction of being in metaphysics is "first philosophy." Hence the interchangeable use of the terms "metaphysics" and "philosophy," and their corresponding adjectives. Clearly then, metaphysics is the foundation, if not the whole house, of philosophy. Also let me add that despite many variant and controversial shades of meaning in contemporary thought, I use interchangeably the terms "metaphysical" and "ontological."

As previously asserted, the fundamental and primary function of philosophy is the articulation of the widest totality of experience. Now, it is in the performance of this function that the metaphysical categories such as being or reality receive their existence and meaning. Moreover, the comprehensive unification of experience is a real and indefeasible human need and human function. Hence the perennial relevance and lure of philosophy. That the need and function are undeniable may best be established by pointing to the difficulty, approaching to impossibility, of denying or avoiding them. Many men, seeing the traditional defects and excesses of metaphysics, have sought to proscribe or deny it. Yet in their effort to deny metaphysics they involve themselves in utterances and reflections that have undeniably metaphysical character. The total denial of metaphysics becomes one more metaphysical system, as the history of modern positivism ironically shows. So philosophy asserts itself in attempts to deny it.

It also sometimes exists unconsciously as an aspect or dimension of the thinking of men who are blissfully unaware of its existence. As the horizon around specific, concrete activities and enterprises widens to approach totality, so thinking takes on an inevitably and inescapably philosophic or metaphysical character whether the person is conscious of this aspect or not. Thus philosophy is at bottom an aspect of the whole life of the human mind before it is an explicit and defined activity or intellectual discipline.

To be sure, such philosophic reflection is never better and is often much worse for being unconscious. For unconscious means uncriticized and uncritical. Uncriticized totality utterances often constitute very bad philosophizing. So, as we shall soon see, it is an essential feature of the method of explicit philosophy to dig out such unconscious assumptions and expose them to the clear sunlight of rigorous criticism. To an understanding of this difficult but unavoidable aspect of the mind's life which is philosophic thinking and speaking we must now turn, looking first at some of its identifiable traits and then to the method by which it may best be carried on.

1. *Some Traits of Philosophy*

The primary data of philosophy are a particular body of writings in the Western cultural tradition, augmented by analogous documents from other cultures. To these data we must put the question, What are the significant characteristics of philosophy?

a. What has already been said is sufficient to establish the peculiar historical character of philosophic thinking and speaking. By this is meant that philosophy is an activity that takes place within a particular historical tradition, and locates and defines itself within that tradition. In this respect, philosophic thinking differs from scientific thinking. It is possible to study the elements of natural science quite apart from the history of science. Indeed, a good case can be made for the view that in natural science these two elements are logically altogether independent of each other. Such independence does not appear to be the case in fields like philosophy, where the whole life of man is at the very center of what is studied. Rather, in such fields thinking necessarily takes place in significant relation to a community and tradition. Here we think, with other men of the past looking over our shoulders. Notable among them in the West are such ancient Greeks as Plato and Aristotle.

The Greek origin and character of philosophy are vigorously reasserted in recent papers by Martin Heidegger, who claims not only that the Greeks originated philosophy but that philosophy *is* Greek in nature, and that it finds adequate expression only in the Greek language![1] Surely this is pushing a good idea much too far. The truth in Heidegger's position is that the Western philosophic tradition owes its origin to a particularly limpid spring in ancient Greece. However, it is also important to add that the stream which began there has flowed through many different landscapes, both influencing and being influenced by them, and has been fed by many other tributary sources— Christianity in the ancient and medieval periods, and natural science in more modern times, to mention just two. It is also important to add that other human cultures have their own distinctive philosophic traditions, strikingly different from the West in many ways, but enough like it to make justifiable the common noun "philosophy."

b. Looking over these traditions, we note the observable fact that philosophy has concerned itself with what we have already termed an inclusive vision of the totality of things. Traditional philosophic statements, as frequently argued in these pages, are thus totality statements. There have been many historical variations on this theme. The totality has been envisaged in many ways, and the basic ingredient or ingredients of this totality have been variously conceived. Sometimes this vision of the scheme-of-things-entire has been subjected to critical attack. However, philosophic criticism is criticism in this context, and it differs from other forms of criticism precisely in its reference to this context.

This definition of philosophic statements as inclusive totality statements, which has been presupposed throughout our study, and alluded to frequently, runs the danger of one serious misunderstanding, to which attention may be called at this point. It is the danger that we consider simply the extension of this inclusive class of all beings without its intension, thus gathering all entities within the boundaries of this class and labeling it the subject matter of philosophic thinking. Actually this is only the beginning of the problem. The logical class of *all*—literally and etymologically, *all entities that have being*—is surely a radically unique class, having its own peculiar properties and implications. What takes place is that as the human mind (which is itself within this class) looks out to the horizon of totality which bounds this unique class, there is a kind of reflexive movement of the mind from the horizon to all the individual entities within the class. Thus, they are beings within the field which thinkers from Aristotle to Tillich have called Being-as-Such.[2] By some such process of thought as this, the radically unique concept of Being takes shape in the human mind, utterly singular in its extension, intension, and significance. Such is the subject matter of metaphysics, and the source of philosophic thinking.

c. Philosophy is a form of critical thinking whose nature and criteria can be clearly and explicitly stated. The Greeks, who had words for so many things, had a word for this aspect of mind and world, namely, the word *logos*. Untranslatable in any exact sense, perhaps the word "rationale" best conveys its meaning. Thus the Greeks believed that the world or cosmos had a rationale which human thinking could apprehend, or lay hold of, and set forth in rational speech. This process of apprehension was called "knowing" and its product was knowledge. And philosophy, the Greeks believed, was knowledge; indeed, it was the highest, most synoptic form of knowledge, called "wisdom."

The rational method of philosophic thinking has been

variously conceived, and I shall presently attempt my own formulation. Yet here let us note the peculiar and rigorous formulation given to the critical task of philosophy in semantic analysis as a contemporary illustration of philosophic reason and devotion to reason. Indeed, the rigorous and comprehensive critical analysis of other philosophies, as well as all other types of statements, is often taken by this school as the whole task of philosophy. In devoting itself to criticism, this type of philosophy has often specifically disavowed constructive philosophy, particularly in traditional terms. It has assumed the possibility of critical attack upon other peoples' metaphysics without any metaphysical presuppositions on the part of the critic.

Grateful as we must be for this dedication to the critical work of philosophy, one still cannot avoid the conclusion that this is a one-sided and distorted view. Rather is it the case that in the area of human experience to which philosophy refers, namely, the whole of experience, it is not possible to criticize or reject one proposition or viewpoint without consciously or unconsciously accepting another. Once this is perceived, then it follows that critical philosophy and constructive philosophy are not two distinct and separable types of philosophy, but, rather, two inseparable aspects of the integral task of philosophy. One of these two may receive relatively more or less emphasis, but the other will never be completely absent. Attempts completely to suppress either will simply drive it underground, where it will function unconsciously, and therefore uncritically and probably badly. As already observed, metaphysics is never better, and often worse, for being unconscious.[3]

The duality between analytic and synthetic or between critical and constructive aspects of philosophy is closely related to another duality, namely, that between the activity of philosophizing and its goal or end in philosophic system. The Greek adage, "Not philosophy but to philosophize," expresses a preference for the activity of philosophic thinking over its products or conclusions. Yet if the viewpoint of this chapter is valid, the process is properly inseparable from its goal. If such a violent separation is made, the activity of philosophic thinking becomes inchoate, and its conclusions in philosophic systems become artificial, pretentious, and irrelevant. The latter are so because their human use is lost sight of. Conversely, only as the activity of philosophic thinking and its goal are held in the closest unity does philosophy exist in integrity and power. It is both a system of thought and the activity of inclusively systematic thinking.

d. The reference above to unconscious philosophy leads us to a further characteristic of philosophic thinking, properly so called, namely, to its necessarily self-conscious character. This is a trait that contrasts with both art and science, and that virtually forces consideration of the problem of philosophic method. It is possible to practice scientific thinking without having a conscious theory of scientific method; and one can be an artist without a philosophy of art. But in the case of philosophic thinking, it is doubtful if any man can do it well without some explicit, conscious awareness of what he is doing. In other words, an essential part of philosophy is some account of what philosophy is. We cannot "do philosophy," as the British like to say, at least we cannot do it well, without some conscious, deliberate attention to what it is that we are doing. There is, as previously noted, such a thing as unconscious philosophy, or, in other words, there are beliefs of philosophic significance that do actually inform and guide the life of a human mind but of which that mind is unconscious. However, such unconscious philosophy has the ambiguous character of being uncritical, and therefore to this extent, and in this sense, unphilosophical. An important part of philosophic activity is to dig out such beliefs from their dark hiding places and expose them to critical examination.

e. Traditional Western philosophy, while having an irreducible rational or logical aspect, has nonetheless also had an equally irreducibly expressive, personal or subjective aspect as well. Logical positivism termed this "emotive meaning." The subjective aspect in turn has both its individual and its common aspects. As to the latter, in the ancient Greco-Roman world, philosophy often involved a whole organized way of life not unlike the religious or monastic organizations of many cultures. While this has been less often true in the modern world, philosophy has never succeeded in discarding completely its relation to a way of life. A philosophy expresses the life values of an individual as well as a community. What all this means for philosophic language is that some of its essential terms will inescapably be symbols. This poetic or imaginative aspect is obvious enough in some philosophers, such as Plato. Yet the argument here is that in varying measure it is true as well of all philosophers—of prosaic Aristotle as well as poetic Plato. Aristotle's writings may sing less beautifully than Plato's, but an expressive quality is there in such aspects as his view of being, his depiction of friendship, of the contemplative life and of the life of deity. Indeed, a close scrutiny of Aristotle's writings will disclose certain root metaphors that are the vehicle of this aspect of his thought and communication; and a similar inspection of the writings of other philosophers will bring to light similar aspects.

One part of the content of this imaginative or poetic aspect of philosophic discourse will be a direct expression of what may be termed the philosophic attitude. Individual versions of this emotion or attitude have varied widely. Aristotle called it wonder.[4] Perhaps it will be illuminating to place it in a spectrum of human attitudes midway between religious awe and scientific curiosity. Surely it is a question-asking attitude; indeed, the philosophic attitude is persistently one of inquiry. But it is curiosity or inquiry confronting the whole situation of man in the universe, with its mingled humility and exaltation, of triumph and tragedy, and especially of the mystery[5] which results when the human mind faces its own limits in the universe. Something like this is the distinctively philosophic emotion.

Expressed also in the symbolic aspect of philosophic discourse are the deepest personal values of the philosopher who utters the words and sentences of this philosophy. For the inclusive totality which is philosophy's subject matter includes one's own self or mind and all one's responses to the totality of things. This fact about philosophy imparts an indefeasibly personal quality to philosophic discourse, expressing the fundamental life values, the whole posture in existence of the philosopher.

When this value-oriented aspect of philosophy is put together with its rational character discussed above, what emerges is a systematic criticism or appraisal of fundamental human values, a process of synoptic and rational evaluation. Such reflective valuation is certainly not the least significant aspect of Western philosophy; for in the values which thus emerge in this continuing process of appraisal we envisage and lay hold upon nothing less than the image of man which has sustained his humanity during the centuries of Western history.

From this aspect of philosophic discourse, a further conclusion is forthcoming. It is that in the last analysis every man must be his own philosopher. From another man he may get stimulus and necessary factual help of many sorts, but his philosophizing and his philosophy must be his own. He must do it, otherwise it will have neither validity nor authenticity for him. We can no more philosophize for each other than we can be born or die for each other, or eat another's meal and have it nourish him. In this respect, philosophy differs radically from natural science where impersonal results can be communicated and appropriated in ways separable from personal participation.

f. From these personal and expressive aspects of philosophy also emerges still a further characteristic, namely, the noncumulative character of philosophic thinking and speaking. Here again we see a contrast with the processes of natural science which are clearly cumulative or progressive. It is true that, like natural science, philosophic thinking must be done over and over again, and that there is no finality at any stage in the process. Also like science, a final and absolute truth never emerges in philosophy, despite the illusion of some philosophers that their system is such Absolute Truth. Rather, the truth of philosophies and of philosophy is as relative as that of science. The decisive and crucial difference between these two modes of human thinking lies in the absence in the case of philosophic thinking of precisely the cumulative or progressive character of science. Philosophy shows historic development but not progress. The reason for this absence in turn lies in the essentially personal character of philosophic thinking. Philosophy thus emerges as a continuing conversation concerning persistent and recurrent human issues of great breadth or generality. In this great conversation every man is invited by virtue of his humanity to participate.

2. A Conception of Philosophic Method

The observations of the preceding section may well elicit from the reader this question: How, then, will a man philosophize? By what method will he do this form of thinking? Certainly one part of the answer to that question will be that in view of the personal character of philosophic thinking different philosophers will pursue different methods. Recognizing this individual aspect of philosophic thinking, let it be plainly said that the paragraphs which follow here state the writer's method. Yet immediately I add that I accept and practice this method because I believe it to be most rational or adequate to all the pertinent facts. Thus it is, by implication (as is the case throughout philosophy), an invitation to the reader to join in this method of thinking or at least to consider it seriously.

What has already been asserted about philosophy and philosophic thinking carries clear implications for the proper method of carrying on this activity. For example, if philosophic thinking possesses the historical character here claimed for it, the philosopher will seek as he philosophizes to locate himself in a philosophic tradition and community. If it has the valuational character here claimed for it, he will seek not the exclusion but the responsible inclusion of personal valuation, both individual and social.

Against this background, what are some of the essential features or traits indicated for philosophic method? In answer, two main assertions will be made. The first assertion is that philosophic thinking proceeds presupposition-ally.[6] This means that this kind of thinking proceeds properly by digging into the presuppositions of any and every process of thought and experience, bringing their presuppositions into the open, stating and examining them critically. In this contention there is an important negative implication, namely, that the wrong way to proceed with philosophic thinking is to take some process of objective thinking, scientific or of any other sort that occurs within a definite and specific context, and extrapolate it, or extend it beyond the relevant evidence. Such processes stretch good thinking beyond the limits of intelligibility, and the results are more or less meaningless speculation. Indeed, it is this kind of thinking which has given philosophic speculation so bad a name.

If one is to proceed by the method of presupposition, he must put to himself the question of precisely what a presupposition is. The term and method date from Kant and his *Voraussetzungen,* but both have been used so loosely that we must be concerned with the clarification and establishment of a definite meaning. A presupposition, carefully defined, will be seen to have logical, psychological, and axiological characteristics.

Logically, a presupposition may be said to stand in the relation of implication to a statement of the human concerns or interests to which it is related. In other words, if the truth of the presupposition is granted, the truth of the given or data statement follows from it. A presupposition is thus in this respect logically similar to a postulate, a premise, or indeed to a scientific hypothesis. Among the conclusions to be drawn from this fact is that our knowledge of presuppositions is never more than probable, for, working from a statement backward to presupposition, we can never be certain that we have the only presupposition or set of presuppositions from which the data statement might be derived. It is entirely possible that another presupposition may be discovered which would function equally well to explain or justify the problematic concern.

Yet the decisive feature of presuppositions is not logical but psychological in nature; it is, namely, the fact that presuppositions are more or less unconscious. In contrast to suppositions which are premises or assumptions, they are literally *pre*-suppositions. From this, we are led to a view of philosophy as a rational method for digging into the foundations of human thought and attitude, and setting out and examining the assumptions or premises we find hidden there. As has been pointed out, this definition of the philosophical task owes much to Collingwood's definition of metaphysics as the science of absolute presuppositions of a particular man or age.[7] By absolute presuppositions, Collingwood appears to mean those deepest assumptions which derive from no others but from which all others derive. Such assumptions thus have the characteristics of being both logically and psychologically "primitive," or underived. Moreover, their only possible mode of existence lies, according to Collingwood, in being presupposed. The moment such assumptions, or, rather, more accurately pre-assumptions, are drawn into articulated propositions or statements, they are no longer living but dead presuppositions, and indeed presuppose yet other presuppositions. From this view of the nature and function of presuppositions follow several of the distinctive features of Collingwood's viewpoint. For one thing, the student of philosophy is no longer a metaphysician but rather a kind of archaeologist of past, dead presuppositions—a position which, in effect, spells the end of all living metaphysical thinking. Note too that Collingwood nowhere doubts or questions the capacity of the human mind to stand clear of all metaphysics and perform this task in a neutral, presuppositionless fashion![8]

Collingwood's emphasis on the unconscious character of presuppositions yields another implication, unintended by him, yet conceivably fruitful for contemporary philosophizing. It is well known that psychoanalysis and related types of depth psychology have placed great emphasis upon unconscious areas of the mind's life. Therapy for mental illness is frequently conceived as a process of bringing such unconscious elements up to the level of conscious awareness where an individual can at least begin to cope with them. To be sure, philosophic analysis is not therapy (at least it is not so in any ordinary sense of the word), yet are there not here similarities between these two processes of analysis, such that each might learn from the other? A tentatively affirmative answer to this question is given by an increasing number of contemporary philosophers.

A logical comment on the nature of unconscious assumptions may also pertinently be inserted at this point. There have been occasions in the history of mathematics where an unconscious postulate or assumption has significantly influenced mathematical thinking. Later generations have been able to articulate the unconscious postulate and describe its influence. There are similarities between such occurrences in mathematics and logic, on the one hand, and the wider philosophic situation here under consideration.

As a beginning in the critical understanding of philosophic presuppositions, let us note two distinguishable aspects of the process of becoming aware of them. First is the act of digging a presupposition out of the subconscious depths of the mind and exhibiting it in propositional form, and second is the critical activity of affirming or denying its truth. In other words, we ask of presuppositions: (a) Can we become aware of them? and, (b) Will they stand the light of critical analysis? Collingwood gave a negative answer in both cases, but in both cases I believe that a fuller view of the situation will lead us to disagree with him and answer both affirmatively. At least I see no reason why some presuppositions may not pass either or both of these tests.

Can philosophic analysis really get at presuppositions? Surely the task is extremely difficult, particularly when we realize that, as someone has said, there are no real presuppositions except the last—or first, i.e., those lying deepest in the mind. The task of analysis becomes even more difficult when one becomes aware that he must examine and lay bare an actively functioning part of his and others' minds' life, like the surgeon who must operate on the heart without impeding its vital operation. Yet difficult as it is, there is no inherent impossibility in the process.

Yet even conceding the possibility of laying bare such an absolute presupposition, can a man still affirm it philosophically? Or, as Collingwood believes, will he necessarily deny it? This question is crucially important, for it involves nothing less than the possibility of undertaking explicit conscious metaphysical thinking. Again we must say of Collingwood that he gives no reason for his crucial negation. Nor does critical examination turn up any such crucial negation. To be sure, some philosophic affirmations and utterances will surely not stand the light of day. But why is this necessarily true of any or all such assumptions or pre-assumptions? Why is it not at least a possible mental activity to examine such propositions in the light of all the available factual evidence, and still to accept or affirm them? Why is not an explicit metaphysical affirmation at least an open possibility? This chapter is written from the viewpoint and conviction that this is not only possible but that it is the center of the philosophic task. It is so particularly if we keep the nature of this task clearly before us. The task, it will be recalled, is the synoptic unification of experience; and the first aspect of this task is to dig out and appraise the deepest and most general assumptions lying at the foundation of the mind's life.

A further criticism of Collingwood is invited by his view (everywhere assumed, yet nowhere argued) that it is a possible act of the human mind to stand altogether clear of all metaphysical statements, studying and discussing them in neutral objectivity. This is clearly impossible for several good reasons, chief among which is that we are here dealing with an inescapable aspect of the relation of each man's mind to its world, namely, with the horizon of totality around it. The analyst of other men's presuppositions has his own presuppositions which observably influence his own thinking. Thus, if we recognize the fully developed human mind in all the varied aspects of its integral life, a metaphysics of some sort is inescapable or unavoidable.

Thus arises a peculiar aspect of metaphysical thinking and speaking to which attention has already been called. In common sense and natural science it is entirely possible to criticize or reject one idea or statement without accepting or affirming another. Indeed, it is possible to stand clear of all such views. In philosophy this is not possible. Here, in the philosophic situation, if we criticize or reject one statement, we do so in terms of another which consciously or unconsciously we accept or affirm. It is possible to affirm or deny a metaphysics only from a metaphysical viewpoint.[9]

The second main assertion to be made concerning philosophic method is that it takes place by means of a peculiar use of metaphor or analogy. So far we have been largely concerned with the process of envisaging presuppositions; now we must turn to their articulation. As we do, let us be aware of the fact that in philosophy, seeing and saying, while distinguishable, are in fact not separable elements. Indeed, this duality of elements is similar to that already discussed between the critical and constructive, or the analytic and synthetic, aspects of philosophic activity.

Turning to the process of philosophic saying or articulation, we confront a grave difficulty. Human speech has its origin and its primary function in distinguishing specific elements within the totality of common experience, but clearly the totality of things is a referent far beyond such common objects of experience. The difficulty is how speech may be used for a purpose so different from that which is the primary function of language. Seeing this predicament, one may understand the attitude of those who assert that in such a situation the silence of agnosticism is the only wise course. Any attempt to speak in this situation constitutes, they argue, a violent misuse of language.

As an alternative, I propose here a language of deliberately stretched or expanded metaphor. In Chapter III the function of metaphor in the mind's apprehension of new and unique entities was discussed, and a foundation was laid for the philosophic and religious use of metaphor. The metaphorical dimension of language is the way the mind lays hold of new elements of experience, and also of unique elements. What is here proposed is that philosophic language properly consists of certain highly distinctive metaphors drawn from within experience and then deliberately expanded or stretched to depict and characterize totality. A particular system of philosophy will thus consist of the systematic exfoliation and elaboration of the metaphor which lies at its roots.

This proposal for the nature of philosophic discourse, or, more specifically, for the articulation of presuppositions, is by no means unique. It is similar to the idea of analogy or analogical prediction in Thomism. The similarity consists in the deliberate stretching of words for a new use. Yet the present proposal differs from Thomist analogy in two respects. It does not carry the heavy baggage of Thomism's whole system of categories, and it emphasizes the expressive quality of metaphor as well as the referential functions of analogy. It is for this latter reason that the term "metaphor" or "root metaphor," rather than "analogy," is preferred and used here.

Beginnings have been made in a root-metaphor approach to philosophic thinking and saying by men as different as Austin Farrer and Stephen Pepper. The former does much to bridge the gap between metaphor and Thomist analogy.[10] The latter, Pepper,[11] argues that metaphysical systems begin with the statement and elaboration of a root metaphor. Metaphysical thinking consists accordingly of the application of this metaphor to all the various aspects of experience. It may well be questioned whether there are, as Pepper asserts, only four such metaphors, namely, form, mechanism, context, and organism, or that any philosophy is limited to a single root metaphor. One might also wish that the expressive as well as the referential qualities of root metaphor might be developed. Nonetheless, here is at least a significant beginning in the study of the metaphorical character of philosophic utterance.

For such an approach, philosophic or metaphysical thinking will consist in the total process of stating and judging the adequacy to all the facts of existence of the root metaphors which are the fundamental terms of this language. The function, once more, of this whole process of thinking and speaking is synoptic unification of experience. It is not important whether the process is called metaphysics or ontology, or, as Aristotle called it, first philosophy. Indeed, it is ironical to note that Collingwood used the word "metaphysics," and rejected the term "ontology" in ways precisely opposite to the usage of Heidegger, Tillich, and others. What matters here is not words but their meanings.[12]

3. Philosophy, Theology, and Religion

At several points in this chapter we have approached the border between philosophy and religion. This disputed border territory over which so many wars have been fought and so many claims and counterclaims entered may be described as the field of fundamental life values which give meaning to human existence. It is obvious on the basis of our previous study that this aspect of human experience is of crucial importance to both philosophy and religion, each of which accordingly lay claims to authority and jurisdiction.

This observation may easily be confirmed by a look at historical relations between philosophy and religion. In the first place, in many human cultures as different as Greece, India, and China, it is religion in one form or another that gives birth to philosophy. The historical development of philosophy out of religion is thus an observable phenomenon at many different times and places in human history. The precise nature of the relations between religion and philosophy vary widely in different situations, extending from a desire to communicate and understand a new religion or to defend a religion that has been attacked to the desire to attack any or all religions with a view to radical change or abolition. Historical illustrations of these various attitudes will come readily to mind. The attitude of hostile and critical attack is so frequently assumed as axiomatic in the modern West, particularly in the intellectual community, that it is necessary to point out that other relations do in fact exist and have significance in human history.

If it is asked why religion should at times give birth to philosophy, the answer lies precisely in the ultimacy of ultimate concern or valuation. As previously argued, religious experience consists of concerns or valuations that have the quality of absoluteness or ultimacy in the lives that experience them. In sharpest contrast to all the immediate or proximate values that claim only a partial or qualified response, at the heart of religious experience are values to which men respond with complete or absolute attachment. It is precisely this quality which creates philosophy, for a part of the experience of ultimate concern is the demand that this concern or its object be related to all things whatsoever. In this way there comes into being the idea of an altogether inclusive totality, variously called Being, Being-as-such, or Reality, which becomes the defining feature and philosophical statement and reasoning.

This observation enables us to understand the fact frequently alluded to in these pages that philosophy and religion, alone among the forms of human discourse, involve a completely unrestricted use of the word "all." In the case of religion, it denotes a top-priority concern, or in alternative and opposite metaphor, one that bottoms all other concerns. The appropriateness of such height or depth metaphors lies in the location of the religious interest in personality, and its relation to the whole structure of interests or concerns that constitute a personality.

In contrast to what may perhaps be called the vertical quality of ultimacy or absoluteness in relation to religious experience, stands the horizontal quality of philosophic ultimacy or absoluteness. The latter is totality in an extensive, all-encompassing sense. Religious experience is, as Joachim Wach remarked, "the most intense kind of experience of which an individual is capable,"[13] while the defining characteristic of philosophic thinking and speaking is the widest totality of which man's mind is capable. It is what Jaspers has termed the *Umgreifende* or comprehensive.[14]

Once philosophy is born, it goes its own way and lives its own life. It may be born into a household of faith, but presently it grows up, leaves home, and, as it were, sets up housekeeping on its own. Its origins may be sacral, but its adult life is likely to be quite secular. In no culture is this more true than the post-Renaissance or modern West; and in no human concern has the massive secularization of Western culture been more influential than in philosophy. Philosophy appears here as a child that has been alienated from its parent. Yet the fact of parenthood remains. Incidentally, parental resemblance is sometimes most clear at just the points at which a child seeks most strongly to avoid or renounce it.

There is a middle term between religion and philosophy, namely, theology. In the next chapter, religious statements will be distinguished from theological statements, the former being symbolic statements whose use is the direct expression of religious experience, and the latter conceptual statements whose purpose is not direct expression but the understanding of religious experience. Theological statements thus constitute the linguistic vehicle for the study of religion. In the next chapter, we shall look in detail at this somewhat controversial view of theological statements, attempting both defense and explanation. Here we note that despite differences of emphasis and attitude, there is no clear or sharp discontinuity between theological and philosophic statements.

Meanwhile, this chapter may be concluded by calling attention to the relation of faith and philosophy, and of their respective forms of utterance to each other. Elsewhere I have asserted that "all philosophies have religious foundations and all religions have philosophic implications."[15] This double assertion has been attacked by other philosophers and theologians. While I cannot here undertake the full task of response and rebuttal, I may perhaps speak to certain misunderstandings. First, no intention is either expressed or implied to lure or coerce any philosophers into religious communities which they find uncongenial. Equally, no assertion is here either made or implied about any particular religion. All that is here either said or intended is that at the foundation of all philosophic utterances is some attitude of ultimate concern, which thus forms the foundation upon which the philosopher as a man stands. It will thus function as an assumption, explicit or implicit, conscious or unconscious, of his philosophic thinking.

Conversely it must also be asserted that the conscious having of an ultimate concern entails philosophic responsibilities. For this concern demands relation to all that is. Yet once such philosophic thinking emerges, it is likely to turn its criticism upon its religious source. So it is that religious people and groups have frequently been hostile and defensive in their attitudes toward philosophy. To such people (as to the philosophers of the previous paragraph) let it be clearly asserted that whichever end of the stick one picks up, he picks up the whole stick.

IX Religious and Theological Statements

❖ ❖

1. *Two Forms of Religious Discourse*

In Chapter IV a distinction was proposed between religious statements and theological statements. These two kinds of religious language differ fundamentally in both form and function. First-order religious statements, or faith statements, are expressive in form, their main terms being images; their function is the direct expression of religious experience. They seek to articulate and communicate the immediately and directly experienced quality of religion from the participant's viewpoint. Thus they are statements "in" religion, in contrast to theology, whose statements are "about" religion. Second-order religious statements, or theological statements, are conceptual rather than expressive or symbolic in form; their main terms are not images but concepts, and their purpose is not direct expression but the understanding of religion. Hence, according to this viewpoint, theological statements are the linguistic vehicle for the study and understanding of religion.

While no claim is here made for any originality or uniqueness of this distinction between faith statements and theological statements, it must be pointed out that the distinction does not occur in any explicit or developed

form either in the classical works of Western theology or
in the contemporary literature of this field.[1] Moreover, the
failure to make the distinction seriously confuses much
of the contemporary semantic analysis of religious and
theological language. The distinction does appear to have
a basis in common experience and common language; the
man in the pew has no doubts about the matter when the
preacher shifts from religious language to theological language. He is clear that the Biblical commandment, "Hear,
O Israel: The Lord our God is one Lord; and you shall
love the Lord your God with all your heart and with all
your soul and with all your might" is a firsthand expression of faith rather than a theological statement, and that
the statement "God exists," asserted as the conclusion of
an argument, is by contrast theological in character. The
task of this chapter is to assert this distinction and to develop a few of its implications.

2. *Some Main Forms of Religious Language*

It will clarify the distinction to look first in detail at
some of the different forms of first-order religious language, or faith language, as they may be observed in the
religious communities of human history and also in religious experience as an aspect of individual life. The list
that follows here may well not be complete or exhaustive,
and at times the categories or forms tend to overlap. Nevertheless, here are seven significant and recurrent forms in
which men have expressed and communicated ultimate
concern. Not all of them find exemplification in all religions, yet they do recur widely. It may also be observed
that if we focus attention on a particular religion, studying its witness, its prayer, its commandments, its myth and
ritual, we shall often find the unifying force of a common

image which is expressed in many or all these different kinds of utterance.

a. Confession or witness is perhaps the most elemental form of religious utterance, for it consists of the spontaneous cry of the heart, expressing or declaring the meaning the speaker has found in existence. It is a direct expressive statement of the attitude of conviction that is central to religious experience. Vital convictions of all sorts generate a demand to be declared or expressed. The form of this witness or confession will be that of luminous and powerful images, and its content will be a distinctive configuration of life values which are the content of faith or ultimate concern.

Confessional statements of a distinctive sort may be found in the literature of all the world's faiths. The Shema of Judaism, "Hear, O Israel . . ."; the New Testament confession, "Jesus is Lord"; the statement of the Buddhist monk, "I take refuge in the Buddha, the Dharma, and the Sangha"; the Muslim confession, "There is one God Allah, and Mohammed is his prophet"—are but a few examples of this recurrent type of utterance. While obviously not original for each individual adherent, these statements become confessions of the individual heart wherever conviction is authentic. In monotheistic religious traditions like Christianity, confession is interpreted theologically as the content of revelation. It is the content of what God says to man.

b. Closely related to confession is prayer. One of the few features in which all the many faiths of mankind seem to agree is that man does not stand alone. Rather, he is dependent on a Power not his own, however this be understood and whatever the attitude toward this Power.[2] In its most elemental sense, prayer is man's direct address and appeal to Power. The mood and spirit vary widely with the individual man, with his religion, and with the situation. In the midst of peril it may be a cry for security. In the midst of darkness and weakness it may be an appeal for light and power. It may be a cry of the heart for help and for fellowship. Its language, like that of confession, is direct, expressive, and personal; and its contents are the needs and aspirations deepest in man's heart.

c. Both confession and prayer soon become formal and stylized in the various communities and traditions in which they occur. They congeal into fixed bodies of expressive words and nonverbal symbols, to be repeated on stated occasions. Prayer and confession are thus transformed into ritual. Rite or ritual consists of a configuration of expressive images in word, in act, and sometimes in other media, to be repeated at set times. Ideally these images are to be appropriated spontaneously and authentically by each individual participant, though the fixed character of ritual always carries the peril of empty formalism. The content of ritual is the life values by which the individual or community get life orientation. What goes on or takes place in rite is thus a direct, expressive statement and celebration of these values.

However, other elements soon creep into ritual. Sheer love of repetition is a powerful motive. A mimetic impulse, a human need for expression, as real as the need for daily bread, also plays a part. Magic frequently enters the scene. If only these words are said or that symbolic action performed, desired results will take place and undesired ones will be averted—such is the magician's claim. Similarly an aesthetic or artistic motive soon finds significant expression here. How many rituals in different cultures of the world have been the fruitful sources of dramatic art! Out of sacred ritual comes drama, in Greece, in Japan, in medieval Europe and elsewhere. So it is that ritual maintains its many-sided fascination. Its religious origin, we repeat, is the imaginative statement of life values or life orientation.

d. Closely related to rite is myth, or sacred story. The life values that are acted out in rite are sung out in myth. Whether myth or ritual is first is indeed a chicken-and-egg question. They must be regarded as two expressions of the same concern, namely, of the values by which a man or a community lives and declares life meaningful.

In recent theological and philosophic discussion the term "myth" has been used frequently and in such a bewildering variety of ambiguous meanings that the waters of discussion have been seriously muddied. So vast and so serious are these ambiguities that any single writer would be presumptuous to think he can clear things up. Yet one can at least begin the large task of clarification, so necessary in this issue, by listing a few of the questionable uses, noting both their justifiable and unjustifiable features. First of all, I offer a commonsense definition of myth as a sacred story that expresses the life values or life orientation of a person or a community. All three features—the sacredness, the narrative, and the function of expressing and justifying human values—are necessary to myth, and taken together, they are sufficient to define it.

One group of writers, illustrated by Santayana[3] and Niebuhr,[4] uses the term "myth" as a synonym for all first-order religious language. This use calls attention to the imaginative, expressive character of this language, as well as its relation to poetry; but by its excessive breadth it blurs the distinction between myth and other forms of first-order religious language.

Another group of writers equates myth either expressly or tacitly with fiction, or a story that is not true.[5] Such interpretations point out the obviously unfactual, fantastic aspect of myths. Also they are often strongly under the influence of modern natural science, and so tend to regard myth as prescientific attempts to formulate explanatory hypotheses concerning natural phenomena. A candid reading of many myths indicates the inescapable element of truth in this view, yet primitive attempts at etiology are seldom the sole or main aspect of myth. Other different kinds of meaning also find expression in myths. Thus if one distinguishes the religious from the scientific meaning, he is able to affirm the former aspect of a myth while avoiding or discarding the latter. This distinction Reinhold Niebuhr has formulated as the difference between "primitive" and "perennial" elements in myth.[6] It is one of the achievements of the modern naturalistic outlook on man's life in the universe that it has forced us to make this distinction more clearly and forthrightly than ever before in human history.

A variant of this naturalistic view is the assertion of Gilbert Ryle,[7] who defines a myth as a categorial mistake, as, for example, when one speaks of a concept or an idea as a thing, or when Truth or Beauty are personified. Such a mistake might be formulated by Waismann as a mistake in language levels or strata. In general, for all the benefit of their disinfectant criticism, many naturalistic views display a philistine ignorance and imperceptiveness of the whole field of human experience with which myth deals.

Another group of writers, such as G. E. Wright,[8] H. Frankfort,[9] and E. Cassirer,[10] seeks to limit the term "myth" or "mythology" to a particular type of religion that concentrates attention on nature and culture. Such religions, from Greece and Babylonia to China, have produced a luxuriant variety of tales of gods, half-gods, and heroes. In contrast to such mythologies, Biblical religion is regarded by this viewpoint as antimythological. The term "myth" in this usage is applied to the origin story of ancient Babylonia, but denied as a description of the Genesis story of creation. These views have the virtue of pointing to a significant and fundamental discontinuity between these two types of religion and the literatures they have produced; but this is hardly sufficient grounds for denying the mythical character of the Biblical stories. Rather, we shall argue that the Biblical narratives constitute a new and different type of myth.

A fourth group of writers,[11] for the most part social scientists, looks upon myth as a story that is used variously to justify, validate, or rationalize some form of social power or authority. A myth is, thus, a story which, if accepted, leads men to accept the authority of this or that system of power in state, church, or any other human community. This approach calls attention to the important feature of myth which we have described as the imaginative statement of and justification of values, but it often does so to the neglect of other essential features. There is also a serious pitfall not always avoided by this view. To perform this function of justification, a myth must be accepted as in some sense true. If it is to perform the function of validation effectively, the myth must be accepted as valid. Stories contrived by propagandists, public relations men, and other ideologists to control public opinion are surely spurious and not authentic myths.

A fifth and final use of the terms "myth" and "mythology" is associated with the name of Rudolf Bultmann and the controversy that has swirled about his name and writings in recent years. The most notable feature of Bultmann's use of the terms is the perilous ambiguity of its use of these terms. A close inspection of Bultmann's writings will show that he has run together one or more of the four preceding views of myth and mythology in his pages, and very often without any clear notion that the various meanings have been blurred. In other words, the whole "demythologizing" controversy vividly illustrates the evil results of ambiguity; and a first step in resolving these vexed issues is the clarification of the basic terms "myth" and "mythology."[12]

e. A fifth type of religious language is commandment or moral imperative. Beginning with "thou shalt" or "thou shalt not" (or, from the human viewpoint, "I ought"), it consists of prescriptions or proscriptions for human action. In its most primitive form it is tabu, but among the developed and civilized religious traditions, such statements develop into the various patterns of morality characteristic of the particular traditions. Such moral traditions exhibit the greatest variety in their specific commands, but commandment or imperative of some sort there always is as an aspect of religious experience. The life values that constitute the content of religious experience assume the form of commandment as they impinge upon the active life of man. The values imaginatively celebrated in myth and rite become in morality norms for conduct. Life orientation in this context takes on the meaning of morality. It is this close relation which leads many writers, from Comte to Braithwaite, to equate religion and morality. The relation is certainly close and significant, but the terms "religion" and "morality" are by no means equivalent.

f. A sixth type of religious language, namely, "homily" or "sermon," has as its purpose the communication of direct experience from one person to others. Its purpose

is thus one of propagating a faith, or, in the strict sense of
the term, "propaganda." The terms "homily" and "sermon" in popular speech often carry the connotation of
exhortation. While this form of discourse is frequently in
the hortatory mood, this is by no means invariably the
case. Often, indeed, the purpose of propagation is better
served by the indicative or declarative rather than the
hortatory mood. Often, too, sermon or homily engages in
didactic or teaching functions. Sometimes the sermon
moves away from first-order religious language toward
second-order or theological language. Some sermons sound
or read like theological treatises. Yet despite these various
tendencies, the essential features of this type of religious
language may still be characterized as the use of expressive
language for the purpose of propagating, stimulating, and
sustaining a particular religious faith. It is a purpose of
arousing, persuading, and stimulating this form of experience.

g. A final type of religious language occurring in diverse
ways in most of the religions of the world is scripture or
sacred writing. It is a type that varies greatly in its meaning
and significance from religion to religion, and that in a
baffling way overlaps other forms of religious language.
Many of the preceding six types, and others too, are to be
found within the pages or scrolls of sacred scriptures.
Scripture probably emerges from the oral tradition and
communication that precedes it through the practical mo-
tives of preserving these sayings for posterity or making
them available to a wider community. But once in existence, scriptures assume a religious significance of their
own. This fact, true of various religions, in their own
ways, assumes a unique significance in the Biblical religions, as we shall see in Chapter XI.

Not only do these seven forms of religious language

emerge recurrently in the various religions of the world, but it is also both somewhat amusing and illuminating to note their emergence among the various religious substitutes of the modern secular world. Communists, humanists, adherents of "religions" of science, of democratic values, and of art for art's sake, may sometimes be observed to engage in witness, in ritual, in mythmaking and myth telling or recital, in scripture, in sermon or homily, and in the moral commandments appropriate to their respective systems of life orientation.

3. *The Religious-Theological Spectrum*

From the various kinds of first-order religious utterance we turn now to a consideration of the distinction between faith and theology, and their respective forms of utterance. Once the distinction has been made, questions and disagreements press in upon us from all sides. Plainly the thesis is controversial, and if it is to be maintained successfully, it will have to be carefully guarded against misunderstanding. It will also have to be significantly qualified if it is to be at all useful in understanding many actually occurring forms of religious utterance that appear to lie intermediately between theology and the direct expressions of faith.

To get the issue before us, let us attempt a summary restatement of the thesis or hypothesis. It is that there are two distinguishable kinds of religious utterance, faith statements and theological statements, together with certain intermediate types to be described below. While the function of the first kind of utterance is the direct expression of faith from the participant's viewpoint, the second or theological type of utterance may be characterized as the linguistic vehicle of the study of religion. This last assertion leads to another, namely, that theology is properly nothing less than the comprehensive and all-embracing study of religion. In other words, the proper function of the second kind of utterance is the comprehensive critical study of the first kind. This will lead us to some controversial conclusions concerning the nature of theology, which will be set forth briefly in the final section of the present chapter.

As a device for visualizing and summarizing the thesis and the qualifications to be discussed, the reader is asked to imagine a spectrum or continuum, at one end of which is placed first-order religious utterance, and at the other end of which is placed philosophic discourse. The various kinds of theological language, as well as such intermediate types as creed, catechism, and apologetics, may then be understood as points or ranges along the straight line that extends between these two extremities. The implications of this diagrammatic representation will be drawn out and discussed in the pages that follow.

It is necessary to guard the thesis by pointing to several possible plausible misunderstandings. Precisely what does the hypothesis claim or propose, and what does it not claim or propose? First of all, let it clearly be said that it is not a thesis about any particular theology or theologian of the past or present. So understood, it would be clearly false. For in the first place, in a great many existing theologies there is no distinction between what has here been termed "first-order" and "second-order" religious discourse. Furthermore, in the case of many theologies, the activity of theologizing is conceived to take place entirely within a particular community of faith, as that particular faith's effort at self-understanding. Also, in addition to critical understanding, theology often includes defense and advocacy of a particular faith. So from this viewpoint our definition of theology as the study and understanding of religion is woefully inadequate.

Yet if the thesis is not about individual theologies or theologians, what then is its proper domain or scope? The answer is that it is about a whole subject matter as contained in the tradition of classical documents, and in the whole present discipline or study. Looking at the total common enterprise of theological study, past and present, and embracing the full range of religious viewpoints as well as of criticisms of these viewpoints, we ask what are its defining characteristics. One possible answer to this question, and the one here proposed, is that theology is, quite simply, the comprehensive and all-embracing study of religion. To be sure, other recurrent or common elements are also empirically observable in this wide field of theological study. There is no small amount of defense and advocacy of this or that faith, not to speak of special pleading. But there is also the activity of study aiming at understanding; and it is the recurring presence of this element that justifies our present definition.

Yet is not this definition of theology a "persuasive definition,"[13] i.e., a partisan conclusion smuggled into an argument as a definition? The only candid answer is Yes and No. To the extent that the activity of study aiming at understanding of religion is factually a common feature of theological study, past and present, the answer is No. Yet let it be plainly said that the present hypothesis is *for* some trends or tendencies and *against* others in theological study. Hence it is not only persuasive but openly contentious. Among the various present trends and tendencies of theological study the view here presented proposes that this form of study be frankly open to all competent persons who wish to participate, regardless of religious or intellectual viewpoint or affiliation.

There is a final misunderstanding of the hypothesis of this chapter to which brief attention may be called. If we distinguish between direct faith statements and theological statements, the question arises whether there is or is not a rational structure of faith statements. Do first-order religious utterances have a rationale? The answer is that of course they do. The simplest religious confession or witness is stated in the grammar and syntax of a language and has at least this degree of rational structure.[14] Further, the person who utters it does so presumably because he believes it is true and is thereby bound, perhaps unwittingly, by these implications of his utterance. Even more fundamentally, the same self that expresses its allegiance in first-order religious utterances is also a mind committed to critical understanding, which extends equally to religion and to other aspects of experience. It is literally schizophrenic to posit any fundamental dualism between these two aspects of the life of a mind or self.

If it is true that direct religious experience has its own kind of rational structure, this means that this experience involves as an aspect of itself a form of cognition or thinking. If one asks what kind of rational structure and process this may be, the answer, in brief, is that it is image thinking rather than conceptual thinking. In other words, the terms of this distinctive form of cognition are not ideas but the images that form so central a part of religious experience. Religious experience may be said to be a form of rational activity just in the measure that it is a search for images that are consistent, coherent, and adequate to the facts of existence. In the measure that religious experience seeks images that meet these criteria, it may properly be regarded as a form of cognitive activity.

Now let us turn attention to some of the details of the religious-theological spectrum outlined above. One of the most important points along this spectrum or continuum is that which separates religious language, with its implicit theological structure, from explicit theological utterance. This point may be recognized by the clear emergence and predominance of conceptual terms in the language. Instead of powerful images, the terms of speech tend to be the neutral, highly abstract, and technical terms of theology. A technical language is also accompanied, here as in other fields of human experience, by professional students of the subject matter. When these two conditions occur, we have what may be termed explicit theology. The task of explicit theological thinking may be said to consist of digging out the rational structures of primary religious utterance in order that they may be examined and tested by means of all pertinent logical and factual criteria. In short, second-order religious statements or theological statements have as their function the examination and understanding of first-order religious statements. Once more, theological statements are the linguistic vehicle for the study of religion.

The metaphor of a spectrum of the different forms of religious utterance points to another significant relationship. Beginning at one end of the spectrum, as we move away from direct religious utterance we begin at once to encounter intermediate or mixed types that still retain some characteristics of direct religious utterance but combine with them varying amounts of explicit theologizing. In general, these forms come into being when men are led with varying degrees of explicitness to think conceptually and propositionally about religion, as well as directly to have religion or to be religious.

A clear and simple illustration of such an intermediate linguistic form is creed or creedal statement. Confession, we recall, is a form of direct religious utterance. A creed may be said to develop out of a confession when the confession is challenged by various conflicting interpretations and understandings, and in the ensuing struggle a group seeks to set forth what it believes to be a sound interpretation against unsound or heretical interpretations. Creeds, in other words, invariably begin in conflict. Their motive is to defend or protect the original confession against interpretations that would undermine or subvert its authentic meaning. Against such views, creeds seek to set forth criteria or standards for belief, acceptance of which is accordingly required or demanded. Often associated with such conflicts are the anathemas pronounced upon false views and the excommunication of those who hold them. In linguistic structure and significance, a creed is a mixed type, partly religious and partly theological.

In the light of this origin of creeds, which might be illustrated with any of the creedal statements of any significantly creedal religion, it is ironical to observe the subsequent destiny of many creeds. Originating as formulas in conflict, they sometimes come in the course of time to be chanted in church or recited as part of a ritual. In other words, they capture or recapture an original confessional function. It is also pertinent to observe of such statements as the Westminster Confession, the Heidelberg Confession, or even the Tridentine Confession, that there are present in these documents varying amounts and combinations of both religious and theological language.

Another significant intermediate type of religious statement is catechetical teaching. The catechetical situation may be described as one in which the aim of teaching is to clarify and stabilize as well as to illuminate a faith which the recipients are assumed already to possess. Since a part of the aim is directly religious, the language will still exhibit the luminous and powerful images that are the vehicle of faith. However, since a part of the aim is clarification and explication, it will also exhibit a rational structure, sometimes implicit and sometimes explicit, and at still other times a mixture of both.

As we move along the spectrum from the religious toward the philosophic end, it is a pertinent observation that human reason becomes a kind of inevitable hazard for any and all religious faiths and communities. In view of man's stature as a mind, it is inevitable that all religious discourse should exhibit some degree of rational structure. Yet, once the reasoning process has begun, it is literally impossible to tell how or when it will end. So it is that some religious individuals and groups shrink from reason. Yet it is an encounter that more vigorous and vital faiths seek out and develop to their great advantage.

There is still another and different kind of religious peril in these new forms, namely, the peril of intellectualization. It is an easy but fatal step to say that if only a person accepts a doctrinal formula, then he has true religion. In this manner the faith of the heart becomes identified with the belief of the intellect, a false identity that often spells the betrayal and degradation of religion. For while religion extends to the whole self and mind, its true center is the heart or will rather than the intellect.

Still another form of intermediate religious utterance is dogma or doctrine. In general, it may be said to have two functions, normative and intellectual. In the first place, it is or claims to be an authoritative statement of correct belief, to be received and followed by all members of the community. It is literally a rule of faith. But statements of dogma or doctrine also clearly exhibit the intellectual motivation of stating and explicating what the content of implications of faith may be. If a person accepts a given faith, to what has he committed himself? Dogma and doctrine attempt to answer this question.

If doctrine or dogma is addressed to the religious community, there is still another intermediate type of utterance, namely, apologetics, which is addressed to the outsider. It is a combination of religious and theological utterance designed to explain the religion to the outsider in terms he will understand, and also to recommend it to him. Such apologetic forms of statement occur in a wide variety of ways in many different religious communities. They differ from homily or sermon in their frank combination of expressive and conceptual terms, in their combination of religious and philosophic motivation, and in their general spirit of accommodation toward those to whom these statements are addressed.

4. *Theology Redefined*

While still more intermediate types of religious utterance will undoubtedly come to mind, we must now turn attention to another aspect of our problem, namely, the origin and significance of theology and the kind of utterance in which it finds expression. The etymology of the word, as well as its Greek origin, suggests the broad view of a critical inquiry into religion. Yet many writers, past and present, argue for an exclusively Christian definition of theology and its distinctive forms of reflection and study.[15] This view has historical support in the fact that some religions are notably more theologically minded than others. Christianity, for example, is a much more theologically minded religion than Judaism. It also claims support in the historical fact that much, if not most, theology in the West has been Christian and has claimed for itself a position internal to Christianity and Christian faith. Yet as we look farther afield to other religions of mankind, we see processes of thinking which bear significant analogy to those of Christian theological study. Furthermore, in an age when the religions of the world confront one another and present themselves for rational study as never before, the crucial question is whether the traditional Christian definition of theology is not absurdly and impossibly restrictive.

The key question is whether theology invariably occurs within and is limited to a particular religious community. As we have seen, from this viewpoint, it is held that theology is a particular religion's attempt at self-understanding; and it is often further stipulated that the theologian must be an adherent of the religion that he studies. So it is that the theological universe of discourse is located entirely within a particular religious community.

This view of the role of theology is often assumed not only by adherents but by critics as well. Indeed, the latter assert that this limitation is one of the things most wrong with theology as a form of understanding and study. Critics often allege that this limitation throttles genuine intellectual freedom, and commits the theologian in advance to the inglorious task of rationalizing a preconceived position. For if he questions the validity of his faith, if he steps out of the closed circle of faith, he ceases to be a theologian. From this critical viewpoint, theological statements are conceived to be the vehicles not of genuine rational inquiry but of rationalization.[16]

The educational implications of this criticism are particularly damaging in contemporary America. It is alleged that theological study violates the commitment to objectivity and freedom which is the great glory of the modern mind. My experience is that this is a false charge, that indeed on the contrary there is as much objectivity and freedom in this as in any other major form of human inquiry. But the point that must be asserted here is that the traditional view of the relation of theology to religion lends color to this false criticism, whereas a clear avowal of the full freedom of the theologian would greatly help in the rehabilitation of theology as a reputable form of liberal study. Incidentally, this avowal of full freedom ought not to prohibit religious allegiance on the part of the theologian, and for the critic of theology to assert such a position is an extremely odd application of the freedom he claims. Here, as elsewhere, in the life of intellect, it is the part of common sense to say that freedom and knowledge are where you find them.

From early medieval times, the germ of an alternative to the traditional view has existed in Christianity in the distinction between revealed and natural theology. This distinction has been variously conceived and developed; but in one preeminent interpretation, namely, the writings of Thomas Aquinas, natural theology consists of the study of religion from the viewpoint of natural human reason, whereas revealed theology is reflection or study carried on within the community that accepts as valid the Christian revelation. In its Thomist formulation, this distinction carries the implication of two distinct realms of nature and supernature, and two distinctly different kinds of statement within each realm. Thus natural knowledge is held to be possible on the basis of human reason, interpreted in generally Aristotelian terms, and without assumptions derived from any supernatural source; while the statements of revelation are assumed to be divinely communicated and certified statements of information necessary for salvation and available to man within the one true church. Despite its great tradition, the difficulties of this philosophic-theological position are so great that a new beginning on these matters is altogether imperative.

Such a new beginning is possible in terms of the categories set forth in this and preceding chapters of our study. Indeed, such a fresh start was suggested two decades ago in William Temple's *Nature, Man and God,*[17] in which it was proposed that natural theology be redefined as "all study of all religion," pursued with the rigor, freedom, and comprehensiveness of science. Further, it was suggested that all religious experience, regarded from the viewpoint of the adherent or participant, is in some sense revealed religion. That is to say, it is the faith he holds as valid. It will, I think, be immediately apparent that these redefinitions are congenial to the idea of the religious-theological spectrum as set forth in this chapter. It will also be apparent that this redefinition of basic categories will make possible an altogether free and open study of all religious experience. Thus it goes far toward meeting the charges of partisanship of theological study.

This redefinition leaves us with the problem of the nature of revealed theology. If all religious experience from the viewpoint of the participant is revealed religion, what then is revealed theology? Thomism and other traditional Christian viewpoints regarded it as rational study of the divinely revealed text of scripture carried on within the Christian community. The answer I wish here to make is that it is natural theology, as redefined by Temple, adapted to the study of one particular religion. It follows also that such study must proceed freely by whatever methods and tools are likely to yield success, and that it is open to all men who wish to participate, regardless of religious affiliation or allegiance.

A further question which this redefinition of categories leaves with us is the relation of natural or rational theology to philosophy. The answer is that between these two forms of study and statement there are no fundamental discontinuities. A natural theologian is simply a philosopher whose center of intellectual interest is religion; and, conversely, a philosopher is simply a natural theologian whose basic concerns extend from religion to other aspects of man and the world. The only differences are those of interest and emphasis.

Thus we arrive at the farther end of the religious-theological spectrum, or, more precisely, the religious-theological-philosophic spectrum. As we have moved along it, undoubtedly the reader has noted many problems and issues to which only scant attention, or no attention, has here been given. Yet if the discussion has served to raise and pose some of the fundamental issues in the relation of religious practice to theological study in contemporary context, our goal has been achieved.

X Root Images and the World's Faiths

❖ ❖

1. *Paths of Life*

In the final two chapters, we shall seek to relate the results of our study of religious language to actual or existing religions. In this chapter the relation will be made to the religions of mankind, and in the next chapter more specifically to religion of the Bible and the Biblical tradition. In both cases, we shall in effect be treating our main results concerning religious language as hypotheses to be tested on factual data. At least we shall begin the process of application and testing, which needs to be carried much farther than is possible here.

We begin by recalling briefly what has been established concerning the nature of religious language and symbolism. Primary religious language, it has been argued, consists of symbols or images used to express total life orientation or life valuation; to this it may now be added that the images of any particular religion are of an entirely particular or specific sort. Indeed, the particularity of its images is a good way to characterize the particularity of any religion.[1] Taken together, these images of any one religion form a more or less unified and coherent structure or configuration which provides life orientation for adherents of the

248

religion. In other words, the structure provides answers to the perennial human questions, Whence? Whither? Why?, forming what C. W. Morris has termed a path of life.

Now we must test this idea by applying it to some of the religions of the world. Will these existing faiths permit us to regard them as paths of life, or systems of life orientation or life valuation? If so, what are some of the significant paths, and kinds of paths, which men have trodden in the course of human history? Again, what are some of the aspects and components of these paths? As we cast an eye over the panorama of the world's religions, past and present, what ideas are necessary in order to relate the main thesis of this book to the facts we encounter there? It is with this question that the present chapter is concerned. To answer summarily, we see three kinds of pertinent data. In the first place we observe a large number of root images that recur frequently among the faiths of mankind. These expressive images are common elements in different religions. They constitute the basic terms of religious language. Yet, common as they are, these images show sharp differences of meaning in different contexts. These differences will lead us, in the second place, to a threefold classification of kinds or types of religions. If an analogy with music be permitted, the recurrent images are similar to themes, and the threefold classification of types, to musical pitch or key. Themes recur, but they do so in different keys, and hence they have profoundly different significance. Still a third point of significance will also be observed, namely, recurrent life situations. These may be characterized as recurring occasions and types of occasions, of sufficient significance to demand religious interpretation. They range from the birth and death of human individuals to social events of ultimate concern such as war and peace, plenty and famine, disaster and well-being, law and crime, and many more. Different religions will be distinguished by the differing ways in which they deal with such recurring life situations.

2. *Recurrent Images*

What are some of the root metaphors of the faiths of mankind? What is their origin, and how do they function as bearers of meaning? Which ones recur most frequently in different religions? The base of all metaphors is man's common daily experience of nature and society. This experience provides him with the raw materials for all of his imaginative extension of language and experience. What other source could there be? What the human mind (or, as argued in Chapter III, that primal aspect of the mind called imagination) does is to take striking or significant aspects of this experience and use them to express or articulate new or unique facets of human experience. Thus, a metaphor—any metaphor—is an image that has been stretched or extended for this purpose. As argued in Chapter III, such is the metaphorical dimension of language.

In the case of philosophy and religion whose respective objects are quite literally out of this world—that is to say, beyond the common secular world in which language originates and to which it primarily refers—a second extension or stretching takes place to fit the image to this doubly new and special use. The language of both philosophy and religion in their respective ways thus consists of doubly extended or stretched images.

As we look at the clusters of images to be found in the world's religions, what are some of the most important recurrent images or image clusters? An exhaustive answer to this question is not possible within present limits of space. We can, however, make a brief sampling of such images as they occur and recur in the world's religions. It is to be noted that in each actual occurrence an image is an element in a configuration or ordered structure of images.

Among the most persistent images of the world's faiths is that of height.[2] In a great variety of ways the religious object is regarded as high. Literally or physically, height means distance from the surface of the earth, but height is not slow in gathering new and extended meanings to itself. It has done so in two widely different ways. The heaven or sky above man has been an object of mystery. Hence it has frequently been regarded as divine, or the home of the gods. High mountains present a similar remoteness and inaccessibility; hence, they also are sacred or divine or the residence of deity. But human society as well as nature presents significant height situations. Small children must look up to their elders in a quite literal sense; kings elevate their thrones and require men to bow low before them. Metaphorical extension of such situations readily assumes religious meaning. Doubtless both social and natural sources of the height metaphor contribute to the religious meaning of height.

Height is, to be sure, not an altogether universal metaphor; chthonic gods and faiths as well as sky gods find exemplification in human history. But in a variety of very widespread ways men have regarded their gods as high and lifted up, dwellers in the sky or in heavenly bodies or on high mountains. Similarly, man's destiny, and occasionally even his origin, has been envisaged in this way. It is also interesting to note occasions where depth as well as height provides a metaphor. In many languages the same word means both "high" and "deep." Objects of religious devotion are thus deep as well as high. In the next section, we shall employ this root metaphor as a key to the three main types of religion, the object of ultimate concern being located *in* the common world of nature and culture, *above or beyond* it, or dialectically *above and within*.

A second root metaphor of widely recurring incidence is that of light, and, at times, its opposite, darkness. The physical facts of light and darkness are so familiar and pervasive that conscious attention and effort are necessary to separate literal fact from metaphor. Who first spoke of an idea as enlightening, or of an experience as illuminating, or of mystery or bafflement as an experience of darkness? The world's religions have picked up these metaphors and used them in a wide variety of ways to express many different aspects of religious experience. There are gods and goddesses of light or of light-bearing objects such as the sun and moon. Deity is often said to dwell in light, though at times darkness is similarly used. Light and darkness are also used to express different aspects of man's destiny both here and hereafter. Human beings are classified as men of light and men of darkness. Heaven is depicted as a place of light with no darkness at all, and hell is a place of darkness. Light imagery also gets combined with that of sun, moon, and stars, not to speak of the light of sacred fires, torches, mirrors, and other shining bodies. To see its meaning in any given situation, it is of course necessary to examine it in specific context.

Still a third widely recurrent metaphor is that of duration through time, or a kind of exemption from change denoted by saying that something is above or beyond time and change. Gods and goddesses are frequently thought to enjoy some such status, and upon occasion human heroes are said to achieve it. Particularly they are thought to be elevated above the human prospect of death. Eternity is frequently ascribed to sacred objects that are said to be unchanging or to exist forever. Socially conservative references frequently relate religious objects to an immemorial and unchanging past, while radical references sometimes make a corresponding eschatological appeal to futurity. We may also note that such references to duration through or above time acquire widely different kinds of valuations ranging from absolute negation to absolute affirmation. In traditional Christianity, for example, both heaven and hell are forever. Unending existence is sometimes regarded as a blessing, but sometimes as a curse, as in many forms of Indian religion.

Another cluster of metaphors centers in the earth, and its vegetation and fruitfulness, often with the closely related patterns of sexuality and reproduction in human life. How often and in what a variety of ways men have envisaged the religious object as a great mother, or have symbolized the religious relation as one of sexual love! Religious eroticism is a persistent pattern in the world's faiths, particularly those of the first type to be described in the next section. Even more widely recurrent is that of mother to child, or of parent to child.

Still another kind of metaphor is derived from social and political experience. Because all functioning social groups entail authority, the root image here is one of authority, whether of father, king, or, more generally, of sovereign will. How often and how variously the religious object is envisaged as lord! So pervasive is this pattern that we must remind ourselves that to call deity lord is, in fact, a social metaphor; literally, a lord is a social superior who exercises authority over us. Frequently the whole religious realm is a kind of transcendental mirroring of the social relations of a people, as in ancient Babylonia, looking like nothing so much as a transcendental feudal order. As we shall see in the next chapter, the Biblical Hebrews developed their own radically unique interpretation of the image of sovereignty.

Social relations, however, exhibit another and more amiable quality, whether described as comradeship, fellowship, or love, and whether illustrated by family or other wider social groups. In either case, such relations provide a metaphor for a significant and persistent aspect of religious experience, in which man is said to seek comradeship or love of God or gods, and vice versa. Indeed, man often regards himself as desperately dependent on this relation for life orientation and fulfillment.

This sampling of images and patterns of images does scant justice to the full range and variety of actual religious language and symbolism. Hence it is perhaps in point to add that no act or word of common daily life is so commonplace or trite that somewhere men have not used it to express religious meaning. Eating, drinking, sleeping, waking, sexual union and sexual abstinence, pleasure, pain— all these and many more commonplace daily experiences have been picked up and used symbolically in word and deed. Yet also it must immediately be added that no word or experience is so bizarre or deviant but that men have somewhere and somehow used it for a similar purpose.

3. Choice and Criterion of Images

A series of questions that have been with us throughout our study obtrude themselves upon the discussion at this point. Granted that religions are paths of life constituted by root images, how are these images to be chosen? What is the criterion of choice? How can men know which

images are right or true? Indeed, by what rational standard, if any, is it possible to answer these questions? Or
again, do the adherents of any particular faith know that
they are speaking metaphorically and not literally? And,
coming to an awareness of the metaphorical character of
faith, will they not give it up as false or illusory?

It would be entirely false to the situation of human faith
to suppose that all men necessarily choose or decide consciously or deliberately. However, it is the case for thought-
ful people that, confronted by many different possibilities,
choice does in fact arise, and demands and deserves a reflective answer. Even here it must be asserted that men choose
not as buyers at a fruit counter selecting oranges but,
rather, as travelers at a crossroad choosing the path they
will tread.

In Chapter V it was argued that truth may be defined
in terms of consistency, coherence, and adequacy to fact.
This view must be applied to the present situation. In a
strict sense the question of truth cannot be raised concerning images, but rather concerning statements con-
taining images as their terms. However, we are confronted
here with just such faith statements composed of images.
They are statements or assertions, either explicit or implicit, concerning the meaning of man's existence, and as
such they claim validity or truth. At the point of this claim
to truth, criticism becomes pertinent. Thus men examine
the images of any and all faiths for consistency and coherence, and they appraise their images for adequacy to existence in all the manifold ways in which existence is confronted.

So far, this epistemological task is not different from that
of appraising other varieties of cognition as discussed in
Chapter V. However, an extension and adaptation are re-

quired to take account of at least one distinctive element
in the faith situation. In this situation the mind is not in
an attitude of detached observation but of action. It is not,
so to say, in the grandstands but on the playing field.
Accordingly, adequacy here means adequacy to encountered facts. Here, as elsewhere, a fact may be characterized
as what the mind finds, and does not make, in its active
encounter with the world. Facts are pieces of reality; but
the pieces of reality here confronted may well be different
from those of supposedly detached neutral observation.

The nature of the faith situation can be put in terms
previously discussed. Reinhold Niebuhr has asserted that
the meaningful character of existence is the common assumption or postulate of all religion. (From a different
viewpoint Santayana once remarked that life has a meaning—how impossible a conclusion yet how necessary an assumption!) If this is true, then those are true faiths whose
images articulate or express the meaningful character of
existence without contradiction or incoherence or inadequacy to fact. To this extent and in this measure a faith is
true; contrariwise, to the extent that it fails to meet these
tests it is false or inadequate. Indeed, it is not too much
to say that precisely this is the meaning of truth and falsehood for human faiths and the configurations of images in
which faiths are articulated.

4. Three Types of Religion

Let us turn from the recurrent elements of religious
expression to the three main ways in which they are combined, or to the three main types of religion.[3] It is important, incidentally, to note at the outset that they are
types and not stages in development. Each of the three has
been regarded as final by large numbers of people, and no

claim is here either expressed or implied that one of them is necessarily a stage on the way to other higher forms.

The three types of religion may be designated and classified in a variety of ways. As previously noted, the metaphor of height applied to the religious object yields three possibilities; this object may be located (a) within the common world of nature and culture, (b) above or beyond it, or (c) dialectically both above and within. The first type finds its god or gods within the common world. In most cases these objects are plural, or in other words, type-one religions are polytheistic. This first type may also be characterized as nature-culture religion since, as we shall soon see, the life values that it embodies and expresses are those of nature and culture combined in many varieties of ways. The many gods of polytheism are apotheoses of these life values.

Of the three types, the second raises the most serious difficulties for the height metaphor. In its various manifestations this type is commonly acultural and also monistic, finding a single source of meaning above or beyond the common world of nature and culture, which are correspondingly devaluated. Yet it must be readily conceded that in many instances of this type there is little or no explicit reference to height; in some the whole emphasis is on descent into the inner self. Yet throughout the historical illustrations of this type of faith there is an unvarying rejection of the common world and a consequent search for meaning which is, in some way, beyond. There is in all instances of this type some sort of "Archimedean point" outside the common world of nature and culture in terms of which that world can be judged. Perhaps the term "transcendent," with its clear etymological intimation of "going beyond," is the least misleading appellation for the second type of religion. Since it places a high value on unity, let us call it transcendent monism.

The third type makes unequivocal and radical use of the height metaphor, locating its one God both above and within the common world of men and nature. As we shall soon see, in this type as well as in the others, many other significant traits cluster around this defining characteristic.

The threefold typology may be clarified by specific examples. The ethnic religions of mankind, from ancient Greece and Rome, or ancient Babylonia or Egypt, to ancient China and Japan, are clearly faiths of the first type. Modern nationalism often tends to take on religious quality of this sort. The "religion" of extreme American nationalism is thus also a type-one religion. Perhaps the purest historical illustrations of type-two religions are Buddhism and Hinduism, particularly in their intellectual formulations. The more monistic kinds of mysticism of both Orient and Occident are also clearly type-two religions. The third or monotheistic type of faith is illustrated by Judaism, Christianity, and Islam. However, in all historical examples it is well to remember that ideal types are seldom, if ever, perfectly illustrated in reality; most actual historical religions are mixed types.

There is little doubt that man's first religions were those of the first type. Prehistoric and primitive religions have as their objects more or less personified values or aspects of nature and society. Man worshiped this river or that tree, or this or that object or aspect of tribal life. When one considers the precarious or hazardous situation of prehistoric and primitive man, this form of religion is altogether comprehensible. For one thing, man's continued life was dependent upon an environing nature that was often capricious and sometimes hostile. Hence, it was natural for him to appease its threatening aspects and to celebrate its benign aspects. The slim chance man had for survival in this environment depended also upon the solidarity of his social group. Hence, the tribal life or some of its aspects was also an object of religious devotion. As we have previously argued, religion in such circumstances expressed man's will to live. There was a kind of realism in man's statement of the meaning of his life in these terms of nature and culture; these objects did in fact constitute the ultimate meaning of his life.

Such nature-culture religions have persisted throughout human history. Indeed, it is a safe generalization that the actual functioning religion of most human beings in history has been of this type. The type has shown enormous variety, flexibility, and development within an overarching unity and similarity. Often, as these religions develop, they reflect and express large, complex, and civilized cultures. Often, too, the pantheon seems indefinitely expansible. In the case of ancient Greece and China, a sensitive, perceptive humanism is carried within such a religious vehicle. In their more developed phases, such religions frequently contain cosmopolitan and rational values of a wide variety of kinds. As we have noted, this type of religion continues in unbroken continuity in many human cultures throughout the whole history of the culture. Yet, in others, there has occurred a radical change or breakthrough from nature-culture religion to a religion of the second or third type.

We must briefly glance at this process of breakthrough or discontinuous change. Something of this sort took place between the Vedic age in India and the period of the Upanishads, whatever be the date we assign to these periods. The teachings of Gautama Buddha reflect a similar change from a religion of the first to that of the second type. In ancient Iran we see another kind of breakthrough from a religious orientation of the first to the third type. For the Western cultural tradition the most important breakthrough was that which occurred in the ancient Near Eastern world when Israel emerged from the traditional pattern of nature-culture religion to a religion of the third or monotheistic type. Similarly, the early Christian movement in the Greco-Roman world exhibited many of these same discontinuities with its environment. It is perhaps necessary to repeat that history invariably blunts the sharp edges of these typological distinctions. Historically existing religious groups tend to be more or less mixed types. This is particularly true of a group or organization that has been in existence for a long time.

These three types of religions present significant similarities and differences. Types two and three are similar to each other and unlike the first type of religion in their common devotion to a single religious object. Thus the second type is often termed monism, and the third type monotheism, in contrast to the luxuriant polytheism of the first type. Both monism and monotheism find a single religious object above or beyond the life of nature and culture. Thus, in both cases, the deification of nature or culture (or particular objects therein) is broken. Yet here the similarity ends, for monism finds the common secular world a valley of shadows or appearances. By contrast, monotheism, while it denies the absolute reality or goodness of the common world, does treat it as seriously real and as seriously good. In their affirmation of the reality and goodness of the common world, types one and three are alike, though it must be added that the ways in which this real world is understood in these two situations are profoundly different. The type-three understanding of the world is epitomized in the Biblical Creation story in the comment that "God saw everything that he had made, and behold, it was very good"—a sentiment quite alien to the more consistently otherworldly attitude of type-two monism.

A distinguishing feature of the third type is the absolute uniqueness of deity, which is often expressed by means of the height metaphor. God is here the Most High in a sense radically different in kind from the other types of religion. This trait generates a difference between what may be termed the principle of continuity, which is a trait of religions of types one and two, and the principle of discontinuity, which is characteristic of type-three religion.[4] The former asserts the continuity or homogeneity of all objects within the encompassing totality of the universe or world. In many cases there is in these outlooks a kind of participation of each in all, and also in some cases a relation of "free substitution," whereby any object may be said to represent any other object. Hence, one god is often taken as representing another god or all gods. And thus, too, an image or idol authentically stands for or represents the god, or indeed, all the gods. In such a continuous and homogeneous world, it is logical to assert that the image *is* the god, since all things participate in each other. Hence, too, with a certain inner logic, anything can represent anything else. Again, since there is among gods a principle of free substitution, any god can in a way stand for or represent other gods or all gods. Obviously such situations place a low value upon individual entities. Religiously speaking, the assertion of the principle of continuity is that gods, men, cultures, and objects of nature all are members together of the homogeneous and continuous universe.

In contrast to the principle of continuity is the principle of discontinuity, which is the distinctive characteristic of type-three religions, and which asserts that between God and all else there exists a fundamental and radical difference. There is, as it were, a radically asymmetric relation of dependence between God and world. To state the issue in metaphors of the Bible, this relation is between the Lord and his dominion, or between Creator and creation. Many observable traits of type-three religion may readily be shown to follow from the principle of discontinuity. We shall be concerned to discuss several of these in the next chapter. Here a single illustration must suffice. There is in type-three religions an idea of idolatry or false religion for which there is no parallel in the first two types. The essence of idolatry is to deify some aspect of the created world, to take for God some object short of the absolutely unique Lord and Creator of heaven and earth. It is, in Reinhold Niebuhr's phrase, to absolutize some relative interest or concern.

What truth there is in the popular notion of an idol as a "heathen god" (or a statue of such a god) derives from these distinctions. In religions of the first and second types there is a continuity both between deity and the rest of the universe, and also between deity and sculptured likeness. From the viewpoint of the third type of religion with its emphasis upon radical discontinuity, there is a tendency to rejection, more or less total, of all visual representation of deity. There is also a rejection of false views or ideas of deity. From the viewpoint of type-three faith, the deities of type-one and type-two religion are false because they find the whole meaning of existence in some limited, relative, and creaturely object or concern. From the type-three viewpoint it is this quality which most basically constitutes their idolatry.

Other differences among the three types of faith or paths of life might also be pointed out. For example, their views of death and the hereafter differ profoundly. The Nirvana of type-two religions differs from the heaven of type-three religions. It may also be remarked in this connection that images of the "hereafter" deeply influence men's valuations of the "herein." This is also true of the life values, moral, aesthetic, and of other sorts, which are brought into being by the different faiths, and which in a sense constitute the path of life. Accordingly, the process of study must consist of sensitive, careful, and adequate description of particular values and value configurations as they may be found among the three types.

5. Recurring Life Situations

To the ideas of recurrent patterns of images in the three different religious types must be added one further concept, namely, that of recurrent life situations.[5] Despite the much-emphasized differences among human individuals and societies, there are certain recurrent situations that become religiously significant, and demand expression in many or all religions. In every case, their meaning is depicted or interpreted by expressive images, verbal and nonverbal, which we have found characteristic of religion as such. Yet as we have observed, the expressed content of the images varies from religion to religion. Hence there are profound differences in the way in which the various religions understand and interpret these recurring aspects of the human situation. The point to note here is that it is by a careful analysis of the relevant images, verbal and nonverbal, that we learn what each religion has to tell us about the human occasion or situation that is characterized and interpreted by the images. For example, the ways in which Buddhism and Christianity understand and interpret death might be fruitfully approached by an analysis of the images for Nirvana and heaven and also of the images in their respective funerary rituals.

What, in general terms, are the recurrent life situations? Here we cannot make even a catalog of them, let alone a comparative study of the ways in which the various religions interpret them. We can, however, glance quickly at a few illustrations, pointing to the ways in which the religious experience of ultimate concern related itself to such life situations. Man's faiths are in large measure constituted by statements of these experiences in luminous and powerful symbols. The religious concern gets applied to the career of the human individual in a series of rites of passage,[6] beginning with birth, and moving on to coming-of-age, marriage, selection of lifework, and coming at length to death. In the case of almost every religion of the world, such occasions are placed in religious perspective and interpreted through appropriate symbols. Similarly recurrent are the ways in which such common human besetments as illness, misfortune, grief, as well as the various forms of success and achievement, are drawn within the scope of a religious interpretation of existence. Again the symbolic expression and interpretation of such experiences is a large part of the content of man's religions.

Religion, however, is social as well as individual in its nature and functioning. The nature of the religious community and its relation to society, the intrinsic significance of the society as a human community, and the relations of the individual to all its groups—these are only a few of the

social situations that are frequently understood and lived
out in religious terms. This is particularly true of family
life and sexual relations—fundamental as they are to the
whole life of society and of man. In the case of many societies and religions we might add to this list such social
experiences as war and peace, the organization of political
life, economic life, and many more aspects and occasions.
In each case it is entirely possible to find many societies
that interpret this aspect of common life in religious terms.

There is still another group of recurring life situations of
great religious significance that cut across the distinction
between individual and group life. For example, there is
man's experience of his dependence and limitation. In this
mixture of strength and weakness, men press at the limits
of their powers and become anxiously aware of their little-
ness. Out of this aspect of his situation springs the anxiety
that is a permanent part of the human predicament. So,
too, is guilt, for men inevitably do actions that violate their
own professed standards and values. All these elements and
others unite to evoke the desperate cry for salvation, for
healing and wholeness, which is so insistent a feature of
the world's religions. In their various ways, religions express their answers to these mortal questions. The points
that are pertinent to note here are the recurrent nature of
these questions, and the symbolic character of the various
answers given by the world's faiths.

In the case of any particular faith, if we put together its
characteristic responses to life situations, we have further
significant verification of the idea of religion as a path of
life. The path becomes specific for the individual as it
offers understanding of the road from cradle to grave, not
to speak of the claim of many religions to blessedness
hereafter. For the social group, it is a path of duty and

meaning, embracing many of the significant aspects and events of the common life. So it is that the images of religion express or body forth in concrete and specific ways the meaningful character of human existence. This, indeed, is the proper and distinctive function of religion in human existence. To repeat once more the main thesis of this book, religions may be construed as symbol systems whose function is total life orientation. In this chapter we have sought to indicate ways in which the thesis may be applied to the comparative study of the world's religions.

XI Images of Biblical Faith

❖ ❖

1. *Traits of Type-Three Religion*

In this final chapter we shall be concerned with the language and symbolism of the third type of religion, namely, monotheism, or, as it has recently been characterized, radical monotheism.[1] Historically speaking, this type of religion probably emerged independently both in ancient Iran and in ancient Israel. The living religions that fall into this type are the remnants of Zoroastrianism of India and Persia, together with Judaism, Christianity, and Islam. Yet for all practical purposes in contemporary Western discussion, type-three religion is Biblical religion. Religiously speaking, though not culturally or historically speaking, it may also probably be maintained that Islam is a derivation from the Biblical tradition.

Some of the similarities and differences between this type of faith and the other two types have been sketched in the previous chapter. As we have seen, monotheistic faith is similar to type-one religion and unlike type-two religion in its affirmation of the world of nature and culture. However, in agreement with the second type and in disagreement with the first, this third type finds a single source of meaning above or beyond the world of nature

267

and culture. So it is that monotheism rejects the deification of any object within the world, but asserts the reality
and goodness of the created world. In other words the
world is asserted to be good, but not God. The Biblical
creation story is a mythical statement of this characteristically monotheistic attitude.

One consequence of this view of creation is a higher
estimate of matter and material things on the part of
monotheism than is characteristic of the religions of the
second type. Against monistic devaluations, William Temple has remarked that Christianity is the most materialistic
of the world's great religions.[2] It is so in its recognition that
matter and material things are seriously real, and are essential to the realization of human goods. Temple might well
have added that in this sense Judaism is even more consistently "materialistic" than Christianity. True, Temple's
assertion concerns the doctrine of the incarnation which
Judaism rejects, but it can be made equally in terms of the
doctrine of creation, which is common to Judaism and
Christianity, and to Islam as well.

A further feature, common and peculiar to monotheistic
religion, and close to its essence, lies directly across the path
of any study of religious language. It is, namely, that these
are scriptural religions, faiths based upon a book—their
respective Bibles, in the case of Judaism and Christianity,
and the Koran, in the case of Islam. Sacred writings of
many kinds exist in other faiths, but nowhere else do they
assume the central significance that they possess in type-
three religion. Indeed, it is possible to approach many of
the distinctive features of this type of faith from this viewpoint.

Speaking from such a viewpoint, students of religion
have often characterized monotheism as religion of revela-

tion. By this is meant that in these religions, the one God is held to reveal or disclose himself and his will to mankind, and that conversely man finds the meaning of his life in receiving this revelation or disclosure from God. So it is that the fundamental form of religious experience is here understood metaphorically in terms of speaking and hearing; religious experience consists of man's hearing and doing the will of God.

Whereas in monotheism the dominant metaphor for the relation of man to the religious object is clearly that of hearing and doing, this is not the case in the religions of the first two types. In these types there appears to be no one clearly dominant metaphor, though in the case of the second type vision persistently recurs. In this type of religion man is asserted to see the religious object. This is of course by no means to deny that audition as a metaphor occurs in the first two types of religion, or that vision occurs in the third type. It is rather only to insist upon the dominance of auditory imagery in the monotheistic religions. In the Bible, God calls, and man's role is consequently to hear and do the divine will.

The idea of revelation imparts to type-three religions a distinctively linguistic emphasis. If God's relation to man may be understood in terms of words, then indeed words assume a new and unique religious significance. From this fact many consequences have flowed in the course of history. Judaism, for example, has never ceased to assert that Hebrew language is the indispensable vehicle of both Jewish faith and Jewish culture, and that for this reason it must be cherished and studied.

Perhaps, however, the most significant consequence of this feature of monotheism is literalism, with all its attendant problems and evils. If God has spoken to man, it is only a small step to assert that the contents of the divine utterance are contained within a particular document. Accordingly, this document is often regarded as verbally inerrant, and as exempt from critical analysis. Rather, it must be accepted without questioning and without thinking. In this manner arises the phenomenon of bibliolatry, or the deification of a collection of human words. The manifold problems of bibliolatry, ranging from legalism in ethics to obscurantism in science and philosophy, are amply illustrated in the history of all scriptural religions.

If, however, we turn our attention from the problems of the past to contemporary theology, these issues cease to vex. For it is one of the great achievements of critical theology of the contemporary West to have produced a view of revelation at once free of literalism and faithful to the monotheistic tradition. Indeed, it is not too much to say that a critical reformulation of the idea of revelation has played a central and crucial role in what is often called the contemporary theological revolution. While a complete description of this idea lies beyond the province of this discussion, we must take cognizance of two points at which it makes contact with our subject matter. In the first place, the new formulation of the idea of revelation has successfully avoided the pitfalls of traditional verbal or propositional revelation with its accompaniment of verbal inerrancy and infallibility. It has done so by relocating revelation in particular historical events and the apprehension of the meaning of the event by individuals and groups. In the new view, God speaks to man through man's apprehension of the meaning of historical events, rather than by means of supernatural communication of propositions. So, for example, Karl Barth[3] has suggested a threefold understanding of revelation as follows: (a) God speaks to man, (b) under divine obedience, man speaks and acts, and (c) someone writes a record of (a) and (b). So the text of the Bible is not, strictly speaking, revelation, but the record of revelation. In a similar vein, Emil Brunner[4] has described the event of revelation as a divine-human encounter. According to Brunner, it is this, rather than a literal conversation between God and man. H. Richard Niebuhr[5] has located the Christian revelation in the whole event of Christ's life, and the contrasting Old Testament Hebrew revelation as the events of the exodus and Mt. Sinai, as apprehended by those men who responded to them. Thus, to receive revelation means to apprehend the full significance of these historical events, rather than to hear supernatural propositions spoken by deity.

While it is not difficult to see great gain in these reinterpretations, the new view faces no lack of problems. To the solution of at least one of these problems the thesis of this book relating to expressive images can make a significant contribution. If one gives up any idea of propositional revelation, that is to say, the notion that the content of revelation consists in the supernatural communication of propositional knowledge, then surely the question remains: What are the crucial features of the revelatory experience? To this question our theory of expressive images affords at least a significant part of an answer. For it asserts that revelation involves the occurrence in the receiving human mind of new, powerful, and luminous images. Indeed, the revelatory character of the event consists in the authoritative and illuminating character of these new images. Thus, in a word, we may assert that what Moses received on Mt. Sinai was not any set of propositions, written or oral, but a new set of images. In terms of these images a new understanding of faith was articulated. These images, being received and transmitted by Moses and his followers, constitutes the core of Hebraic religious tradition.

To be sure, the term "image" carries the suggestion of visual perception, in contrast to what we have already asserted as the decided preference of monotheistic faith for the metaphor of audition over vision. However, it may be pointed out that in both cases these are metaphors and not literal fact. Further, there are such things as auditory images as well as visual images. In any case the revelatory situation presents us with the situation of direct perception plus a conviction of absolute authority. Such a situation is apparently more readily expressed by the metaphor of hearing than seeing. Yet against any assertion or suggestion of literal hearing we must clearly assert its metaphorical character.

This approach to revelation presents both definite limitations and new possibilities for the study of religion. First, as to the limits, the observing student cannot penetrate into the inner life of the religious person to check on his images, though he can note the person's report of them; and he can study the images of the religious person's expressive words of confession and witness. Still less is it possible for the modern student of Hebraic religion to study in any direct way the religious life of men of the past such as Moses. However, what he can and should do is to focus attention upon the powerful images of the religious tradition that stems from Moses, as they are contained in the Biblical documents. He can, in other words, approach this close to the events of Mt. Sinai; he can see their impact on a tradition, as that impact and tradition are contained and expressed within the documents of the Bible. He can, in effect, observe the results of revelation;

and those results include the powerful expressive words and statements that articulate the experience of receiving revelation.

Similar possibilities and limits open before us if we take the role of theologian rather than phenomenologist of religion, seeking, in other words, normative evaluation rather than observation and description. There is obviously no way in which theologian or philosopher can, as it were, jump out of human existence in history, and from some neutral and objective vantage point assess the validity or invalidity, the veracity or falsity, of the images that lie at the heart of revelation. For the theologian and philosopher remain finite, mortal minds—even as other men. However, what they properly can do is to begin with the claim which the experience discussed in previous chapters. Indeed, precisely this kind of critical and normative evaluation is their business. By tracing the implications of this experience, seeing its wider relations, noting its consequences, they can and do come to some conclusions as to the validity and veracity, or the invalidity and falsehood, of the experience. The point that we note here, once more, is that at the heart of the experience which theologians study are the lively images in terms of which revelation takes place.

Two further traits of monotheistic religion may be observed to stem from its nature as religion of revelation; and, in turn, both of these features exert an influence on the expressive forms of this type of religion. Monotheism has sometimes been termed historical religion. By this is meant that in monotheistic religions may be found what may be termed a linear and dramatic view of human history in contrast to the cyclic views characteristic of the first two types. Most of the world's faiths, of all three types, deal in their respective ways with the problem of history or historic destiny; but the problem is clearly larger and more central in the religions of the third type. Furthermore, they alone appear to insist that history has a singular, once-for-all character. For them it is a drama played through just once. This view also carries the implication that a human self is a piece of historic destiny. Obviously the implications of this feature of monotheism extend to all aspects of religious experience and religious expression.

Closely related to the historic character of monotheistic faith is its indefeasibly social and ethical quality. If revelation consists of hearing God speak, then obediently to do God's will is the ethical conclusion of faith. From this viewpoint, man is no solitary visionary but a member of society, bound together with his fellowmen by the necessity of their common obedience to God. While some attention to morality is an altogether general feature of man's religions, many faiths are more aesthetic than ethical, and more individual than social. For monotheistic faiths, their ethical and social character pervades their entire structure, including their forms of expression.

2. *Biblical Faith and Paradox*

An additional trait of monotheistic faith, namely, paradox, bears so closely upon problems of language as to call for special comment. To be sure, paradox is by no means an exclusive feature of the discourse of monotheistic religion, but rather is a trait of human language in general. It also has special meaning for both philosophic and religious language of many kinds. In most general terms, a paradox may be defined as an apparent contradiction. Often it is the linguistic means of asserting a factual statement incompatible with a previously held theory. The problem set by the paradox is then to discover which of the two incompatible assertions is true, for to continue to assert two or more logically incompatible propositions is to violate the logical rule or law of noncontradiction and thus to stultify the mind's life. For, logically, if two contraries or contradictions are both asserted, then all propositions are true.

In both philosophy and religion, paradox may be characterized as a way of pointing out or indicating some odd or peculiar kind of fact that is not readily assimilable in ordinary logical terms. Such paradoxes may perhaps be termed significant contradictions, though it must immediately be added that the contradiction involved is apparent and not real. For here as elsewhere, really to assert a contradiction is to stultify thought. In these terms, paradox is a frequent device of many forms of philosophic and religious discourse.

Yet paradox in a further and special sense is a feature of monotheistic faith. The fundamental paradox of this type of faith may be expressed in any one of several ways. In terms of our threefold typology, the third type is faith which asserts paradoxically that deity is both above and within the world. The assertion of both divine transcendence and immanence surely constitutes an apparent and significant contradiction of a special sort. The writings of Kierkegaard develop the theme of paradox in characteristically polemical fashion. Thus, for example, *Philosophical Fragments*[6] speaks of the great king who comes incognito to woo a humble maiden. This parable may be regarded as a particularly poignant and forceful statement of divine transcendence and immanence. The *Concluding Unscientific Postscript*[7] attributes paradox to all religion, and asserts the "absurd" as the special category of "religiousness B." We may, I believe, understand Kierkegaard to mean by the absurd the radical paradox which is the special and distinctive characteristic of that form of religion here characterized as radical monotheism, Biblical faith, or type-three religion. It is indeed precisely what we have here termed the dialectical relation of the God who is at once above and within the world.

Yet in what terms can and must paradox be responsibly asserted of monotheistic faith? First of all, it must be clearly asserted by the theist that there are no contradictions in the mind of God. However paradoxical an aspect man's world may present, the theist must assume that ultimate reality is not self-contradictory but is rather self-consistent, coherent, and rational. Yet to man, the creature and sinner, many features of his experience will remain paradoxical till the end. Paradox may thus be regarded as a result of man's creaturely and sinful view of the world. Indeed, man's own finite-infinite nature is the fundamental paradox, which is then subsequently compounded by sin. In the mortal situation the final allegiance of the human mind must be to the facts, and not to one's own finite systems of coherence, which are forever being shattered and remade in the light of new experience. In some such way as this we may understand the paradox which is an observable characteristic of the language and expressive forms of type-three religion.

3. *The Hebrew Breakthrough*

One of the great achievements of contemporary critical Biblical study is that it has enabled us to see the Bible "against its environment"—in the case of the Old Testament, the ancient Near Eastern world of Egypt, Mesopotamia, and Syria—and in the case of the New Testament, first-century Judaism and Greco-Roman culture with its numerous and various faiths and philosophies.[8] In both cases, we observe a radical discontinuity. The term "breakthrough" asserts this discontinuity with particular emphasis on the emergence of new forms of thought and expression. It is used here without prejudging the value or validity of old or new forms, but, rather, simply to assert the historic fact of discontinuous change.

The religions of the ancient Near East which formed the environment of the Old Testament were invariably those which are called type-one religions. There was, of course, considerable variety among them, and many of them exhibited a high degree of civilization. Yet, of all of them it may be asserted that their gods remained more or less personified objects of forces of nature or culture. The values that formed the content of these religions were invariably those of a particular culture or of man's immediate relation to environing nature. The limits of nature and culture were for these faiths the limits of the world, or of reality.

As the student makes his way from this world to the strange new world that opens before him in the pages of the Bible, the breakthrough becomes evident.[9] Gone is the closed, bandbox world of nature and culture of which gods, men, and all the creatures and objects of nature alike are members. Gone is the closed world of the city-state and its civic ritual and ethic. And before us in the Bible unfolds the open world of the one God and the universal history in which he calls all men to live and labor. Gone, too, are the stories of the gods and goddesses with their loves and squabbles, their adventures and misadventures. Instead, in the Bible we meet myth in a radically new key. It is the story of the one God who calls a people to his service, together with a realistic account of the obedience and disobedience of this people, and of the word that God speaks through this people to all mankind. Here is radically historicized and universalized myth.

A similar discontinuity is to be observed as Hebraic or Biblical religion in its Christian form confronted its Greco-Roman environment. The faiths and philosophies of that world may be characterized as a miscellany of type-one and type-two religions. As the Christians made their way throughout this world with their gospel of the God who, having spoken through Moses and the prophets, now spoke a new, decisive, and saving word in the figure of Jesus Christ, the result again was a new breakthrough. It was so in the sense of the emergence of type-three religion with all its characteristic forms and features from an environment of type-one and type-two religion.

This assertion of a Hebraic breakthrough must be guarded against several sorts of misunderstanding. In the first place, it was not an event that took place all at once, but, rather, over a period of centuries. Indeed, as to historical circumstances we are entirely dependent upon the work of historical scholars; and the sketch given here has simply presupposed as background the consensus of scholarly conclusions in this matter. Also, the idea of a breakthrough does not preclude extensive borrowing on the part of the new religion from its environment. Neither ancient Israel nor the early Christian church lived in a vacuum; and, in fact, the evidence of extensive borrowing of ideas, themes, practices, and other forms is overwhelming. To cite just one of a great many possible examples, the dependence of Genesis upon the Mesopotamian world at such points as the creation story and the flood story is apparent from even a superficial reading of the analogous documents. But this kind of comparative study also yields the further significant conclusion that the ancient Hebrews radically transformed what they borrowed. Hence, where the Babylonian creation story presents a luxuriant polytheism, the Biblical creation story is characteristically monotheistic in its outlook. An analogous observation of similarity within radical difference of viewpoint might be made of the Babylonian and the Genesis flood stories.

Similarly, in the case of early Christianity, there was extensive borrowing of ideas, images, and other forms. Stoic and Platonic philosophy were soon appropriated and used by Christians. The early Christian missionaries must have seemed to their contemporaries very similar to the itinerant teacher-preachers of other faiths and philosophies. Likewise, the mystery cults and Gnosticism exercised important influence. Yet, again, the essential point is that these borrowed or appropriated elements were radically transformed as they found expression in the new context.

This same conclusion of similarity within radical difference may be drawn from a close study of the images of the text of the Bible and those of its environment. Not one of the great images of the Bible is altogether new. The images of sovereignty, height, light, eternity, and the like, are common to the Bible and its environing religions. Indeed, as we have already seen, these images are recurrent throughout the world's religions. If there is anything unique about the Bible's use of them, it must be sought in the way in which they are brought together and used.

4. Images of the Bible

The limitations of space and the nature of our study prevent us from undertaking any of the many possible and illuminating kinds of detailed analysis of the images of the Bible. We can, however, point briefly to a few salient aspects of this imagery which verify the hypothesis of a Hebrew breakthrough. The Biblical literature taken as a whole from Genesis to Revelation shows a development of imagery and themes that might be compared to the plot of a drama. There is a main theme, which is stated and developed as it confronts other themes and new situations, coming at length to climax and then to conclusion. Or, if we may again employ a musical analogy, the Bible is like a symphony in which there is the statement of a main theme, followed by the development of this theme as well as the introduction of other subsidiary themes, all moving on to climax and then to resolution or conclusion.

The root image or major theme of the Bible is clearly the kingship or sovereignty of God. God is understood throughout the Bible as king, sovereign, or supreme authority. The confession "God is King" or "God is Lord" runs through the Bible like a refrain from beginning to end. This statement in any of its many and variant formulations may be taken as the basic claim or assertion of Biblical faith. As we have seen, the metaphor of lordship or sovereignty is by no means unique to the Bible. The world that surrounded the Bible was, as Paul remarked, a world of "gods many and lords many," from Marduk of Babylon and the god-kings of Egypt, to Dionysius or to the Roman Caesars. Yet the theme of sovereignty assumes in the Bible a centrality and is accorded a development that is unique among the world's religions. Again, all deities are in some sense ultimate or absolute, but in Biblical religion this relation of man to God is developed in a way more intense and more single-minded than in any other religion in human history (with the possible exception of Islam).

The development of this uniquely monotheistic theme

provides the inner unity and coherence of the Bible. It begins with the first chapter of Genesis, in which God speaks with regal voice, calling the world into existence. From this point onward the absoluteness of the heavenly king continues and develops throughout the Bible. It is underscored and developed by subsidiary metaphors. For example, the height metaphor is pressed with the greatest vigor: God is the Most High. So, too, the metaphor of power or might, in the sense of strength necessary to accomplish one's goals, serves the same function: God is almighty, or all-powerful. Similarly, the light metaphor is applied to deity: God dwells in light unapproachable. Thus, sovereignty seldom occurs as a solitary image but rather as the center of a cluster of images. Around it are grouped, in ordered fashion, light, power, existence through time, and many others. And what is pertinent here is that they all serve to assert and develop the central theme of the absolute lordship of God.

From a very early period of Biblical history, another metaphor, that of fatherhood, supplements and counterbalances that of king. Both king and father, let it be clearly said, are authority figures in the Biblical world. But father includes also an element of friendship, fellowship, or love which is often (though not always) lacking in the metaphor of kingship. Thus, the relation of God to man includes not only sovereign rule but love as well. Let it be asserted in passing that for the modern man there is here a real danger of misunderstanding; the term "love" is a perilously vague word as we move from language to language. It is also extremely ambiguous within the English language and tradition. In the Bible it means the fulfillment of personal or interpersonal relations in the Bible's own distinctive understanding of those relations.[10] Yet with these cautions and qualifications in mind, if there is a single phrase that sums up the Biblical understanding of deity, it is sovereign love. It is an understanding set forth or expressed in the characteristic metaphorical images of Biblical faith.

Not only is there great variety in the imagery of the Biblical documents, but in the approximately fourteen centuries of Biblical history there is very significant development. From the Song of Deborah (Judges, ch. 5), and its desperate cry to the Lord of battle, or from the Song of Miriam (Exodus 15:21) and its cry of triumph over the Egyptians, on to the final chorus to the heavenly king in the book of The Revelation, extremely significant developments are perceptible in the Biblical imagery. These developments are of two kinds: first, a broadening and deepening of the image of sovereignty; and second, a generation of other subsidiary images implied by sovereignty. However, in both cases, it is the absolute or unqualified quality of the divine sovereignty which literally pushes or drives the Biblical writers to develop new implications. In the ever-new situations of Israel's history, new implication and new images appear, articulating new understandings (or misunderstandings) of her sovereign Lord, and his relation to his people.

In the earliest days of Israel's religion, the Lord's sovereignty does not appear to differ greatly from the authority of other lords or gods over their peoples. However, even here a new and radical element is present in the relation of the Lord to Israel in the sheer absoluteness of this relation of God to people. As the reader moves onward in the Bible from book to book, the implications of this lordship are developed in both breadth and depth. In other words, the people of Israel learned much in both breadth and depth concerning the meaning of God's lordship from earliest to latest days.

In these lessons the prophets played a crucial role. The prophetic movement as a whole sought to vindicate the lordship of God over the common life of the nation and then over the world, as well as over religious ritual. Also, in the writings of men like Hosea and Jeremiah, God is also understood as lord over the individual man and over his innermost heart, as well as over the public doings of the nation. In the prophetic viewpoint, God was lord of the human heart as well as the great events of history.

In a similar way, God's lordship was broadened to include the whole world. As horizons widened and men of Israel were drawn into contact with men of other nations, the question was raised, Was God also lord of these peoples? In general, the logic of prophetic thought was that God was not lord at all if he was not lord of all. Hence, the prophets were led to assert that God was lord equally of all men and nations. In this manner was born the idea of mankind or humanity. The inference was from one God to one world. In all this development the driving force was the absoluteness of the divine sovereignty.

The lordship or sovereignty of God not only pushed toward broadened and deepened meanings, it produced new subsidiary images. Here we can offer only two or three illustrations of this process. Imbued with the absolutely unique lordship of God, as Israel's thinkers deliberated concerning the beginning of things they produced the image of creation. In other words, the fundamental meaning of the Creation story is that God is lord of beginnings. His sovereignty is extended temporally to first things; and the stories of creation are the result. This logic is particularly apparent in the writings of Deutero-Isaiah (Isa., chs. 40 to 55) whose influence is apparent on the priestly editor who wrote the Creation story of Genesis, ch. 1.

If the implications of sovereignty were pushed backward

toward the beginnings of time, there was also a "turning to the future," as Martin Buber has put it.[11] The Biblical writers were sufficiently realistic in their observation of history to see that the sovereignty of God was not at all apparent in the present. In the present age, other kings than God exercised dominion or lordship. The sovereignty of God was therefore extended into the future. There would come a time when the lordship of God would be manifested for all to see! So asserted the prophets. The result of this line of thought was the whole eschatological orientation of the Bible. In the last times God's lordship would be manifested. So it is that the Bible argues that God, who is the absolute lord, is accordingly sovereign over first things and last things, over creation, and of Judgment Day. The images of creation and consummation may thus be understood as corollaries of God's sovereignty.

A similar logical development is exhibited in still another image of the Bible, namely, that of the Messiah or Anointed One. The literal meaning of the term was "one who had been chosen as king," symbolized by the ceremony of anointing; and its first use is in reference to Saul as the Lord's anointed, or chosen king of Israel (I Sam. 10:12). But in the course of time this meaning was extended to an ideal ruler who would be the divine agent in bringing in the great age of fulfillment. This "good time coming" was envisaged as an age of universal peace and justice. Thus, the Messianic king or Messiah came to be regarded as the agent through whom God's whole will for mankind was to be done, or through whom the divine sovereignty would be manifested over all the world. Once more, the new image may be understood as a corollary of the absolute sovereignty of the one God.

In the course of time, all these notes increased in intensity as prophecy developed into apocalypse. Apocalypse, with its bizarre imagery, was a definite religious and literary form in the later Old Testament period as well as the New Testament period. Apocalyptic literature may be said to consist of tracts for bad times. In effect its religious message is that even in desperate times God is still lord. In highly stylized and often bizarre images, it depicts the present evil age as through ascending series of woes it approaches a climax of evil. At this point, God will intervene, sending his Messiah to conquer the forces of evil and bring in the great good age of the future, thus vindicating his own sovereignty over human history. Again, the point that is pertinent here is that behind all the strange imagery of apocalypse stands the basic image of the Bible, namely, the absolute lordship of God. What in effect the Bible says is that God is Lord of history; and these apocalyptic images are the terms in which this assertion is made during a long and troubled period of Biblical history.[12]

It is obviously impossible in a sketch of this sort even to hint at the richness and variety of the Bible's imagery. One can only plead that many of the images that could not be discussed here because of space might be fitted into the structure outlined in this section, as variations or developments of these basic themes. For example, man is understood in the Bible essentially as a servant of the Lord, his obedience is the root image for faith, and his disobedience or obedience to other masters is the root image for sin. This understanding of man is in turn filled out by many other images such as those of God's love for and fellowship with his creature. But again, what is pertinent here is that it is in terms of this cluster of images that the Biblical understanding of man takes place. By means of its images the Bible achieves its own distinctive view of existence.

5. *Biblical Images in Western Culture*

As repeatedly suggested in these pages, no living religion is ever completely cooped up in its institutional forms; rather, it has implications for the whole life of the human cultures with which it interacts. Conversely, the business of creating and sustaining the life of a culture, or, for that matter, the death of a culture, is never without religious significance. Paul Tillich has remarked that no great work of human culture can hide its religious source.[13] These relations between religion and culture are altogether general, being applicable to all religions and all cultures that happen in point of historic fact to interact. Illustrations of the different kinds of interaction may be had from many parts of the world and many ages of history.

Here, however, we are concerned with the interaction of Biblical faith and Western culture. A caution is necessary at the outset. It is as easy as it is false to think of Biblical faith in either its Christian or Jewish form as a culture faith of the West having the same relations as any type-one religion to its culture. Indeed, there are times and places when adherents of Biblical religions have themselves fallen into this false view. But it is accompanied necessarily by violence to essential elements of Biblical religion. Both Judaism and Christianity are properly universal religions whose God is Lord of all mankind and not just of one people or culture. Yet it is also a historical fact that both of these religions have interacted significantly with Western culture, and it is this fact which claims our interest.

The term "Western culture or civilization" is not without its serious ambiguities and problems. We shall endeavor here to follow the usage of practicing historians. So conceived, Western culture had its origin as a new synthesis that took place in the ruins of classical Greco-Roman culture somewhere between 500 and 1000 A.D. It is, of course, patently impossible to assign precise dates to the birth or death of cultures, despite the fact that these are real facts of human history.

Many elements combined to form the new culture. The mind of Greece in philosophy, science, and the arts was a rich heritage, as also was the practical administrative genius of Rome embodied in her law and empire. A new infusion of energy was given by the barbarian tribes that swept over Europe during this formative period. But in addition to these three, there was also a significant Hebraic contribution which is often neglected or overlooked alike by historians and philosophers of history. Moreover, it is much too easy and too simple to say that the Hebraic contribution consisted of the Christian religion, and to let the matter rest at that. True, the Biblical or Hebraic contribution was religious and ethical in nature, but if we say this, we must keep in mind the wider relation of religion to culture and the distinctive role of religious faith in creating and also in sustaining a culture and its characteristic forms of expression.[14]

If we do this, we shall be able to appreciate the deep and pervasive impact of Biblical religion on Western culture in its formative period, and throughout its history. The men who stand at the beginning of the West were, for the most part, adherents of this faith. Many of them were new converts to it. So it is that the Biblical images for God and man, for historic destiny, for life and death, penetrated and infused their minds. Often their understanding of the faith was unsophisticated and crude, and in no case was this the only element in their minds. Rather, it existed alongside many other factors, conditioning them and being conditioned by them. There was then, in summary, a clearly Hebraic or Biblical ingredient in the new culture, and the medium by which this ingredient was communicated was the Biblical images. The four elements, Greek, Roman, Teutonic, and Hebraic, flowed together to form the new stream of Western culture or civilization. The stream thus formed has maintained its continuity from its origin to the present time.

The point of these observations for our study is that we may observe the Hebraic or Biblical element in the Western cultural tradition by noting its images as they have been carried by this tradition and have impressed themselves in power and vitality upon the minds of men in successive generations of Western history. Perhaps the most obvious and sometimes the most superficial application of this truth is the use of Biblical images, themes, persons, and ideas in Western arts. Western literature, music, and painting all in their respective ways show this influence. For example, from the earliest medieval days onward through the emergence of national literature to the present time, such influence is clearly visible in the great works of Western literatures.

The impact of the Bible on the Western mind, however, goes far deeper than simply a use of Biblical subject matter and images, pervasive though that use may be. Rather, Biblical imagery might be said to have seeped into men's minds during the formative centuries of the West, affecting and influencing its most basic forms and processes. One sees here a significant illustration of the primacy of imagination, the place of images, among the functions and aspects of the mind. Thus the Biblical influence was decisive on the mind's image of itself, of who and what man is, why he is alive, of the nature of the world and man's relation to it, and of the life values which give his existence meaning. All these issues are the stuff of which religions are made, and, as previously argued, they come to us through the mediation of root images. It is through such processes that the root images of the Bible found their way into the mind of Western man.

We cannot here undertake detailed analysis of any particular historical writer or work, intriguing as such tasks would be. Rather, such study must here be indicated only as agenda for future study. One might, for example, study the impact of the Bible on the mind of Augustine by means of a study of Biblical images in his writings. One could undertake similar studies of other figures such as Donne, Shakespeare, Milton, or Eliot. This study must, of course, be prepared to find many degrees and kinds of influence, and indeed to find some minds and some works where it is negligible or nonexistent. In other words, the thesis here asserted might well be treated as a hypothesis to be tested on specific bodies of relevant facts. Our point is that expressive images are the vehicles of this influence, which therefore can be studied by a study of the images.

Erich Auerbach's monumental volume, *Mimesis, The Representation of Reality in Western Literature,* marks at least a significant beginning in this kind of analysis.[15] Auerbach illustrates the epic style of the Bible by means of a comparison of the Genesis story of Abraham's sacrifice of Isaac with the episode of the scar of Odysseus in Book 19 of the *Odyssey,* and by a similar comparison of the story of Peter's betrayal of Jesus with a Hellenistic document contemporary to the New Testament. Here, in both Old Testament and New Testament, is a kind of realism and temporalism or historicism profoundly different from contemporary Greek or Roman literature. By similar comparative studies, Auerbach works his way through the ancient world to the formative period of Western culture and Western mind, and thence by a consideration of representative works through significant periods of the various Western literatures.

His term for the distinctive kind and use of expressive image involved in the nascent literature of the West is *figura*.[16] Such *figurae* are illustrated and described from the literature of successive periods of the West. It will not be false to Auerbach's idea to say that *figurae* are expressive images set in historic time and taken as interpreting the meaning of the historic process. They occur in the minds of men immersed in history who have ceased the vain effort of the great classical thinkers to find the timeless order and peace of some supratemporal or nontemporal, eternal realm, and who seek meaning in time. So it is that existence in time is not to be regarded as an alienation from God or from reality; rather, it is the kind of reality distinctive to human creatures of the Lord of history. *Figurae* are also the terms in which the meaning of historic time is articulated or depicted. More specifically, they are images which have their basis in one moment of time and refer to another subsequent moment which thus fulfills their meaning. Thus they might be termed allegories which have the function of interpreting the temporal or historical process. In the light of our previous analysis, the impact of the Bible is clear in the idea or concept of *figurae*.

Here we cannot follow Auerbach through his long and scholarly study of works of Western literature extending from Homer and the Bible to Virginia Woolf, and embracing works in no less than eight national literatures of the West; we can, however, remark that the term "historical realism" describes the thread of continuity which he traces through this long and varied tradition, and that his work goes far to establish the thesis of a continuous cultural tradition in Western literature together with the impact and influence of the Bible on this tradition.

The massive impact of the Bible upon Western culture is by no means limited to men who are professed Christians or Jews or members of any religious institution. Indeed, it appears at times more strongly and significantly in those who disavow any relation to institutional religion. Apparently once a great faith finds it way into a cultural tradition, it operates in ways of its own, somewhat heedless of human distinctions and limits.

This influence operates pervasively upon many or all the significant aspects of the mind's activities. In the case of the influence of Biblical faith on Western culture, the influence is observable and significant in all the major areas of intellectual or cultural activity, ranging from the arts through the social sciences and philosophy, and extending even to the natural sciences. Surely this is a primal and major influence upon the Western tradition. The point that is relevant here is that the vehicle of this influence is the imagery in which Biblical faith is articulated.

6. *Faith, Images, and the Individual*

The central contentions of this chapter and of our entire study may perhaps be brought home more clearly by a final glance not at large cultural issues but at factors that are decisive in the individual's own mind and life. I must plainly add in this connection that the original motivation for this study was a desire for self-knowledge concerning my own religious language. At a time when the study of different forms and functions of language were becoming an increasing preoccupation to students of philosophy, I found myself, along with many others, asking about the nature of religious language. As I went about the practice and study of religion, the question increasingly forced itself into my attention: What goes on in these uses of language? What is the function and significance of the language of prayer and worship, of witness, confession, and command-ment, of Scripture and sermon? What, too, is the use or significance of those other kinds of words so essential to the study and critical understanding of one's own faith and the faiths of other men? These questions which motivated the study have continued with us throughout its course.

For the Jew or the Christian, the Biblical words and images are dominant in the whole religious life. Hence in both of these faiths the seminal religious or devotional practice is a distinctive kind of reading of the Bible. From this practice the Biblical images find their way into all the other forms of experience and expression which to-gether constitute religion. If one asks what is the distinc-tive character of religious reading of the Bible, the answer is that in this kind of reading the person opens himself existentially to the images presented to him. He puts him-self under the authority of these images, seeking from them, and through them, light and power, or, as we have previously put the matter, total life orientation.

As we saw in Chapter VIII, this religious way of reading is similar, though by no means identical, to the reading of poetry, or indeed of any literature. In both religious and literary experience the focus of attention is upon the ex-pressive images of the writing. It is through the perception of these images that the process of reading is fulfilled, and the meaning comes home to the reader. The difference is that in literary or aesthetic reading the end or goal is con-templative enjoyment, while the end of faith is action.

Literary experience does not seem to involve the claim to authority which is so central a feature of religious experience. Religious discourse usually includes or entails direct commandments or moral imperatives in a way seldom true of literature. With these qualifications in mind, it may be said that religion is the poetry men live by.

Stated once more in individual terms, a man engages in devotional or religious reading precisely at the point at which he places himself under the authority of the images presented to him (or, more precisely, of the reality mediated by images) and seeks to trace their implications and significance for all of his life. To be sure, the Bible is not the only book in the world that is read thus religiously or devotionally. Comparable practices will come to mind from all functioning faiths and faith substitutes. Accordingly, all faiths may be said to live in their major images. By means of these images they are articulated, and by this means they are aroused, communicated, and sustained.

Questions continue to spring up around these issues. What book shall I read devotionally? Why the Bible rather than the Bhagavad Gita or the Koran or Shakespeare or the Communist Manifesto? What is the precise and detailed nature of the authority asserted for images of faith? Here it must suffice to answer that for each man the issue is ultimately experimental—if we may use the word "experiment" for a form of experience in which the self is not a more or less detached observer but is totally engaged. It has been wisely said that every value and value system is addressed: To whom it may concern. Certainly this is true of those value systems which are the religious and religious substitutes of mankind. It is only necessary to add in the present context that the address takes place through the images of faith or ultimate valuation.

Notes

❖ ❖

CHAPTER I

1. Ernst Cassirer, *An Essay on Man* (Yale University Press, 1944), p. 26. This book is now available as an Anchor Book.

2. George H. Mead, *Mind, Self, and Society* (The University of Chicago Press, 1934), p. 140.

3. Walt Whitman, *Leaves of Grass,* ed. by Malcolm Cowley (The Viking Press, Inc., 1955), pp. 55–56.

4. Reinhold Niebuhr, *The Nature and Destiny of Man* (Charles Scribner's Sons, 1941), Vol. 1, p. 13.

5. Gilbert Ryle, *The Concept of Mind* (paperback edition, Barnes & Noble, Inc., 1959), p. 15. The original edition of this book was published by Hutchinson and Co., Ltd., London, 1949.

6. Cassirer, *op. cit.* See also Cassirer's *Philosophy of Symbolic Forms,* trans. by Ralph Manheim (3 vols.; Yale University Press, 1953–1957) and *Language and Myth,* trans. by Susanne Langer (Dover Publications, Inc., 1946).

7. Cassirer, *An Essay on Man,* p. 24.

8. Susanne Langer, *Philosophy in a New Key* (Harvard University Press, 1942), p. 42.

9. See *inter alia* M. Cohen and E. Nagel, *An Introduction to Logic and Scientific Method* (Harcourt, Brace & Company, Inc., 1934), p. 21; J. S. Mill, *A System of Logic,* 8th ed. (Longmans, Green & Company, Inc., 1930), pp. 11, 29.

10. Cohen and Nagel, *op. cit.,* p. 32.

11. See A. J. Ayer, *Language, Truth and Logic* (paperback edition, Dover Publications, Inc., 1950), Ch. VI, pp. 102 f. The original edition of this book was published by Victor Gollancz, Ltd., London, 1936. Rudolph Carnap, *Philosophy and Logical Syntax* (Kegan Paul, Trench, Trubner & Co., London, 1935), pp. 26, 58, 78.

12. Philip Wheelwright, *The Burning Fountain* (Indiana University Press, 1954), p. 49.

13. For a criticism of the idea of perceptual immediacy, see Ryle, *op. cit.*, pp. 201 f. I do not believe that Ryle's criticisms apply to my use of the term, which I believe appeals to the ordinary prephilosophic usage of both words. See also A. N. Whitehead, *Symbolism* (The Macmillan Company, 1927, 1955), for a discussion of "presentational immediacy."

14. Leonard Linsky (ed.), *Semantics and the Philosophy of Language* (University of Illinois Press, 1952). See especially the essay by Carl G. Hempel entitled "Problems and Changes in the Empiricist Criterion of Meaning."

15. F. Ernest Johnson (ed.), *Religious Symbolism* (Harper & Brothers, 1955), p. 109. This point recurs in many of Tillich's writings.

16. Wheelwright, *op. cit.*, pp. 55, 60.

17. *Ibid.*, pp. 58, 74.

CHAPTER II

1. Rudolph Carnap, *Meaning and Necessity* (The University of Chicago Press, 1956; Phoenix Book, 1956). See appendix on "Pragmatics."

2. Ludwig Wittgenstein, *Philosophical Investigations,* trans. by G. E. M. Anscombe (The Macmillan Company, 1953), p. 51 e.

3. For discussion of the uniqueness of human language, see *inter alia* the articles by Edward Sapir on language and communication in the *Encyclopedia of Social Sciences.* See also *Selected Writings of Edward Sapir in Language, Culture, and Personality,* ed. by David G. Mandelbaum (University of California Press, 1949); A. Kroeber (ed.), *Anthropology Today* (The University of Chicago Press, 1953); A. Kroeber, *Anthropology* (Harcourt, Brace & Company, Inc., 1948).

4. A. J. Ayer, *Language, Truth and Logic;* Carnap, *Philosophy and Logical Syntax.*

5. As illustrations of this tendency, see the works of Ayer and Carnap cited above, as well as the following: Charles Stevenson, *Ethics and Language* (Yale University Press, 1944);

G. E. Moore, *Principia Ethica* (Cambridge University Press, London, 1922), contributes to this tendency by its characterization of value as a logical indefinable property. Aspects of this issue are discussed in P. A. Schilpp (ed.), *The Philosophy of G. E. Moore* (Northwestern University, 1942). Critical essays 1–6 deal with aspects of it. The writings of John Dewey and his followers with his view of values as rooted in natural liking or preferences offer similar illustration. Truly this view is a pervasive feature of contemporary philosophic thinking and writing.

6. As illustrations of this preoccupation of semantic philosophy with problems of logic and the methodology of science, see *inter alia* H. Feigl and W. Sellers (eds.), *Readings in Philosophical Analysis* (Appleton-Century-Crofts, Inc., 1949); Linsky (ed.), *op. cit.* None of the papers in these volumes is concerned with philosophic issues or problems in which human values are central; every one of them has to do with aspects of the methodology of logic and science. Such issues are both interesting and significant, but the point is that in the minds of many contemporary philosophers they appear to have crowded more traditional issues and problems completely off the stage.

7. Carnap, *Meaning and Necessity,* especially pp. 64 f., on the material mode of speech. See also Ayer, *op. cit.,* especially Chs. 1 and 2.

8. The Introduction to the 1946 edition to Ayer, *Language, Truth and Logic* contains an elaboration and defense of the verification principle. Also Ayer (ed.), *The Revolution in Philosophy* (The Macmillan Company, 1956), contains an interesting retrospective essay on the same theme.

9. F. Waismann, "Verifiability," *Essays on Logic and Language,* ed. by Antony Flew (First Series; Philosophical Library, Inc., 1951), p. 118.

10. See as illustrations of this tendency, John Dewey, *Experience and Nature* (The Open Court Publishing Company, 1958). See also Carl G. Hempel, "Problems and Changes in the Empiricist Criterion of Meaning," Linsky, *op. cit.* I feel quite certain that Hempel means empiricism in the more rigorous and narrow sense, but he never explicitly says so in this essay. Ernest Nagel, "Naturalism Reconsidered," *Proceedings and*

Addresses of the American Philosophical Association, 1954–1955, pp. 5 f., also illustrates this double use of the term "empiricism."

11. Ludwig Wittgenstein, *Tractatus Logico-Philosophicus* (Routledge and Kegan Paul, London, 1922), p. 189.

12. Wittgenstein, *Philosophical Investigations.*

13. Waismann, "Language Strata," in *Logic and Language,* ed. by Antony Flew (Second Series; Philosophical Library, Inc., 1953), pp. 11 f.

14. *Ibid.,* p. 18.

15. *Ibid.,* p. 12.

16. *Ibid.,* p. 19.

17. *Ibid.,* p. 28.

18. M. Cohen and E. Nagel, *op. cit.,* pp. 133 f.

19. *Encyclopedia of Social Sciences,* Vol. 9, pp. 155–169.

20. Langer, *op. cit.,* pp. 94–95.

21. Schilpp, *op. cit.* See in this volume critical essays 12 and 13. The former by C. H. Langford is entitled "Moore's Notion of Analysis" and the latter by Norman Malcolm is entitled "Moore and Ordinary Language."

22. Basil Mitchell (ed.), *Faith and Logic* (George Allen & Unwin, Ltd., London, 1957), pp. 194 f.

23. Samuel Laeuchli, *The Language of Faith* (Abingdon Press, 1962).

CHAPTER III

1. See *inter alia,* Plato, *The Republic,* Bks. III, VII, X. The role of images and ideas in the mind's life is a recurrent problem for Plato. Readers familiar with Plato's thought will think of many other references.

2. B. Spinoza, *Tractatus Theologico-Politicus.* See especially Ch. I, entitled "Of Prophecy." For the role of imagination in the life of thought, see *inter alia* Joseph Ratner (ed.), *The Philosophy of Spinoza* (Modern Library, Inc., 1927).

3. G. F. W. Hegel, *Philosophie der Religion.* As in the case of Plato, Spinoza, and others, the relation of image and idea is a persistent theme of Hegel's thought. See Carl Friedrich (ed.), *The Philosophy of Hegel* (Modern Library, Inc., 1953).

4. Whitehead, *op. cit.*

5. Langer, *op. cit.*

6. Augustine, *Confessions,* Bk. 10, Ch. 8.

7. *Augustine: Confessions and Enchiridion,* ed. by Albert Cook Outler (The Westminster Press, 1955), pp. 208–211.

8. Richard Kroner, *The Religious Function of Imagination* (Yale University Press, 1941).

9. Sidney Hook (ed.), *Psychoanalysis, Scientific Method and Philosophy* (New York University Press, 1959).

10. Sigmund Freud, *The Future of an Illusion,* trans. by W. D. Robson-Scott (Liveright Publishing Corporation, 1949).

11. H. Richard Niebuhr, *The Meaning of Revelation* (The Macmillan Company, 1941), pp. 99 f.

12. Aristotle, *Posterior Analytics,* II, Ch. 19, 100a 5, 6; 100b 4, 5.

13. *The Works of Henry Vaughan,* ed. by L. C. Martin, p. 466. (Oxford: At the Clarendon Press, 1957). The line is from a poem entitled "The Vision," which is a part of *The World.*

14. Edna St. Vincent Millay, *The Harp Weaver and Other Poems,* p. 70 (Harper & Brothers, 1920). The quotation is the first line of a sonnet that bears the same title. It is sonnet xxii in pt. iv of *The Harp Weaver.*

15. Aristotle, *Poetics,* 1457b–1458a. It may be found in *Aristotle on the Art of Poetry,* trans. and ed. by Ingram Bywater (Oxford: At the Clarendon Press, 1909), or in *The Works of Aristotle Translated Into English* (Oxford: At the Clarendon Press, 1924), Vol. XI.

16. Allen Tate, *On the Limits of Poetry* (William Morrow and Co., Inc., 1948). See especially the essay entitled "Tension in Poetry."

17. Wheelwright, *op. cit.,* pp. 100 f.

18. Jacques Barzun, *The House of Intellect* (Harper & Brothers, 1959), pp. 15 f. Barzun speaks disparagingly of creativity as a banal and trite word leading to the betrayal of intellect. Granting fully the justice of his charge, one wonders if he is able to dispense completely with the category in his work as scholar and teacher.

19. J. S. Mill, *op. cit.,* pp. 253 f. Mill's methods of intellectual discovery or induction here set forth are critically ap-

praised by Morris Cohen. See Cohen and Nagel, *op. cit.*, pp. 245 f.

20. George Bernard Shaw, *Saint Joan of Arc*, Scene One.

21. Emil Brunner, *The Divine-Human Encounter*, trans. Amandus W. Loos (The Westminster Press, 1943).

22. Austin Farrer, *The Glass of Vision* (The Dacre Press, London, 1948).

CHAPTER IV

1. See Carnap, *Philosophy and Logical Syntax*, pp. 68 f. Ayer, *Language, Truth and Logic*, Ch. VI.

2. For a useful summary of recent currents in semantic philosophy, see J. O. Urmson, *Philosophic Analysis: Its Development Between the Two World Wars* (Oxford: At the Clarendon Press, 1956). It might also be added that Ludwig Wittgenstein's later philosophy as seen in *Philosophical Investigations* has also been a powerful influence toward a multi-valued conception of language.

3. Antony Flew and Alasdair MacIntyre (eds.), *New Essays in Philosophical Theology* (SCM Press, Ltd., London, 1955), pp. 96 f.

4. Plato's arguments for God may be found in *The Laws*, 891C *et seq.* (G. P. Putnam's Sons, Loeb Classical Library, 1926), pp. 319 f.

5. Aristotle's arguments for God are to be found in the *Metaphysics*, Book Lambda 6–10.

6. Thomas' fivefold argument for God is to be found in both the *Summa contra gentiles* and the *Summa theologica*. For an accessible source of the latter formulation, see A. Pegis (trans. and ed.), *Introduction to St. Thomas Aquinas* (Modern Library, Inc., 1948), pp. 25–26.

7. Flew and MacIntyre, *op. cit.*, pp. 99 f.

8. *Ibid.*, pp. 103 f.

9. R. B. Braithwaite, *An Empiricist's View of the Nature of Religious Belief* (Cambridge University Press, London, 1955).

10. John Hick, *Faith and Knowledge* (Cornell University Press, 1957).

11. Frederick Ferré, *Language, Logic and God* (Harper & Brothers, 1961).

12. Hick, *op. cit.*, p. 127.

13. *Ibid.*, p. 150.

14. Willem Zuurdeeg, *An Analytical Philosophy of Religion* (Abingdon Press, 1958).

15. *Ibid.*, pp. 13 f.

16. *Ibid.*, pp. 23 f.

17. *Ibid.*, p. 27.

18. *Ibid.*, pp. 28 f.

19. Paul Tillich, *Systematic Theology I* (The University of Chicago Press, 1951), pp. 105 f.

20. Paul Tillich, *The Protestant Era* (paperback edition, The University of Chicago Press, 1958), p. 32. The original edition of this book was published by The University of Chicago Press, 1948.

21. Cassirer, *Language and Myth*, pp. 18–22.

22. Randall has made this suggestion in many unpublished lectures and discussions. It is also suggested repeatedly in *The Role of Knowledge in Western Religion* (Starr King Press, 1958).

23. Rudolf Otto, *The Idea of the Holy*, trans. by John W. Harvey (Oxford University Press, London, 1928). This book is also available in the Galaxy paperback series of the same publisher.

24. Mircea Eliade, *The Sacred and the Profane*, trans. by Willard R. Trask (Harcourt, Brace and Company, 1959).

25. John Wood Oman, *The Natural and the Supernatural* (Cambridge University Press, London, 1931, 1950), pp. 59 f. I am also indebted at this point to an unpublished Ph.D. dissertation on Oman's philosophy of religion by John Morris. It is being prepared under the Joint Committee for the Ph.D. in Religion at Union Theological Seminary and Columbia University.

26. Cassirer, *An Essay on Man*, Ch. VII. Also in this connection, see *Philosophy of Symbolic Forms* by the same author. Volume II of this three-volume work deals in these terms with mythical thinking.

27. George Santayana, *Reason in Religion* (Charles Scribner's Sons, 1905), pp. 49 f.

28. Reinhold Niebuhr on "The Truth in Myths." This essay

appeared in E. Bewkes (ed.), *The Nature of Religious Experience* (Harper & Brothers, 1937), pp. 117 f.

29. Bronislaw Malinowski, *A Scientific Theory of Culture* (University of North Carolina Press, 1944).

30. The term "creative intelligence" in John Dewey and his many followers begs this question by loading human intelligence with all the values which more traditional philosophies derived from God. See *inter alia* John Dewey and others, *Creative Intelligence* (Henry Holt & Company, Inc., 1917). For further illustration of this same tendency, see Dewey's other writings. Or see Y. H. Krikorian (ed.), *Naturalism and the Human Spirit* (Columbia University Press, 1944). The essay on "Naturalism and Democracy," by Sidney Hook is an especially illuminating illustration. Many of the values are sharply different, but a similar process takes place in Barzun, *The House of Intellect.*

31. Charles W. Morris, *Paths of Life* (George Braziller, Inc., 1956).

32. Henri Bergson, *The Two Sources of Morality and Religion,* trans. by R. Ashley Audra and Cloudesley Brereton (Henry Holt & Company, Inc., 1935).

33. Bronislaw Malinowski, *Magic, Science and Religion* (paperback edition, Anchor Book, Doubleday & Company, Inc., 1955). The title essay of this volume was originally published in Joseph Needham (ed.), *Science, Religion and Reality* (The Macmillan Company, 1925).

34. *Ibid.,* pp. 49–51.

CHAPTER V

1. See *inter alia* Y. H. Krikorian, *op. cit.*

2. The phrase "existential meaning" is an attempt to state precisely the idea of meaning which recurs in the writings of Reinhold Niebuhr. Niebuhr gives explicit attention to this issue in an essay entitled "Coherence, Incoherence and Christian Faith" in the volume entitled *Christian Realism and Political Problems* (Charles Scribner's Sons, 1953).

3. Tillich, *Systematic Theology I,* p. 120.

4. Ryle, *The Concept of Mind*, pp. 25 f.

5. Bertrand Russell, *Scientific Method in Philosophy* (Oxford: At the Clarendon Press, 1914), pp. 25, 144.

6. John Herman Randall, *Aristotle* (Columbia University Press, 1960), pp. 15–16 f.

7. Johannes Pedersen, *Israel: Its Life and Culture* (Oxford University Press, London, 1926–1940), Vol. 1, pp. 106 f. H. Wheeler Robinson (ed.), *Record and Revelation* (Oxford: At the Clarendon Press, 1938). See especially the essay on the language of the Old Testament.

8. See *inter alia* Cohen and Nagel, *An Introduction to Logic and Scientific Method,* p. 27, where a proposition is defined as anything which can be true or false.

9. Carnap, *Meaning and Necessity,* p. 27.

10. These three laws of thought, associated with traditional or Aristotelian logic, are not explicitly formulated in Aristotle.

11. Y. H. Krikorian (ed.), *op. cit.,* pp. 210 f. Nagel's essay in this volume, entitled "Logic Without Ontology," is an attempt to state Aristotle's law as logical rules for language without involving the referent of language.

12. Cohen and Nagel, *op. cit.,* p. 27. Logical validity according to these writers means at least consistency within a pure or uninterpreted logico-mathematical system, while material truth is a trait of statements in interpreted or applied systems.

13. Jean-Paul Sartre, *Existentialism,* trans. by Bernard Frechtman (Philosophical Library, Inc., 1947), p. 27.

14. *Ibid.,* pp. 28 f.

15. Søren Kierkegaard, *Concluding Unscientific Postscript,* trans. by David Swenson (Princeton University Press, 1941), p. 182.

16. See Paul Tillich, "Existential Philosophy," *Journal of the History of Ideas* (1944), pp. 44–70.

17. Jacques Maritain, *Existence and the Existent,* Eng. ver. by Lewis Galantière and Gerald B. Phelan (Pantheon Books, Inc., 1949).

18. Réné Descartes, "Discourse on Method," *Descartes Selections,* ed. by R. Eaton (Charles Scribner's Sons, 1927), pp. 30 f.

19. Among such systems of philosophy, those of Jaspers, Heidegger, and Tillich come readily to mind. Yet other names might also claim inclusion in such a list. The range is from Sartre to Marcell, from the Niebuhr brothers to Buber, Mounier, or Berdyaev, any and all of whom are surely existentialists.

20. I am aware of the efforts of sociologists such as Parsons and Shils to categorize action. See their *Toward a General Theory of Action* (Harvard University Press, 1951). What I believe they produce is phenomenological description and not logical definition or explanation.

21. This view was initially suggested to me by John Macmurray and is expressed in his volume, *The Self as Agent* (Faber & Faber, Ltd., London, 1957).

22. Austin Farrer, *Finite and Infinite* (The Dacre Press, London, 1943), pp. 106 ff.

23. Wittgenstein, *Tractatus Logico-Philosophicus*, p. 31.

24. Wolfgang Köhler, *The Place of Value in a World of Fact* (Liveright Publishing Corporation, 1938).

25. Michael Polanyi, *Personal Knowledge* (The University of Chicago Press, 1958).

CHAPTER VI

1. Malinowski, *Magic, Science and Religion* (Anchor Book, Doubleday & Company, Inc., 1955). This notable essay may also be found in Joseph Needham (ed.), *Science, Religion and Reality* (The Macmillan Company, 1925).

2. See E. Nagel and J. R. Newman, *Gödel's Proof* (New York University Press, 1959).

3. For further detail on the falsification principle, see Karl Popper, *The Logic of Scientific Discovery* (Hutchinson & Co., Ltd., London, 1959), pp. 40 f. For an application of it to theological discourse, see Flew and MacIntyre (eds.), *New Essays in Philosophical Theology* (The Macmillan Company, 1955), pp. 96 f. The symposium that follows here is entitled "Theology and Falsification."

4. See J. S. Mill, *A System of Logic.* For a critical discussion,

see Cohen and Nagel, *An Introduction to Logic and Scientific Method,* p. 45.

5. Karl Pearson, *The Grammar of Science* (J. M. Dent & Sons, Ltd., London, 1943).

6. F. Waismann, "Verifiability," *Essays on Logic and Language,* ed. by Antony Flew.

7. Michael Polanyi, *Science, Faith and Society* (Oxford University Press, London, 1946).

8. Carnap, *Philosophy and Logical Syntax.*

9. See, for example, John Dewey, *Experience and Nature.* Or see Krikorian, *Naturalism and the Human Spirit,* for many striking illustrations of this stretching of nature to a totality concept.

10. See S. Toulmin, "Science and Scientific Mythology," *Metaphysical Beliefs,* ed. by A. MacIntyre (SCM Press, Ltd., London, 1957).

11. George A. Lundberg, *Can Science Save Us?* (Longmans, Green & Company, Inc., 1947).

CHAPTER VII

1. T. M. Greene, *The Arts and the Art of Criticism* (Princeton University Press, 1947).

2. I first encountered this idea in courses in philosophy of art of the late Professor Irwin Edman. See his *Arts and the Man* (W. W. Norton & Company, Inc., 1939). It is developed in more detail in the writings of John Dewey, especially *Art as Experience* (Minton, Balch & Company, 1934).

3. George Santayana, *The Sense of Beauty* (Charles Scribner's Sons, 1936); Irwin Edman, *op. cit.*

4. My first acquaintance with this way of understanding art was T. M. Greene's *The Arts and the Art of Criticism.* However, it is Philip Wheelwright, *The Burning Fountain,* that I prefer for the best overall exposition. It may be seen in the philosophies of art of R. G. Collingwood and Benedetto Croce.

5. Leo Tolstoi, *What Is Art?* trans. by Aylmer Maude (Oxford University Press, London, 1932).

6. T. M. Greene, *op. cit.,* pp. 317 f.

7. Martin Buber, *I and Thou,* trans. by Ronald Gregor Smith (T. & T. Clark, Edinburgh, 1937). While this book is Buber's definitive statement of this idea, it is necessary to add that the idea is a persistent theme in a great many of Buber's voluminous writings.

8. Maurice Friedman, *Martin Buber: The Life of Dialogue* (The University of Chicago Press, 1955). The phrase "life of dialogue," which Friedman uses as title for his biography of Buber, is a recent formulation by Buber of the major theme of his philosophy.

9. T. M. Greene, *op. cit.,* pp. 369 f.

10. Tillich, *The Protestant Era.* I am particularly indebted to Tillich for his analyses of the relation of art to religion and of both to culture. While Section II of *The Protestant Era* deals with this theme, so also do important chapters of Tillich's *The Religious Situation,* trans. by H. Richard Niebuhr (Meridian Books, 1932, 1956), and more recently his *Theology of Culture* (Oxford University Press, Inc., 1959).

CHAPTER VIII

1. Martin Heidegger, *What Is Philosophy?* trans. by William Kluback and Jean T. Wilde (Twayne Publishers, Inc., 1958).

2. Tillich, *Systematic Theology I.*

3. Morris Cohen, *Reason and Nature* (Harcourt, Brace & Company, Inc., 1931).

4. Aristotle, *Metaphysics* 980ᵃ 21–983ᵃ 32. The passage may be found in W. D. Ross (ed.), *Aristotle Selections* (Charles Scribner's Sons, 1927), p. 43.

5. See *inter alia* Michael Foster, *Mystery and Philosophy* (SCM Press, Ltd., London, 1957); Gabriel Marcel, *The Mystery of Being* (Henry Regnery Co., 1950).

6. Robin G. Collingwood, *An Essay on Metaphysics* (Oxford: At the Clarendon Press, 1958), pp. 21 f.

7. *Ibid.,* pp. 34 f.

8. *Ibid.,* pp. 49 f.

9. I encountered this viewpoint first in a lecture by Paul Tillich, though I am not sure he would approve this formulation of it.

10. Farrer, *The Glass of Vision*. See especially Chs. IV and V.

11. Stephen Pepper, *World Hypotheses* (University of California Press, 1942). See also by the same author the article entitled "The Root Metaphor Theory of Metaphysics," *Journal of Philosophy*, XXXII (July, 1935), 368.

12. Collingwood, *op. cit.*, Ch. I; Heidegger, *op. cit.*

13. Joachim Wach, *Types of Religious Experience, Christian and Non-Christian* (The University of Chicago Press, 1951).

14. Walter Kaufmann (ed.), *Existentialism from Dostoevsky to Sartre* (Meridian Books, Inc., 1956), pp. 184 f.

15. John A. Hutchison, *Faith, Reason and Existence* (Oxford University Press, Inc., 1956), p. 29.

CHAPTER IX

1. Frederick Ferré, *Language, Logic and God* (Harper & Brothers, 1961). The preface asserts a union of what are here called religious and theological language, but Chs. XI and XII make the distinction sufficiently clear.

2. G. van der Leeuw, *Religion in Essence and Manifestation*, trans. by J. E. Turner, (George Allen & Unwin, Ltd., London, 1938), p. 23.

3. George Santayana, *Reason in Religion*.

4. Niebuhr, in E. Bewkes, *op. cit.*

5. For interpretations of myth as mistaken science, see discussion in H. Frankfort and others, *Before Philosophy* (Penguin Books, Ltd., Harmondsworth, Middlesex, 1951; originally published as *The Intellectual Adventure of Ancient Man*, The University of Chicago Press, 1946). For further details and bibliography on this etiological view of myth, see the articles on "myth" in the *Encyclopaedia Britannica* and the *Encyclopedia of Social Sciences*.

6. Niebuhr, *op. cit.* Niebuhr's "sermonic essay" entitled "As Deceivers Yet True" in *Beyond Tragedy* (Charles Scribner's Sons, 1937) further elaborates his view.

7. Ryle, *The Concept of Mind* (Barnes & Noble, Inc., 1949), Introduction, p. 7.

8. For vigorous statements of this view, see G. Ernest Wright, *The Old Testament Against Its Environment* (Alec R. Allenson, Inc., 1954). And also by the same author, *God Who Acts* (SCM Press, Ltd., London, 1952).

9. Frankfort, *op. cit.*

10. Cassirer, *Philosophy of Symbolic Forms.*

11. R. McIver, *The Web of Government* (The Macmillan Company, 1948), Ch. III, pp. 39 f., expresses this view of the function of myth. Myths thus become myths of authority. Frankfort, *op. cit.*, develops a similar view as one of the functions of myth.

12. H. W. Bartsch (ed.), *Kerygma and Myth,* trans. by Reginald H. Fuller (S.P.C.K., London, 1953). This book contains Bultmann's now-famous essay on demythologizing, together with critical essays by other writers. It is a particularly good example of the bad results of different uses of the term "myth." No less than three or four such usages can be found in Bultmann's essay alone. See pp. 1–44.

13. Charles Stevenson, *Ethics and Language* (Yale University Press, 1949), p. 206.

14. I am indebted for the point to Professor Paul Tillich, who has repeatedly made it in controversy with other theologians who seek to make an exclusive disjunction between faith and reason and the respective forms of utterance which articulate them. See his *Systematic Theology I*, Introduction and Part I, for his statement of this point.

15. Tillich, *Systematic Theology I* (The University of Chicago Press, 1951), pp. 3 f. Tillich also makes this point more forthrightly in unpublished lectures on the nature and history of theology.

16. Morton White, *Religion, Politics and Higher Learning* (Harvard University Press, 1959). See especially Chs. 8 and 9.

17. William Temple, *Nature, Man and God* (The Macmillan Company, 1935), Ch. 1.

CHAPTER X

1. Santayana, *Reason in Religion,* contains convincing arguments for the particularity of living religions. Santayana is

especially convincing on this point, since his philosophic view-point might well have led him on to an opposite conclusion.

2. In the exposition of recurrent metaphors that follows here, I have been deeply and principally indebted to two volumes: Edwyn Bevan, *Symbolism and Belief* (Beacon Press, Inc., 1955; original edition published by George Allen & Un-win, Ltd., London, 1938), and Mircea Eliade, *Patterns in Comparative Religion* (Sheed & Ward, Inc., 1956). My classification and illustrations are, however, different from those of either of these writers. Some readers will also correctly detect indebtedness to Farrer, *The Glass of Vision*.

3. As to documentation of the idea of three types of religion, I first encountered it in the religious thought of Reinhold Niebuhr. See, for example, Reinhold Niebuhr, *The Nature and Destiny of Man*. Niebuhr is concerned to indicate the distinctiveness of type three, or monotheistic religion, as well as to see its implications for Western culture and thought. However, the idea of both types one and two is discernible in his thought. Elements of this same distinction recur throughout the writings of Paul Tillich. See, for example, the essay "Historical and Nonhistorical Interpretations of History" in *The Protestant Era*. See also Mircea Eliade, *Cosmos and History* (Harper & Brothers, Torchbook, 1958).

4. For the principle of continuity applied to a single type-one religion, see John Wilson's chapter on Egyptian Religion in H. Frankfort and others, *Before Philosophy*. Wilson speaks of the continuous universe of things, men, and gods which characterizes ancient Egyptian religion.

5. My sources in this section have been almost too numerous for documentation. The life-situation viewpoint was suggested to me first by Reinhold Niebuhr, for whom religion and religions have always been ways of understanding human existence. H. Richard Niebuhr's writings, notably *Christ and Culture* (Harper & Brothers, 1951), are also extremely suggestive for this kind of analysis. These writings have been supplemented by reading of various anthropologists, notably Malinowski and Benedict. Also the writings of Christopher Dawson, *Religion and Culture* (Meridian Books, Inc., 1958) and *Religion and the Rise of Western Culture* (paperback

edition, Doubleday Image Book, 1958; originally published by Sheed & Ward, Inc., 1950; German edition, Berne, 1946), deal with many of these issues on creative and significant fashion.

6. Arnold van Gennep, *The Rites of Passage,* trans. by Monika B. Vizedom and Gabrielle L. Caffee (The University of Chicago Press, 1960; originally published in French in 1908).

CHAPTER XI

1. H. Richard Niebuhr, *Radical Monotheism and Western Culture* (Harper & Brothers, 1961).

2. Temple, *Nature, Man and God,* introduction.

3. Karl Barth, *Church Dogmatics* I, 1 (T. & T. Clark, Edinburgh, 1936), pp. 98 f.

4. Brunner, *The Divine-Human Encounter.*

5. H. Richard Niebuhr, *The Meaning of Revelation.*

6. Søren Kierkegaard, *Philosophical Fragments* (Princeton University Press, 1936), pp. 20 f.

7. Kierkegaard, *Concluding Unscientific Postscript.*

8. G. Ernest Wright, *The Old Testament Against Its Environment;* Floyd V. Filson, *The New Testament Against Its Environment* (SCM Press, Ltd., London, 1950).

9. Frankfort, *Before Philosophy.* See especially the last chapter.

10. Buber, *I and Thou.*

11. Martin Buber, *The Prophetic Faith* (The Macmillan Company, 1949), pp. 96 f.

12. See *inter alia* A. Wilder, *Eschatology and Ethics in the Teaching of Jesus* (Harper & Brothers, 1939).

13. Tillich, *The Protestant Era,* p. 57.

14. See *inter alia* Dawson, *Religion and the Rise of Western Culture.*

15. Erich Auerbach, *Mimesis, The Representation of Reality in Western Literature* (paperback edition, Anchor Book, Doubleday & Company, Inc., 1957; original edition of the English edition of this book, Princeton University Press, 1953).

16. *Ibid.,* pp. 42, 64–66.

Index